Being **BLACK** in the Ivory

Being
BLACK
in the
Ivory

Truth-Telling about Racism

in Higher Education

Edited by Shardé M. Davis, PhD
Creator of the viral Twitter hashtag #BlackintheIvory

THE UNIVERSITY OF NORTH CAROLINA PRESS

Chapel Hill

This book was published with the assistance of the Authors Fund of the University of North Carolina Press.

Designed by Richard Hendel
Set in Miller and Klavika types
by Rebecca Evans
Manufactured in the United States of America

Cover art: Chalkboard background, courtesy of Adobe Stock.

A version of Asmeret Asefaw Berhe's essay, "Convenient Narratives Holding Back #BlackintheIvory," originally appeared as "Amplifying Black Voices: The Convenient Narratives That Perpetuate Racism (Parts 1 and 2)," *Springer Nature Blogposts: Life in Research*, October 1, 2020, SpringerNature.com.

Portions of Carolyn Desalu's essay, "Navigating Natural Hair in Academia," appeared in slightly different form in "The Pandemic Prevents White Preoccupation with My Hair," *The Movement Blog*, March 8, 2021, Medium.com.

The poem in Rosamond S. King's essay, "Community and Commiseration," was originally published as "(after depart meant," from *All the Rage* (Brooklyn, NY: Nightboat Books). Copyright © 2021 by Rosamond S. King. Reprinted with the permission of the author.

Library of Congress Cataloging-in-Publication Data
Names: Davis, Shardé M., editor.
Title: Being Black in the ivory : truth-telling about racism in higher education / edited by Shardé M. Davis.
Description: Chapel Hill : The University of North Carolina Press, [2024] | Includes bibliographical references and index.
Identifiers: LCCN 2023045906 | ISBN 9781469678252 (cloth) | ISBN 9781469678269 (paperback) | ISBN 9781469678276 (epub) | ISBN 9798890887092 (pdf)
Subjects: LCSH: Racism in higher education—United States. | African American college students—Social conditions. | African American college teachers—Social conditions. | BISAC: SOCIAL SCIENCE / Ethnic Studies / American / African American & Black Studies | SOCIAL SCIENCE / Discrimination
Classification: LCC LC212.42 .B45 2024 | DDC 378.1/982996073—dc23/eng/20231024
LC record available at https://lccn.loc.gov/2023045906

To all the Blackademics near and far who have been pushed to the fringes of academia. This book was written just for you. You are seen. You are centered. You are heard. You are believed. You belong.

CONTENTS

PREFACE

On the night of Saturday, June 6, 2020, I sat on the couch in my small rental apartment and watched images of illness, death, and crowded hospitals splash across my television screen, listened to Donald Trump spew his racist rhetoric, and read about Black Lives Matter marches taking place all over the globe. I had just returned from one of those marches despite the mandatory lockdown that was still in effect due to the COVID-19 pandemic. The virus was regarded as the most significant cause of illness experienced in our lifetime. But those who are aware of what James Wallis refers to as "America's original sin" and what Nikole Hannah-Jones's 1619 Project denotes as "America's very origin" recognize that we have been in the midst of another, more deep-seated and longer-lasting pandemic—anti-Black racism. On that one evening in early June, I kept thinking about how the murders of Black people affected *me*. I had no immediate history with police, but that didn't mean I wasn't negatively affected by anti-Black racism—the same powerful force that undergirds police brutality—in another social institution. I thought about how academia, my chosen profession, had continuously beaten me down, squeezed life out of me, and nearly squelched my hopes for a professional future. I thought about how the same bedrock upon which policing, mass incarceration, and criminal (in)justice were built was also the foundation for the academic university, also known as the ivory tower. I needed to talk through these thoughts and feelings. But everyone I knew was mentally and emotionally exhausted from living in isolation and fear; no one had the bandwidth to discuss the current events. So, alone in that apartment, I turned to Twitter, and four words for a hashtag came to mind—Black in the Ivory.

THE BACKSTORY

Undoubtedly, living in lockdown was a time filled with considerable fear and uncertainty, as well as rage and exasperation. But in May 2020 our emotions reached an apex. News outlets reported that Black and Brown people were dying from COVID-19 at disproportionately higher rates relative to people from other racial groups. These statistics flashed across my phone screen alongside other reports of civilians and police officers terrorizing and murdering Black people—sometimes in broad daylight, at other times while phone cameras were recording, and typically when the Black person was unarmed. At the beginning of the summer of 2020, widely known as the "summer of racial reckoning," a string of violence against Black bodies spurred a profound visceral reaction of outrage from Americans and also from people around the world. These events included the chase and shooting of Ahmaud Arbery in a small Georgia town; the weaponization of dialing 911 and use of a white woman's tears as an assault against bird-watcher Christian Cooper in New York City's Central Park; the wrongful murder of Breonna Taylor while she was sleeping in Louisville, Kentucky; and the strangulation of George Floyd by a Minneapolis police officer. These tragic assaults stand in a long line of murders of innocent Black civilians, many of which occurred at the hands of state-funded public servants: Kathryn Johnston, Trayvon Martin, Eric Garner, Michael Brown, Tanisha Anderson, Tamir Rice, Sandra Bland, Philando Castile, Korryn Gaines, and Walter Wallace Jr.

I, like so many people at the time, was reeling. Despite recommendations by the Center for Disease Control to stay indoors due to surging COVID rates, I took to the streets to attend Black Lives Matter marches. Shouting chants like "My Life Matters" at the top of my lungs and pumping my fist in the air certainly assuaged *some* of the rage, but my emotions weren't completely quieted. To my surprise, I turned to social media to express myself. It was a surprise because I prefer to lead a private life, and, as a communication scholar who knows the power and lasting effect of words, over time I had slowly distanced myself from various social media platforms. Yet, during the month of May 2020, when I was locked down, alone in that little apartment, I was bursting with exasperation and rage and couldn't take it anymore. Sharing on social media offered a viable release, and at the time Facebook seemed like the best platform from which to connect and lament with others about the ways in which Black people are consistently treated as expendable and dispensable in the United States and around the world. Of course, anti-Black racism is nothing new. But the events of May 2020—racial disparities in diagnoses and deaths due to COVID-19, disinformation by the Trump administration, lockdowns, and murders of unarmed Black people—felt different.

For the next few days I posted searingly honest messages. They ranged in temperament from texting my white-identified friends to inquire about their support for anti-Black racism and Black Lives Matter to imploring my Facebook followers to consider various ways they could support these movements from home. I even shared in these Facebook posts how tiring it is to be Black in America and that I was experiencing low-grade depression, anticipatory anxiety, and stress. And then the outpouring of text messages from friends expressing gratitude for my social media posts began. I was in awe. The positive affirmations invigorated me to keep being a truth-teller. But I would be lying if I did not admit that I oscillated between feeling proud of myself for speaking my whole truth unapologetically and feeling crippled by the exposure of my words.

I continued to wonder what else I could do outside of social media. How could I create change—even if it was small—within my sphere of influence? I was inspired by a young woman who was the first Black student body president at the University of Minnesota. During her tenure, she implored the university administration to no longer use Minneapolis police officers at large-scale events, and soon thereafter the Minneapolis Public School District cut ties with the Minneapolis Police Department, too. Inspired by her ability to reimagine the university's relationship with police, I wondered whether I could help accomplish something similar at my institution. I joined forces with a graduate student who had been championing social justice issues concerning police divestment for years and asked how I could help him get these efforts up and running. There was great momentum and synergy early on, but soon we received discouraging messages from my faculty colleagues who said that pushing my institution to divest from the police was futile. Their words left me feeling useless and, yet again, reeling.

#BLACKINTHEIVORY®

While my social media activist work in May 2020 took place on Facebook, I was also utilizing Twitter as an invaluable news resource—sometimes I would receive higher-quality and higher-quantity information through Twitter than through local and cable news channels. I also found information about how to prepare for marches and how police officers in my area were responding to protesters. Over time, my use of Facebook decreased and my interest in Twitter increased. On Saturday, June 6, 2020, it changed from a source of information to a source of support, like an old friend I could vent to. I had significantly fewer followers on Twitter than on Facebook, none of whom were my colleagues, so I felt like I could bare my soul on the bluebird platform. Alone, frustrated, and overwhelmed by my confrontations with anti-Black racism in academia, I decided to condense these experiences into 140-character tweets, and that is when four words came to mind—Black in the Ivory. Yes, that sums it up. I am Black in a white space. The "stain" on an otherwise pristine garment. The speck that stands out like a sore thumb. I am #BlackintheIvory.

To my surprise, those four words resonated with the masses. With the help of so many Black academics (or "Blackademics" as I referred to them on Twitter) who bravely stood in their right as truth-tellers to share their stories of anti-Black racism in the academy, #BlackintheIvory became one of the top twenty trending US hashtags on Twitter that weekend. Most people would have been thrilled to have their hashtag go viral, but as an untenured Black woman faculty member, I felt incredibly vulnerable because so many eyes were reading my tweets—my friends, other Blackademics, former faculty in my graduate programs, university administration (including my own), and national press outlets. They had access to the ugly truths that I had suppressed for so many years, especially during my graduate studies. Indeed, there was and still remains a hypervisibility that comes along with being in this body, let alone opening my mouth to speak up and, in the words of bell hooks, "talk back." But I was quickly reminded that #BlackintheIvory is not about me. It's about the hundreds of thousands of Blackademics around the globe who stood in their right to speak truth about the racial mistreatment and trauma that they've experienced in the ivory tower.

What makes #BlackintheIvory unique is the *when, where,* and *why* it occurred. The timing of this hashtag during the "summer of racial reckoning" is key. At that time there was a pervasive conversation about anti-Black racism within law enforcement and mass incarceration. Systemic oppression, specifically anti-Black racism, exists in other social institutions too, including education. My hashtag simply shed a light on this truth. Second, #BlackintheIvory started on Twitter—a real-time online platform that connects many Blackademics who had been living and working in isolation not just during COVID-19 but throughout their careers as "the only one"—that is, the only Black faculty member in a department; the only Black person on a diversity, equity, and inclusion committee; or sometimes the only person of color in the entire campus building. Spending over forty hours a week in an environment where *no one* looks like you can be disconcerting because our very being becomes hypervisible and, thus, more easily scrutinized. The ways that we show up in the world personally (that is, style of speech, facial expressions, clothing and hair choices, conversational topics, movement of our hands) and professionally (for example, way of writing, approach to group work, self-advocacy, display of confidence) are often negatively judged because they contrast—or maybe even subvert—dominant social norms that are steeped in whiteness. Isolation can also mean that we are at risk of being scapegoated when things go awry, of being the mouthpiece for all Black people, of being the "resident expert" on all Black-related topics, or even of being tokenized. Twitter at that time was this connective tissue that enabled us to simply *be* and engage in conversation with one another about this difficult topic. And finally, #BlackintheIvory sparked a conversation about anti-Black racism in academia that had not really occurred on a national level, let alone globally. And that conversation leveraged *narratives* to give credence to a notion that many people inside of academia (and some people outside) knew theoretically but not in effect. Storytelling is such a powerful tool for Blackademics because it encourages us to position ourselves as authors of and authorities on our own experiences.

The emergence of #BlackintheIvory was unplanned. But its virality demonstrates that this conversation needed to happen. The hashtag took on a life of its own outside of Twitter, too: individuals referenced and quoted #BlackintheIvory tweets during summer institutes and workshops on social justice, equity, diversity, and inclusion. And in the fall of 2020, some faculty assigned the tweets as part of their course curriculum. The tweets were not necessarily intended for that type of gaze or consumption, but they were used as such. What I mean is the Blackademics who used the hashtag shared their stories without anticipating that their words would appear in a workshop pamphlet or undergraduate course. Quickly it became clear that a book on #BlackintheIvory was crucial to invoke our sense of agency. I wanted to provide a space where Blackademics could opt in to share their stories, with the knowledge that those stories would be archived for other readers—some who are Black and some who aren't. At the same time, anti-Black racism in academia is a behemoth with many viable entry points to the conversation. How could I leverage my expertise in race, group dynamics, and communication to create a book on #BlackintheIvory that makes a valuable contribution? The following pages try to answer that question. I'm fully aware that there are more narratives than any one book can hold, and this conversation about anti-Black racism in academia can move the needle only so far. But for the first time since those days of feeling powerless, angry, and alone in 2020, I'm starting to see not just the effect of my own efforts but the impact of many others' stories, which are bringing to light what (for too long) has been hidden in the shadow of the ivory tower.

INTRODUCTION

A Black professor is walking down the hallway and is mistaken for a custodial staff person. A Black student is told that she received her medical scholarship only because of her race. A Black research scientist is physically blocked from the university mail room and the police are called, even though she has her university ID with her to access the building. These events are not new; in fact, countless empirical studies, edited books, book chapters, and monographs detail systemic racism in academia. Indeed, Blackademics at all career points and across multiple decades have encountered systemic racism in the academic institution, and #BlackintheIvory allowed for these stories and many others to be circulated on Twitter. The racial reckoning that emerged in the summer of 2020 reiterated a sobering truth: racism—and more specifically, the enduring effects of racist history, ideologies, policies, and practices—continues to be largely unresolved for Black people in the United States. And this is certainly true for people, organizations, and institutions that claim to be "liberal leaning," such as academia.

An open conversation about the effects of systemic racism in academia has only just begun—in large part because Blackademics quite rightly fear professional and personal retaliation as a response to sharing their experiences. This curated collection of personal narratives (or counterstories, as I will refer to them in what follows) from Blackademics spotlights those stories and continues the conversation that started in June 2020 with #BlackintheIvory. Put together, the stories here reveal the through line of how racism eats its way through the ivory tower; how academia can be a place that demoralizes bright, valuable, and essential scholars; and how academic institutions—and its individual members—might make lasting change.

RACISM IN THE ACADEMIC INSTITUTION

According to Michael Omi and Howie Winant (2014), racism is rooted in the beliefs that race is the primary determinant of human traits and that racial differences produce an inherent superiority of a particular race. "Anti-Black racism" is a term to highlight the ways in which Black people, in particular, experience racism; it is defined as a system (consisting of policies, practices, and norms) that structures opportunity and assigns value based on phenotype, or the way people look. It unfairly disadvantages Black individuals and communities. While many racial and ethnic groups experience racism or prejudice, "anti-Black racism" underscores the unique experiences of racism for Black people. This book focuses on the specific exclusion of and prejudice against people who visibly are (or self-identify as being) from the African diaspora. Anti-Black racism is a toxic cocktail that mixes these beliefs with how people with power make decisions, how government policies are made, or how state services are delivered. It prevents us from enjoying or exercising fundamental freedoms on an equal footing—like the freedom to live and work in an environment without discrimination and abuse.

Racism, and more specifically anti-Black racism, is perpetrated by social and political institutions, such as schools, courts, the military, or the criminal (in)justice system. Unlike the racism perpetrated by individuals, institutional racism has the power to negatively affect the majority of people who belong to historically oppressed racial groups, such as Latinx people, Indigenous Natives, and Black folks. The term "institutional racism" was first used in the 1967 book *Black Power: The Politics of Liberation*, written by political scientist Charles V. Hamilton and Stokely Carmichael, a prominent organizer in the civil rights era best known for his leadership of the Student Nonviolent Coordinating Committee and the Black Panther Party. Their book delves into the core of racism in the United States and asserts that while individual racism is often easily identifiable, institutional racism is more difficult to spot because of its more subtle nature. Inarguably, no episode in American history has left a greater imprint on race relations than chattel slavery. Many maintain that the legacy of slavery prevails in the present day, since some of our social and political institutions continue to uphold policies, procedures, and practices that eerily reflect the way African enslaved persons were treated over 400 years ago. Widespread conversations about the legacy of slavery and how it reverberates through the criminal (in)justice system crystalized, for instance, in Ava DuVernay's Netflix documentary *13th* and later in the summer of 2020 when many Americans considered the history of police and law enforcement in the United States, tracing its roots to slave patrols in the seventeenth and eighteenth centuries and police enforcement of Jim Crow laws in the late nineteenth to mid-twentieth centuries. According to Michael Robinson, the first deaths in America of Black persons at the hands of law enforcement "can be traced back as early as 1619 when the first slave ship, a Dutch Man-of-War vessel, landed in Point Comfort, Virginia" (2017, 552). The growing movement to discover institutional ties to chattel slavery has also taken place in American colleges and universities.

Dozens of America's oldest and most revered colleges and universities were, reportedly, established through slave labor and slave trade. In fact, Craig Steven Wilder, the author of *Ebony and Ivy: Race, Slavery, and the Troubled History of America's Universities* (2013), claimed that many American colleges founded before the Civil War relied on money that came from the slave economies of New England and the broader Atlantic world to fund the colleges, build campuses, and pay professors' wages. His book lays bare the unsettling truths about a broader role of slavery in the growth of America's earliest academic institutions, a domain usually considered a pillar for liberal politics, ideology, and thought but recently criticized for its racist past. While many institutions are reluctant to examine this past, some have set forth investigations to understand their entanglement with slavery and to debate viable paths of atonement. The historical connections between the academic institution and slavery came to the fore in 2001, when a group of graduate students at Yale University pursued an independent report aimed at investigating the school's abolitionist past. Then in 2003, Ruth Simmons, president at that time of Brown University, announced a major effort to research that school's extensive historical ties to the American slave trade. Other institutions followed with similar endeavors: Columbia University established the Columbia University and Slavery project created by faculty and students to investigate and publicly disseminate information about the university's connection to slavery; Wake Forest University built its Slavery, Race, and Memory project to reach similar ends. These efforts extended beyond private and ivy institutions to others across the nation with the Universities Studying Slavery consortium, founded by the University of Virginia. According to its website, this consortium, representing many institutions, shares "best practices and guiding principles" as the schools "engage in truth-telling educational projects focused on human bondage and the legacies of racism in their histories. . . . Member schools are all committed to research, acknowledgment, and atonement regarding institutional ties to the slave trade, to enslavement on campus or abroad, and to enduring racism in school history and practice" ("President's Commission on Slavery and the University" 2013).

While some institutions are taking steps to acknowledge these issues, including Harvard University's $100 million pledge to research the university's direct ties to slavery as a means of atoning for the way the college benefitted from it, many more colleges and universities have yet to directly and explicitly acknowledge their own entanglement with slavery, not to mention the implications of slavery for the academic institutions writ large today. That is to say, these gestures of restitution and reparations for descendants of slaves (through scholarships and fellowships) are important and necessary ventures, but money alone cannot account for the way these schools' immoral, unjust, seedy, and unconscionable histories have created grave academic and professional work environments and squelched viable opportunities for the success and advancement of Blackademics. As Craig Steven Wilder wrote in his 2013 book, the education project *itself* benefited from the enslavement of Africans. If we can recognize (especially after the summer of racial reckoning) that chattel slavery and racism have disproportionately stymied the political, economic, and social progress of Black Americans in the greater American society, then shouldn't that logic hold when thinking about Blackademics' participation in the realm of academia?

CRITICAL RACE THEORY, BLACK CRITICAL THEORY, AND COUNTERSTORIES

Critical race theory (CRT) is a theoretical tool with which to examine the experiences of members of the academic institution who collectively have undergone violent, traumatizing, and overt and covert racism. CRT interrogates the role of race and racism in society. The framework was introduced in the legal field by Derrick Bell—considered CRT's intellectual father figure—as well as by other architects, including Kimberlé Crenshaw, Richard Delgado, Gloria Ladson-Billings, and Tara Yosso, among others. Critical race theorists assert that racism is and has been an integral feature of life, law, and culture, and any attempt to address and eradicate racial inequities must be grounded in the sociohistorical legacy of racism. Crenshaw—who reportedly coined "critical race theory"—noted that CRT is not a noun but a verb because it is an ever-evolving and malleable practice. It critiques how the social constructions of race and institutionalized racism perpetuate a racial caste system that relegates people of color to the bottom tiers. Among the five tenets of CRT, one of the best known is that racism is not a bygone relic of the past—that is, CRT acknowledges that the legacy of slavery, de jure and de facto segregation, and the imposition of second-class citizenship on Black Americans and other people of color continue to permeate the social fabric of the

United States. Richard Delgado and Jean Stefancic explain in their 2017 book, *Critical Race Theory*, that the CRT "movement is a collection of activists and scholars engaged in studying and transforming the relationship among race, racism, and power" (3).

At the heart of CRT is a recognition of the experiential knowledge of people of color. CRT scholars have argued for "shifting the frame" or "looking to the bottom" so that the knowledge of people of color is not only exposed and heard but also valued. This has been conceptualized as "counterstorytelling" (or counternarrative), which is defined by Daniel Solórzano and Tara Yosso as "a method of telling the stories of those people whose experiences are not often told" (2002, 26). One of the important functions of counternarrative in CRT scholarship is to counteract the stories of the dominant group, according to Delgado's article "Storytelling for Oppositionists and Others: A Plea for Narrative." The dominant group tells stories that are designed to "remind it of its identity in relation to outgroups and provide a form of shared reality in which its own superior position is seen as natural" (1989, 2240). Dominant stories implicitly and explicitly emphasize negative racial stereotypes, reify a racial hierarchy, promote presumptions of inherent inferiority of racial minorities, and obscure the advantages that white people are bestowed at birth. One function of counterstorytelling is to subvert that reality by presenting a substitute or alternative to the mainstream story or the majoritarian story. It should come as no surprise that storytelling "is often seen as problematic because it is regarded as 'unscientific' and subjective"; Gloria Ladson-Billings, though, maintains that "CRT never makes claims of objectivity or rationality. Rather, it sees itself as an approach to scholarship that integrates lived experience with racial realism" (2006, vii). Thus, Charles R. Lawrence III's chapter in *Critical Race Theory: The Key Writings That Formed the Movement* urges that "we must learn to trust our own senses, feelings, and experiences, to give them authority, even (or especially) in the face of dominant accounts of social reality that claim universality" (Crenshaw et al. 1995, 338). Counterstories allow people who have been oppressed to refuse the identities imposed on them by their oppressors and to reidentify themselves in more respect-worthy terms; these stories usually challenge the prevailing ones and set new examples and perspectives. Cassandra L. McKay has summarized the two primary objectives of counternarratives quite well: first, to confront prevailing cultural ideas about a certain group of people "by providing a context to understand and transform an established belief system," and second, "to authentically represent marginalized people by showing them the shared aims of their struggle" (2010, 27). Thus, counternarratives are crucial for people of color, particularly Blackademics, because we can claim the power of speech, take up space to share and be heard, provide alternative viewpoints, promote our particular knowledge as viable and valuable, and allow for others with similar experiences to learn that they are not alone in their suffering and trauma.

While CRT proves to be a useful framework to serve as a critique of white supremacy and racism (broadly speaking), it is not the same as a theory that is specific to Blackness, anti-Blackness, or the Black condition. In response, Black Critical Theory (BlackCrit) was advanced by Michael Dumas and Kihana Miraya Ross in their article "'Be Real Black for Me': Imagining BlackCrit in Education" as a critical theorization of Blackness that expands upon the tenets of CRT and the work of critical race scholars such as Gloria Ladson-Billings, William Tate, and Kimberlé Crenshaw. The "framing ideas" (a term they prefer to use in place of "tenets") of BlackCrit necessarily confront "the specificity of *anti-Blackness*, as a social construction, as an embodied lived experience of social suffering and resistance, and perhaps most importantly, as an antagonism, in which the Black is a despised thing-in-itself" (Dumas and Ross 2016, 416). #BlackintheIvory is a movement not just about anti-Black racism but also about anti-Blackness, a concept that BlackCrit refers to as a "broader antagonistic relationship between blackness and (the possibility of) humanity" (429). BlackCrit provides the language to richly capture the ways anti-Blackness positions Black people (and, more accurately put by Dumas and Ross, Black bodies) as othered, marginalized, disregarded, and pitted against civility, law, and policy. One of the unique contributions of BlackCrit is that it demonstrates the utility of a Black-specific theory, an endeavor that this book lauds since #BlackintheIvory unapologetically centers and amplifies the voices of Blackademics who decide to share their stories. Moreover, BlackCrit is a particularly helpful framework to ground this book because it theorizes why and how Black people suffer in places that champion issues of multiculturalism, diversity, and inclusion, such as academia and, more broadly, education.

BLACKADEMIC STORYTELLING

Counterstorytelling by Blackademics allows the creation of supportive intellectual spaces in which Blackademics may position ourselves as authors and authorities of our own experiences. This positioning disallows the common rhetoric that sees our realities described and defined by dominant paradigms based on Eurocentric norms. For example, white upper administrators (such as deans, provosts, and department heads) can tell stories that their university has low percentages of Black faculty because the applicant pool for faculty searches lacked "qualified applicants." In *Yearning*, bell hooks (1990) talked critically about the dangers of white interpretations of the Black experience. Counterstorytelling by Blackademics provides agentic power to us, offering competing experiential evidence to confront questions of whether we value the process of producing knowledge and learning information, of our ability to actively participate in this process, and of the extent to which we belong at the institutions where this process is taking place. Continuing with the above example, Blackademic counterstorytelling might expose the prevailing misnomers about unqualified and underqualified applicant pools by sharing stories that reveal the *real issues* for low percentages of Black faculty: Black graduate students do not have enough financial, emotional, and career-related resources to finish a PhD; there are broken and missing pipelines to connect the applicant pool to the faculty job market; and some search committee members uphold definitions of "rigor," "high-quality research," "meritocracy," and "competence" that are all steeped in whiteness, thereby creating standards that Blackademics can never meet, let alone surpass. According to many critical race scholars, these subtle but constant forms of racial discrimination and bias are commonplace for Blackademics. Their covert nature allows institutions to deny that these derivations of racism exist on American college and university campuses, particularly those that tout an agenda for racial diversity, inclusion, and justice. Counternarratives of everyday Blackademic experiences are a viable intervention to dismantle dominant stories in academia that claim its members all have equal (or even equitable) opportunities to enter, advance, be fairly compensated or increase one's compensation, work in a safe (nonhostile) environment, and reach high levels of success.

There are many benefits to counterstorytelling. Psychology research has consistently demonstrated that trauma memories can be insidious and can continue to haunt a person even when the individual makes great attempts to avoid the memory. Keeping the trauma a secret can reinforce the feeling that there is something shameful about what happened—or even about oneself on a more fundamental level. We might believe that others will think less of us if we tell them about our traumatic experience. But by creating spaces for Blackademics to tell a different story about ourselves and to contextualize that story within the dominant narratives, Blackademics can begin to identify ways that we have the power to create change in the institutions that impact us. As such, this book does not debate the events that are told in a contributor's story. Instead, this book intends to open new windows into the reality of being #BlackintheIvory.

THE RISKS OF BLACKADEMIC TRUTH-TELLING

Blackademics who assess the landscape and determine that we have the ability to center ourselves and voice our truth about experiences of anti-Black racism in academia must contend with a series of questions: How many details can I share? Do I "call out" someone in the story? Should I share the sanitized version or the raw version? Will they actually listen to me or hear just enough to compose their retort? Can they handle my truth? Whose version of the "truth" will hold weight? Will they find ways to punish me if I share too much? Do I have a backup plan if I am left on the streets with a degree in tow yet nowhere to go?

After reading thousands of #BlackintheIvory stories on Twitter, a notable pattern emerged—the same stories were being told by different people across professional ranks, disciplines, fields, programs, universities, and age groups. It was glaringly obvious that the problem was and is not us (the people) but the racist system that has been institutionalized by American universities. In fact, various press outlets lauded #BlackintheIvory for extending the rare and unique opportunity for the larger public to hear so many stories of racism in academia at the same time. And because of that, individuals could trace the connections and note that one person's experience of racial trauma was now corroborated by the experiences told by so many other Blackademics. For the first time, white academics could not look away. Yet, many of us know that even by sharing similar stories with significant overlap in the minutiae, we will not be believed (at best), or we will be punished for sharing our truth (at worst).

Indeed, great risk comes with great consequence, and Blackademics can experience many negative outcomes when we stand in our right as truth-tellers and share our stories. What are those consequences? Tenure gets denied, or our dossier for promotion to full professor gets flagged; our retention offer is half the amount of a white colleague's offer—if we are retained at all; our invitations to social outings or research teams are conspicuously missing; personal invitations to apply for vacant leadership positions are nonexistent. Or, for Blackademic graduate students, emails to faculty go unanswered; our theses and dissertations take two or three times longer to complete because committee members shirk much of the responsibility to help push the project along (some even stymie progress altogether by being unwilling to meet, offer advice, or read drafts of the manuscript); our questions during advising meetings are not answered in depth; our advisor harshly and unfairly judges our behavior, assuming the worst intentions rather than the best; and we are left alone to drown silently in the sea of a PhD program. And Blackademic college students are not exempt from the looming consequences: administrators listen to our outcries only enough to retort, revise, deflect, and defend; faculty instructors deem us as problematic for expressing critiques of the material or concerns regarding the course; and teachers put forth less effort to constructively evaluate our work or offer help. For these reasons and many more, some of us will not accept the offer to walk to the center of the ivory tower and share our stories. Sometimes it is safer to remain silent than speak up. Our risk assessment also reveals that we will have to constantly filter our words, experience an acute sense of paranoia that we are taking up too much space, and be burdened with anticipatory stress and anxiety because we know backlash is inevitable—and that is all too extensive and psychologically draining. Our mere survival in academia is subversive, considering that the academy was built upon a bedrock of exploitation, human bondage, and myths of Black inferiority; therefore, speaking about these truths requires more of us than we can spare.

Yet the group of Blackademics who chose to share their stories in this book have accepted the personal and professional risks of doing so, knowing that the potential benefits of counterstorytelling may far outweigh the costs. Do not take lightly what it required to get these stories told.

A CALL FOR STORIES

For this book, I issued an "open call" to solicit 150-word vignettes from Blackademics who would share a specific experience of anti-Black racism or anti-Blackness in the American academy across four profiles—college students, graduate students, faculty and administrators, and people who have reimagined a traditional academic structure. Knowing that we are not a monolith, the call emphasized a desire for a diverse group of contributors relative to one's Black identity (for example, multiracial, Afro-Caribbean, or Afro-Latinx persons), field and discipline, identity intersections (such as LGBTQIA+ persons, socioeconomic status, physical mobilities, learning abilities), and academic position (student, faculty person, administrator, and the like). The call also emphasized a range of topics: how one successfully confronted racism on an interpersonal level, sought retribution for aggressors and oppressors, built resilience, or experienced the negative effects of racism on one's health (to name a few). The intention was to discuss anti-Black racism and anti-Blackness within the academy in a holistic manner, recognizing the threads of resistance, agency, resilience, recompense, and retribution as well as deep-seated trauma, stress, agony, (professional) precarity, hypervisibility, hypervigilance, and pain. From the submissions, I leveraged my expertise in inductive, qualitative methods to choose the stories to be included in the book. During this process, I considered stories that demonstrated the diversity and range of anti-Black racism, as well as a diversity in topics and people.

While much of the book features stories from scholars across the United States who responded to the open call, I also invited renowned Black scholars who could place their stories within a scholarly conversation about intersectional racism to compose lead analytical essays that intellectualize their stories using their own work as well as the theory and research by other, preferably Black, scholars. Additionally, I invited well-known public figures to compose spotlight narratives that detail a specific experience of anti-Black racism that has gained national attention using no theory or research. The invited scholars represent major disciplines (such as social sciences, humanities, fine arts, STEM) and career points to reach a broader audience.

BOOK STRUCTURE

Stories are arranged according to the four sections in the book that represent key moments in academia: Undergraduate Life, Surviving Graduate School, Moving Up the Academic Ranks, and Seeking Alternatives to Academia. There is a natural crescendo to the apex of the book, which is a robust collection of stories from individuals in faculty and administrative positions, and then a swift decrescendo to individuals who have entertained alternatives to academia (however defined). Using an inductive approach to soliciting and selecting stories meant that not every section was going to be equally represented. On a more analytical note, it is possible that the influx in stories about graduate student and faculty experiences reflects the notion that these two groups work in an enclave, such that there is a very small number of people on campus or even in their local area who do similar work. And then from that group, there are Blackademics who have an even more distinct experience. Thus, graduate students and faculty persons are likely thinking more deeply about these issues.

This book privileges depth over breadth. You can go to the #Blackin-theIvory thread on Twitter to (re)read all the stories that Blackademics from around the United States and globally have shared about their personal incidents of anti-Blackness and anti-Black racism. Multiple incidents repeat over and over again. But this book intends to go deeper. I want you to get to know the person behind each story, understand it from his, her, or their perspective, and sit with the emotions that the incident invoked in that individual as he, she, or they lived it (and in you as you read about it).

Contributors composed their own stories and had the freedom to share in the way that made them feel both empowered and protected. Some share details about their identities and the identities of the protagonists. Others made the decision to conceal specific identifying factors, including their college, school, or university, by removing specific references altogether or by using pseudonyms. All contributors received ample feedback from the editors at the University of North Carolina Press and me, but at the end of the day, each story is owned by the individual. Remember, these are real stories told by real people with the potential for real consequences.

THE UNNAMED AND UNTOLD STORIES

For each contributor who accepted the journey to revisit hurt, pain, trauma, and other emotional responses from past incidents and decided to associate his, her, or their name with that story, many had to choose a different path. Because many Blackademics have stories of anti-Black racism and anti-Blackness that can only be shared without a name, contributors had the option to anonymize their stories. Very few exercised this option at the outset, but as the months passed, more inquired about removing their names. Their reasons mirror those of many Blackademics who knew about the original Twitter hashtag and chose not to share in the public platform: fear of retaliation for exposing the ugly truths that their colleagues, program, or institutions have been trying to hide. They also expressed a concern that people would not believe them; a few Blackademics worried that readers might poke holes in their stories to invalidate their experiences altogether. They also did not want the undue pressure of recalling every detail with great accuracy and precision. In fact, there are some contributors who sought legal representation while composing their vignettes because they feared individual people or an entire university would pursue legal action. Many Blackademics also explained how draining it is to revisit these events. In fact, several contributors requested an extension (or multiple extensions) for submitting their vignettes because they underestimated the barrage of emotions that would resurface as they wrote their stories; they needed time away from the vignettes—sometimes days, weeks, and even months—to make sense of the events. The writing process resurrected many traumatic memories and negative emotions, and some admitted that even after writing their stories, it will take a considerable amount of time in therapy for them to speak on, unpack, and process their #BlackintheIvory experiences.

Interestingly, Gabriella Gutiérrez y Muhs, Yolanda Flores Niemann, Carmen G. González, and Angela P. Harris encountered similar concerns while editing their critically acclaimed volumes, *Presumed Incompetent* and *Presumed Incompetent II*. These two books, published in 2012 and 2020, collate essays and empirical studies from women of color with diverse intersectional and transnational identities to discuss the obstacles that women faculty of color encounter in their careers in higher education. In the first book's introduction, Harris and González composed an entire section called "A Note on the Silences Shouting from Within This Anthology," which detailed nine specific reasons that potential contributors decided not to have their experiences included in their book. Some of those reasons are comparable to those of the Blackademics who considered submitting their stories to this project: making one's story public might exacerbate already fragile work environments at the home institution; believing that their experiences are rather mild or benign made them think they don't warrant being featured; and sharing these stories might expose other Blackademics or people of color who have (un)knowingly replicated divisive acts and ideologies or even participated in mistreating a potential contributor. Harris and González of *Presumed Incompetent* concluded that "these silences and omissions magnify the importance of the essays in this volume as timely and valuable contributions to our knowledge about the current state of higher education" (2012, 13). Suffice to say that the academic institution writ large has created a culture of silence that is prevalent among not only Blackademics but also other racial groups who experience systemic oppression within academia. But many are using their voices, in the words of bell hooks (1989), to break the silence and "talk back." These stories are the contributors' truths—ones that rarely get told or held in high regard—and should be handled as such.

AUDIENCE AND GOALS

In many ways, this book replicates a "fish bowl" that was evident when the hashtag was trending in June 2020. The initial conversation was really among Blackademics, but others were able to read, listen, and learn. With that in mind, this book was written for Blackademics because throughout time and across the African diaspora we have been forced to disconnect from our bodies, emotions, and trauma to survive. While I am sure any member of academia (or even those in other professional fields and industries that are structured similarly) may deeply connect with the stories here, this book is about anti-Black racism and collates experiences and practices that are specific to the experiences of Black people in academia. Consequently, the language in this book may be most familiar to those who identify with Black or academic culture because the contributors were encouraged to write in a way that mirrors the style of speech common within Black(ademic) spaces. This is not a discriminatory approach, nor is it exclusive; it is simply unapologetically specific and an intentional response to the Eurocentrism that characterizes the greater American society and academia more specifically.

With that in mind, there are other groups for whom these stories may resonate: other academics of color, white academics, Black professionals outside of academia, and laypersons. I can see these stories resonating with Black staff at colleges and universities, too, or perhaps with Black lawyers and judges who understand all too well what it is like to work within an institution that systemically harms you and your people. Black professionals in industries such as insurance, music, film, and production; in fields like technology and business; and in service and trade-related jobs may also feel the effects of anti-Black racism and anti-Blackness in their day-to-day work life and identify with the stories in these pages. Indeed, there may be times when a reader has a story similar to one shared in this book. The point is not that racism affects only Black people in academia or that Blackademics have experienced more discrimination than scholars from other racial groups. The book does not subscribe to the notion of the "oppression olympics"—a term coined in the 1990s by feminist scholar and activist Elizabeth Martínez (1998) to describe a competition between historically marginalized groups for the title of "most oppressed"—because doing so attempts to "identify one sole casualty of injustice, and consequently establishes an inefficient economy of reform, breeds intersectional resentment, and ultimately perpetuates the very oppression it vilifies," according to a *Harvard Political Review* article by

Amen Gashaw (2021). Rather, the point is simply to share stories from a particular vantage point, knowing that doing so is a critical initial step for healing. Moreover, our struggles are inextricably bound together, a point that bell hooks (2000) advanced in her seminal text *Feminist Theory*. Thus, championing issues of anti-Black racism in academia elevates this issue for Black people confronting racism in other work environments and also supports the fight for liberation for groups who confront other systems of oppression, such as classism, homophobia, and sexism.

The primary goals of this book are to help Blackademics transition from trauma to healing—that is, to provide validation that each person is not "the only one" who faces overt and covert racism in the academy; to assure Blackademics that our experience is not idiosyncratic or a product of our individual wrongdoing; to acknowledge the effects of these instances on one's emotional, physical, and mental health and wellness; and to develop a wellness plan. Whether Blackademic readers decide to stay in academia and devise strategies of resistance, resilience, and success or choose to leave academia to find a profession where they are valued, I want them to know that they have options. I hope that after reading this book, each Blackademic is equipped to think about his, her, or their own experiences and stories and channel that energy in productive ways.

Now that I have shared what this book intends to accomplish, let me briefly clarify what it is not. This is not a self-help book for non-Black people, nor is the book a plea for white people to care. It is not an object for white entertainment or consumption. And finally, this book is not an encyclopedia. It is an introductory resource that people who identify as accomplices in this work on anti-Black racism can utilize as they do their own research, find their teachers, and allow themselves to correct myths underlying their subconsciousness and replace them with new information.

HOW TO READ THIS BOOK

The first half of the book prioritizes stories. And so in the pages that follow, you will read counternarratives that will likely challenge some of your beliefs, inspire lively conversations, invoke a range of emotions, and keep the topic of anti-Black racism active. Along the way, you will learn from Blackademic contributors who reflect the great diversity and range within this community and who show that while Blackademics all experience anti-Black racism, the way it manifests and affects each individual varies. There may be some stories that agitate, upset, and disrupt white comfort. But just know that the acute sting of our righteous indignation as Blackademics pales in comparison to the ceaseless retaliation that we experience for the mere act of speaking out. Anyone who is deeply triggered by a story is encouraged to seek out professional resources in the ways that best help you process these events. Please know that the book should not be used to replace therapy and spiritual counseling if the stories cause overwhelming and debilitating emotional responses. Also, there might be places where you are left with more questions than answers or where you want to know more details. The book is designed to start conversations, so consider reading it in a community of peers so that you have space to discuss the emotions, thoughts, and questions that surface. Perhaps your questions reflect a gap in knowledge that a friend, colleague, peer, neighbor, or the like can help address. The book may also inspire you to enact change, and this is an admirable response. But before acting, I encourage you to sit with these stories and the emotions they invoke. Be still, feel, think, and reflect.

Because I hope to move the conversation from one of trauma and pain to a place of validation, understanding, and healing, there are resources in the back of the book to help facilitate this process. Readers, specifically Blackademics, will encounter advice across the book and affirmations in the appendix that you can hold on to. There is also a glossary with key words and definitions for those who are new to academia (or new to certain aspects of it) as well as a suggested reading list. This glossary will enhance understanding of the stories and allow readers to make sense of the layers of meaning. The Black in the Ivory® website (www.blackin-theivory.net) also has some supplementary materials, including reflection questions you can answer honestly by yourself or within community.

I hope that by the end of this book, with some help from the points highlighted in the epilogue and after conversations with others, readers will devise a thoughtful and intentional strategy about what they can do within their sphere of influence. Everyone has the agency to effect change. Even Blackademics can more fully realize our position within academe, how these stories reflect each person's own experiences, and how we can get on (or continue) the path toward healing. It is my sincere hope that everyone walks away from this book enlightened and more committed to elevate the conversation about anti-Black racism in academia and (more importantly) to serve as a catalyst for lasting change in terms of policy, practices, procedures, culture, bylaws, and various other facets of university life that remain intact even after individuals leave.

References

Carmichael, Stokely, and Charles V. Hamilton. 1967. *Black Power: The Politics of Liberation in America*. New York: Vintage.

Crenshaw, Kimberlé, Neil Gotanda, Gary Peller, and Kendall Thomas, eds. 1995. *Critical Race Theory: The Key Writings That Formed the Movement*. New York: New Press.

Delgado, Richard. 1989. "Storytelling for Oppositionists and Others: A Plea for Narrative." *Michigan Law Review* 87, no. 8 (August): 2411–41.

Delgado, Richard, and Jean Stefancic. 2017. *Critical Race Theory: An Introduction*. 3rd ed. New York: New York University Press.

Dumas, Michael J., and Kihana Miraya Ross. 2016. "'Be Real Black for Me': Imagining BlackCrit in Education." *Urban Education* 51, no. 4 (April): 415–42.

Gashaw, Amen. 2021. "In the Oppression Olympics, Don't Go for the Gold." *Harvard Political Review*, October 24, 2021. https://harvardpolitics.com/in-the-oppression-olympics-dont-go-for-the-gold/.

Harris, Angela P., and Carmen G. González. 2012. Introduction to *Presumed Incompetent: The Intersections of Race and Class for Women in Academia*, edited by Gabriella Gutiérrez y Muhs, Yolanda Flores Niemann, Carmen G. González, and Angela P. Harris, 1–14. Logan: Utah State University Press, an imprint of University Press of Colorado.

hooks, bell. 1989. *Talking Back: Thinking Feminist, Thinking Black*. Boston, MA. South End Press.

———. 1990. *Yearning: Race, Gender, and Cultural Politics*. Boston: South End Press.

———. 2000. *Feminist Theory: From Margin to Center*. London, UK: Pluto Press.

Ladson-Billings, Gloria K. 2006. Foreword to *Critical Race Theory in Education: All God's Children Got a Song*, edited by Dixson, Adrienne D., and Celia K. Rousseau, v–xiii. New York: Taylor & Francis.

Martínez, Elizabeth Sutherland. 1998. *De Colores Means All of Us: Latina Views for a Multi-Colored Century*. Boston: South End Press.

McKay, Cassandra L. 2010. "Community Education and Critical Race Praxis: The Power of Voice." *Educational Foundations* 24, no. 1–2 (Winter–Spring): 25–38.

Niemann, Yolanda Flores, Gabriella Gutiérrez y Muhs, and Carmen G. González. 2020. *Presumed Incompetent II: Race, Class, Power, and Resistance of Women in Academia*. Louisville: University Press of Colorado.

Omi, Michael, and Howard Winant. 2014. *Racial Formation in the United States*. New York: Routledge.

"President's Commission on Slavery and the University." 2013. University of Virginia. https://slavery.virginia.edu/universities-studying-slavery/.

Robinson, Michael A. 2017. "Black Bodies on the Ground: Policing Disparities in the African American Community—An Analysis of Newsprint from January 1, 2015, through December 31, 2015." *Journal of Black Studies* 48, no. 6 (April): 551–71.

Wilder, Craig Steven. 2013. *Ebony and Ivy: Race, Slavery, and the Troubled History of America's Universities*. New York: Bloomsbury Press.

y Muhs, Gabriella Gutiérrez, Yolanda Flores Niemann, Carmen G. González, and Angela P. Harris, eds. 2012. *Presumed Incompetent: The Intersections of Race and Class for Women in Academia*. Louisville: University Press of Colorado.

Part I Undergraduate Life

While twenty-first-century American society engages in critical debates about the utility of attending college, especially considering the hefty costs that many Americans cannot afford, the fact remains that hundreds of thousands of young adults each year decide to pursue higher education of some kind—community college, trade school, or four-year public or private university.

Access to higher education and strategies to retain all students and support them to degree completion remain pressing issues that universities, nonprofits, and the federal government attempt to address through various programs. Despite these systems of support, significant challenges remain for Black students. Published research consistently demonstrates that, from college preparation to student retention, graduation rates, and performance in postsecondary education, institutionalized racism is one of the underlying reasons for the disparity in college success between Black students and their peers. For example, violent racialized acts on campus, discrimination by instructors in the classroom, and underfunded cultural programs that facilitate belongingness for students of color are just some of the issues that mar the quality of life for a Black college student.

Even the most famous and notable public figures have a #BlackintheIvory story related to their undergraduate years. For instance, in her critically acclaimed *New York Times* best-selling book *The Light We Carry*, First Lady Michelle Obama writes about her experience as "the only" during her college days at Princeton University. As one can imagine, being a young Black student at an Ivy League college is daunting, partly because the percentages of Black students are so low. In these spaces, one's Blackness is on display and can invoke insecurities, doubts, or feelings of ostracization.

This section on undergraduate life opens with a story by Jael Kerandi, a young Black woman who made university history as the first Black student body president at the University of Minnesota. During her tenure from 2020 to 2021, Kerandi enacted substantial change regarding policing at her university, thereby demonstrating the importance of student activism. Kerandi's efforts drew national attention during the summer of racial reckoning and even inspired me to take action during a time when I was reeling about what I could do to effect change within my sphere of influence. Kerandi's essay sits at the intersection of #BlackintheIvory and #BlackLivesMatter, serving as a powerful opening to this section. Her narrative is followed by those from other Blackademics who share stories about additional dimensions of undergraduate campus life, including life in the dormitories, socializing with peers, classroom experiences, and contending with the ways one's Blackness intersects with other critical identities. Undergraduate years are a formidable and formative season in one's life, and these narratives reinforce the ways in which early college experiences with institutional racism impact Black students' subsequent education, career, and life choices.

2020 VISION

The Impact of Police Brutality through the Lens of a Student in Minneapolis

JAEL KERANDI

Lead Narrative

> I am my great-grandmother's wildest imagination
> I am my grandfather's greatest hope
> I am the pride of my aunts and uncles
> I am the reflection of my sisters and brothers
> I am the derivative of my father's most optimistic dreams
>   and my mother's whispered prayers
> I was the planted seed of sacrifice from my village—
>   and now their fruit
> I hope to one day be the one the young ones look up to—
> for I looked up to so many and God—I looked up to You.

When I arrived at one of the largest public, predominantly white institutions in the nation in 2017, I—like many—was proud of my acceptance to a prestigious institution. As a Black woman, my mirror was hard to find. I believed my previous efforts and discipline would be validated by future professors, classmates, and the community. The admissions materials were filled with photos of students who looked like me—students I assumed to be representative of the campus community. I was wrong. My first few months were filled with questions of identity, place, and purpose.

Black students enrolled at my institution represented around 6.3 percent of the university population (Institutional Data and Research 2020). The implications of this statistic was stark but common and (unfortunately) expected. In classrooms, non-Black students often excluded Black students from the "harder" work in a group project or passively took work away. Other students moved away from us in working spaces to keep from being in the same group or to seem associated with us. Professors asked questions like, "Do Black people watch movies?" and career advisors steered us away from the competitive opportunities in favor of something "more within [our] reach." No one believed in us because no one expected us to be there. And for those of us who "slipped through the cracks," we were supposed to be grateful that our merit had been validated rather than dismissed.

The small percentage of Black students on campus faced other consequences. Microaggressions toward Black students were an omnipresent reflection of campus sentiment: "Students like you are so lucky to be here." "You speak English so well." "Did you get that job through a diversity program?" Going to an institution where we didn't see ourselves reflected or respected felt like we were paying a tax that was not levied on the entire population. People asked to touch our hair or constantly sheepishly gawked at the artful and colorful patterns weaved in our scalps. Throughout the month of February, everyone seemed to tiptoe around us just a little more. We got weary comments that advised us to steer clear of "walking near THAT side of campus," which just happened to be a part of the city that was majority Black (Cedar Lake Ventures 2018). The pressures of academic work, extracurricular activities, recreation, athletics, and earning income often absorbed our lives and left little room to challenge the status quo. Our Blackness was a part of us, but unless beneficial to them they sought to see us separate ourselves from our own being. But we resisted, through our love of who we are, would become, and were.

In the spring of my first year, our Somali Student Association held its annual Somali Night on campus. As the event came to a close, law enforcement was called, ostensibly in response to some minor incident. Police treated students and their families with flagrant disrespect and blatant disregard. The evening was shattered by tear gas in the air, the brute police presence, and flashing lights as campus and city police took over. I begged a police officer to tell me what was going on, and he yelled at me to move on. It was as if time stood still. I will never forget what I saw in the officer's eyes: terror. Behind law enforcement's loudest bark and bite was fear. We posed such a high threat to the officers' power. Yet, what they didn't see was the same fear reflected in our eyes—for our lives and the threat they posed to our daily livelihood. The very individuals charged to keep us safe were the ones we actually needed protection from.

The following year, I pleaded with our administration to address policing matters on our campus. I put the issue on countless meeting agendas and tried to have the conversation with the right people. But no one seemed to want to have it, and frankly, no one seemed to care. The same students who were frustrated were still paying tuition. Administrators treated the event like it never happened. They didn't get it. I was so frustrated at the administration's response, but my constant questioning bore no fruit. The loss of life is not the commencement marker for trauma, so while there had been no death that night, the true casualty was the depleting faith that our university would keep us safe and the memories we would never forget.

I had a desire to ensure that the experiences we were having didn't become the norm for future students. In the spring of my junior year, I served as the first Black undergraduate student body president, inheriting an organization of over thirty-five staff, my own chief of staff, and more than 100 at-large representatives, senators, and student group representatives. I was responsible not only for leading the organization but also for representing and advocating for the entire student body to our senior administration and Board of Regents. I was humbled to serve in the role, but the position came with different expectations for me as a Black woman. I often felt like I was not allowed to say the wrong thing. My advice had to be delivered in the exact right format and with pitch-perfect tone. During my executive board meetings, if I disagreed with matters, the way in which I disagreed was more important than the argument itself. While this may ring true for most leaders, it felt like a heightened task for me. It was as if mistakes were not allowed. I was a Black woman, and to those watching, that was two strikes. "You have to work twice as hard to get half" was my reality. Administrators ignored my repeated emails, and my peers questioned my decisions. To this day, I have emails that were never responded to. At times, my silence was interpreted as an "attitude" rather than reflective. It seemed that everyone feared what I would say next—would there be an outburst? Yet, I had to remind myself that the work I had been given to do was much greater and those very same passions and mannerisms were paramount to fuel the advocacy for the most important stakeholders: our students.

Neither the stifling university bureaucracy nor tenured intellectuals were prepared to accept the voice of a Black woman. Walking into rooms, I often felt doubted, intellectually suspected, and questioned. I felt even more compelled not only to be present but to ensure that my presence was felt. I was committed to contributing to an environment that did not uphold ideologies that enforce and enable discriminatory and racist policies.

The summer before my senior year, everything changed. On May 26, 2020, we woke up to our social media feed inundated by graphic videos depicting the murder of George Floyd at the intersection of Chicago and

Thirty-Eighth, mere miles from the university where I lived in Minneapolis. The brutality of his murder was clear. Silence was not an option. I wasn't just the undergraduate student body president; I was a Black one. It was my duty to call upon our university to demonstrate that there was no tolerance for the lynching ("the public killing of an individual who has not received any due process" [NAACP 2022]) of our people and that the racist actions of the Minneapolis Police Department (MPD) mandated a clear stance. Our university contracted with the MPD in several ways and had close relations with the University of Minnesota Police Department (UMPD). I wrote a letter to our administration demanding that our university sever all ties with the MPD within twenty-four hours (Kerandi 2020). The final paragraph of the letter read as follows:

> There is no middle ground. The police are murdering Black men with no meaningful repercussions. This is not a problem of some other place or some other time. This is happening right here in Minneapolis. We no longer tolerate the ineffective, inconsistent "bias training" that rarely serves as more than a fig leaf. . . . We clearly and without hesitation DEMAND that the University of Minnesota Police Department ceases any partnerships with the Minneapolis Police Department *immediately*. . . . As a land-grant institution, statements professing appreciation of diversity and inclusion are empty and worthless if they are not backed up by action. A man was murdered. It is our job as an institution to exert whatever pressure we can to keep our students safe and demand justice in our city and state. We expect a reply to this concern within 24 hours of receipt.

The needs of Black students had gone unheard, unrecognized, and, most importantly, unanswered for far too long. Our safety and protection were just as important as they were for our non-Black peers sitting right next to us. Our demand was non-negotiable; we were disproportionately impacted by the actions of law enforcement. We deemed it necessary to ensure that our university repudiated its racist practices and the ones of the MPD. It was important that university officials upheld their outlined values. It was their time to stand on moral ground, invalidate the thoughts of white European forefathers, and uphold our Black ancestors' dreams.

And they did, but not to the fullest extent. Within twenty-four hours, the university cut two contracts with the UMPD: its work with athletic events and K9 units. (A full version of the president's response is available online; Gabel 2020.)

It is not just nominal representation within the institution that matters; it is the evidence that representation provides—evidence that we have for so long been excelling in ways that have often not been recognized. Representation also proves that we are here, and it acknowledges the accolades that have often gone on unappreciated and hidden. Representation is the importance of lecturing on Black Wall Street in business classes and discussing redlining and its impact on our city when we teach urban development. It is the work of Black scholars assigned in courses and read by students across majors. Representation is not a matter of the most apt, but it is a matter of accessibility, removal of bureaucracy, and destruction of the need for rigid control. Representation matters because it can serve as one of the greatest, most blatant reckonings.

Black students deserve the space within the ivory tower.

To all Black students: your education is not the only key, but your ability to learn will unlock doors for you. Your greatest thoughts and aspirations are meant to be recognized, and your wildest dreams are meant to be accomplished and realized. **You don't need permission from anyone to succeed.** All that is needed is your internal will and discipline. I walked away from my institution with hope—the hope that our small steps will turn into strides and then a sprint. I walked away knowing that changes in our funding structure for scholarships had shifted; scholarships remove the financial barrier that so many Black students face to attend higher education, a critical piece considering Black students leave school with more debt than their white counterparts (Hanson 2023). Our institution will be in a better place because we are determined to make it a better place. We have our own backs; we are comrades. The halls of the institutions of higher education are not only for us; they belong to us.

References

Cedar Lake Ventures. 2018. "Race and Ethnicity in Cedar-Riverside, Minneapolis, Minnesota." The Demographic Statistical Atlas of the United States – Statistical Atlas. https://statisticalatlas.com/neighborhood/Minnesota/Minneapolis /Cedar-Riverside/Race-and-Ethnicity.

Gabel, Joan. 2020. "Update from the President on the Death of Minneapolis Resident George Floyd." University of Minnesota, May 27, 2020. https:// president.umn.edu/sites/president.umn.edu/files/2020-06/May%2027 %20Update%20from%20the%20President.pdf.

Hanson, Melanie. 2023. "Student Loan Debt by Race." Education Data Initiative. Last updated September 3, 2023. https://educationdata.org/student-loan-debt -by-race.

Institutional Data and Research. 2020. "Enrollments." University of Minnesota. https://idr.umn.edu/student/enrollment.

Kerandi, Jael. 2020. "Letter to the University of Minnesota." May 26, 2020. https://docs.google.com/document/d/16gq6ZoCIvu5SvEmzQig _rIm68qslGxdT2tfwpc73kpg/edit.
NAACP (National Association for the Advancement of Colored People). 2022. "History of Lynching in America." NAACP. https://naacp.org/find-resources /history-explained/history-lynching-america.

ACCESS DENIED
A Black Student and a Forgotten Identity
ANISHA MELTON

It was sophomore year at an upstate university known for its broadcasting program. The incident occurred at the dining hall where I worked, frequently ate with my suite-mates, and lived close to. My suite-mates and I were rushing to make it for brunch, and by the time we arrived at the entrance to the dining hall, I realized I had forgotten my campus ID. I didn't think much of it as there had been multiple times when students forgot their ID, wrote their names down on a clipboard near the card swiper, and went to eat. When I approached the ID swiper, I saw a red-headed, wrinkly short white woman I had worked with before. She and I never interacted much, but we had worked in the kitchen of the dining hall together numerous times. I greeted her by name, explained my situation, and proceeded to write down my name and ID number. She then stated in a raspy voice that the university would invalidate my ID because I wrote my name on the clipboard. "Wait, why?" I asked. "This is my first time writing my name down." She didn't reply and looked away instead. I thought nothing of it and went to get food.

She proceeded to yell out, "Excuse me!" I thought she was talking to someone else, so I continued to get things to eat. But she chased after me, got in my face, and yelled that I couldn't eat. In that moment, the packed dining hall grew extremely quiet as everyone, including my suite-mates, gawked at us in silence. An array of emotions collided within me, ultimately leaving me feeling embarrassed, guilty, and verbally and emotionally attacked but above all powerless and angry. My mind kept telling me that I was in danger, so I felt scared; but I also wanted to gain control and be strong. Most of all, though, I really wanted someone to stand up for me and console me. The reality was that I was hungry, upset, and scared.

At this point, I hadn't responded to the aggressor since I was trying to brainstorm an exit strategy: *How can I remain strong and not blow this situation out of proportion? How can I get out of this situation as quickly as possible? Why me?*

I tried to reason with the aggressor by speaking in a normal tone, but that failed. She wouldn't listen and didn't stop yelling. In fact, as we went back and forth, she instructed a supervisor, who knew me well, to call campus police because I "wouldn't leave." Once she said that, I walked to the dining hall exit and told the supervisor that I wanted a written apology from the aggressor. I didn't return to brunch that day. The next time I saw the redheaded woman, she tried to avoid me, then delivered a half-assed apology about her having a bad day and taking it out on me. When I further pressed her about her aggression toward me, she replied, "Listen, I said I was sorry," and walked away.

The worst part was the people who left the dining hall on the day of the incident apologizing on the woman's behalf, telling me I deserved better and how wrong she was. I wanted to cry so badly, but I forced myself to hold it together because I didn't want to seem weak. On top of that, my roommate and others close to me at the time invalidated my thinking and even told me that I should let it go. In my roommate's words, "I honestly don't think it had anything to do with race." Others said, "You'll never get her to write an apology letter," and they were right. In the end, I knew I didn't want to work in the dining hall forever, but this propelled me to quickly resign. I applied for and accepted a more uplifting campus position as a desk attendant. Being surrounded by individuals who respected me, my hard work, and my contributions was the fresh start I needed and deserved.

A GRIM ENCOUNTER

JEWELL STEWART LAY

Part of my experience throughout undergrad was being forced to attend classes in a cemetery, or at least a visual representation of one. For weeks every winter, small crosses uniformly covered every inch of the quad as far as the eye could see. It was intentionally intrusive, provocative, and uncomfortable—calculated to illicit discomfort, as is the case in many protests against abortion. Displays of religiosity were not uncommon at my private, white Catholic university situated at the tip of the Bible Belt, but this one was particularly gruesome.

In my junior year, the campus ministry decided to increase the impact of its protest by tying ribbons to represent the races of those most likely to receive an abortion. Hundreds of black ribbons were tied to represent the thousands of abortions had by Black women across the country. This is a university that, at the time, was 95 percent white, with an almost entirely white leadership team. As a Black woman on campus, I felt targeted. During those few weeks, it felt like I was being stared at wherever I went, singled out for the desperate actions other women had taken.

To make it worse, the campus ministry handed out pro-life pamphlets around campus. Black babies in distress stared back at me as I received this pamphlet right in the middle of one of the several theology classes we were required to take. This was a class in which I was one of only two Black students present, both of us women. No other race was included in this horrifying collage on the cover. This moment has been forever seared in my mind as the first time I consciously knew the importance of kinship in academia. This woman and I knew of each other (there were so few of us that we all knew of each other) but had never spoken. However, in that moment, we both knew in our souls that it was us against the world.

This moment also profoundly marked the first time I ever had to fight in class over racial injustice. Sis and I looked at each other and prepared to battle, knowing full well that this protest was about to fall on deaf ears. Right in the middle of class, I attacked. Passionately, though I did not have the language at the time, I brought up the racist history of segregation and economic disenfranchisement, which has contributed to the disparity of upward social and economic mobility experienced today. I brought up how trivializing this message was harmful, as it is the reason such a disparity in abortions exists. I even brought up how racist and stigmatizing those pamphlets were, considering the small percentage of Black students on campus.

After addressing all these points, I was brushed off. The team that was distributing the pamphlets replied that the campus ministry was only addressing the truth of the situation and that "facts don't lie." My compatriot in arms and I went silent after that. Yet the battle took a heavy toll. To be both Black and a woman in a space of hostility is to risk alienation at the first sign of your passion. To be branded with the stigma of being an argumentative Black woman is a death blow for relationship building, social climbing, or anything that requires being "likable." At a very early age, I learned that self-advocacy only brought about more pain.

All these years later, the one thing that still astounds me is how thoughtless such a protest was toward the few Black students (and certainly Black women) enrolled. To create a space of hostility in which any group may be targeted is unthinkably callous. I left class that day feeling despondent, embarrassed, and hopeless—desperately wanting people to understand the truth of the situation yet also fervently hoping everyone forgot I spoke up at all. Unfortunately, neither was the case.

When BIPOC folks (Black, Indigenous, and People of Color) argue that diversity in leadership is fundamental, this is precisely what we mean. Not only was this protest extremely alienating toward the few Black people enrolled at this university, but it wasn't even transformative. No one left feeling more informed or more likely to act. The only thing that was accomplished was that my classmates had a fresh story to share about the Black girl who dared to speak up in class.

MISSED APPOINTMENT

AJ

I was a junior in undergrad in 2017 when it happened.

I had been accepted to two summer research internships and had to decide which one to take. My advisor told me that he knew a professor at the other major university in the area who was well acquainted with researchers at both internship sites and could give me advice. He arranged a meeting for me with that professor the following Sunday. I was ecstatic to meet a renowned expert in my field and elated that my advisor had thought enough of me to take the trouble to introduce me to this person. Determined to make a good impression, I read as much of the University of Chicago professor's work as I could understand, and on that Sunday, I put on my best clothes to go see him.

I arrived at the university address given to me by the professor a good twenty-five minutes early. I wanted to make sure that I would be on time and could review my notes before meeting him. Ordinarily, I would have waited outside an unfamiliar building until ushered in, but my dress pants offered no protection against the midwestern winter, and I was starting to lose feeling in my legs due to the cold. I decided to go in to warm up so that I wouldn't be shivering when I went to shake the professor's hand for the first time. I had been waiting in the lobby of that building for about five minutes when a white student walked into the room, saw me there, and immediately turned around. I didn't think much of it until fifteen minutes later when a police car pulled up to the building. A white officer and a Black officer got out of the car and quickly approached me. The white officer started asking questions and barking orders too fast for me to respond. He had his hand on a black object on his belt the whole time, and I was too scared of it to focus on what he was saying. I froze with a terrified look on my face, unable to utter a word. Then the Black officer cut between us and started calmly asking questions. He politely asked me who I was and what I was doing in this building on a Sunday, so I gave him my driver's license and student ID before showing him the email from the professor clearly inviting me to be in this building at this time for a research meeting. Then the Black officer handed back my ID, told me I was free to wait there, and left with his partner. As soon as they were out of sight, I started bawling. I couldn't keep the tears from streaming down my face, and I didn't want to meet the professor like that. I just went home and emailed him, saying that I had gotten sick and needed to reschedule.

Now, a few years later, I'm a PhD student at a top research university, and I always arrive late to events at unfamiliar places. I hate reinforcing the stereotype that Black people are always late to things, but I don't feel safe going in until I know that someone who can vouch for my being there has already arrived. Making good first impressions is less important to me than ensuring my personal safety, now that I know how harshly I may be received in unfamiliar environments.

DOUBLE MAJOR DISCOURAGED
ANONYMOUS

As I attempted to double major in two heavily related subjects at a large private PWI (predominantly white institution), I was met with discrimination and difficulty after calling out racist and nonfactual rhetoric in one of the programs.

After questioning the teaching staff for saying that you cannot eat certain things (like leafy vegetables) in an African country because it was "unsafe" and "dangerous" (due to ill-founded assumptions about the safety of water and sanitation), I was attacked systematically and institutionally. It began with me being chastised in class and was followed by increased difficulty in completing my studies. I was in the major for the first program, and when I attempted to add the second major, I faced numerous complications (with my faculty advisor being the main instructor in the course). The major was cross-listed across two colleges, and a rule from the opposite college I was enrolled in was then applied to me (that you cannot double major). I was pretty angry about this. I had the fighting spirit in me, so I decided to face this problem head-on. After protesting and having higher-up people connect with a "curriculum committee," I was finally able to enroll in and complete both majors.

Later, when I filed to do a senior thesis, it was temporarily blocked by my faculty advisor, the one who was the lead instructor for the course in which I was having problems. This person believed I would not be able to handle all the things I was doing at the time. While my academic plan was tough, I had shown that I was perfectly able to handle the course load and had previously planned my entire course of study to accommodate both majors. I had to arrange a meeting to "explain the situation," in which I was able to advocate to do my thesis in addition to my other commitments. In the same meeting, when my advisor half-heartedly asked what I would do after graduation, I said I was applying to graduate school. The advisor asked whether I had letters of recommendation, and when I said no, the advisor said, "Thank God." I found other references because this person would not have written one.

Upon receiving PhD program offers, I faced ridiculous and inflammatory hurdles in just trying to attend programs on their visit days. I was taking a course in the major that the faculty advisor was over and needed an accommodation (which was extremely justified): I had been accepted to a few top ten PhD programs in the social sciences and wanted to attend a visit day at one of those departments (in which PhD visit days are standard across disciplines). My professor had scheduled an exam that day, and I asked whether I could have a makeup exam so I could attend the event for my top choice department I had been admitted to. The professor said no because it was not a good reason, but of course I went anyway. Ultimately, the professor forced me to find a proctor and take the exam during the middle of the visit day.

I have spoken once to my faculty advisor since the thesis issue (after running into this person haphazardly in the hall), and the advisor happily congratulated me on being accepted into many PhD programs and having chosen one to attend.

PROGRESS DEFERRED

CHRISTOPHER R. ORTEGA

As an undergraduate, I faced many of the microaggressions experienced by BIPOC students, such as being singled out to represent an entire group, having to listen to ignorant comments from classmates while instructors do not correct them, and all the other things that make some feel unwelcome in the academy. One example that has always stuck with me occurred during a cultural anthropology course. A topic related to Puerto Rico was being discussed, and a classmate used the opportunity to state his opinion that "immigrants" from Puerto Rico are dirty and bring diseases to the United States. The instructor stopped and looked at me and another student whose family originally came from Puerto Rico. The way the instructor left it to us to explain both the factual errors and insensitivity in the student's comment was a frustrating experience. We made our best effort to disabuse our peer of his ideas before the instructor moved on to a new topic without addressing the issue directly. Around this time, my university conducted a racial climate survey, and many of the comments detailed in the report (for example, being put on the spot to represent an entire group, having insensitive comments from peers go unchallenged by instructors, and the like) echoed my own experiences. Twelve years following the 2005 report, I secured a job as an assistant professor at the same institution, and not much had changed. In fact, we just completed another racial climate survey, and many of the comments were the same. But now I'm in a position where I can help enact the change I didn't see from my professors, and that is a triumph, in my opinion.

JUGGLING TWO WORLDS

ANDRAYA YEARWOOD

Spotlight Narrative

I was sitting in my chair in my freshman Biology 101 class at my illustrious HBCU, one that was needed for my major but still enjoyable nonetheless. We were reviewing the intellectual abilities of human beings, specifically determined by race. At first thought, you might assume this conversation to have been one on Black prosperity, highlighting the societal advancements of Black leaders and our overall high intellectual abilities. My Black parents have always instilled in me the importance of Black intelligence. My professor happened to be Black, too.

You might also have assumed wrong.

My Black biology professor proceeded to make a comment so ignorant, all I could do was stare in both awe and utter confusion.

"White people are more intellectually advanced than us Black people . . ."

And then I zoned out. I refused to continue to listen to such blatant dishonesty.

What sense does that even make?

I genuinely could not wrap my head around what I'd just heard because of how contradictory a statement it was. The professor rambled on about how evolutionary bases for disparities in social outcomes between racial groups exist and have existed in our society. In particular, many so-called experts argue that Black people fare worse than white people because they tend to be less naturally intelligent. I tried my best to still be engaged with the lesson, but his words would not stop replaying in my mind.

That experience really made me realize how crucial Black excellence and intelligence truly are. The lack of positive Black and Brown representation within the areas of scholarly intelligence has a detrimental effect on the communal advancement of the Black and Brown community. My professor's comments only motivated me to further my own Black excellence. I began emailing surrounding universities to ask for student internship opportunities and joined clubs that I was genuinely interested in.

I was determined to put myself out there, especially due to the competitiveness of today's society. It was, and still continues to be, imperative for Black trans women like me to be seen and heard in spaces that we are consistently denied. It has been very difficult for me to find someone similar to me in my future career field, as there is seldom representation of Black trans women in positions of policy and government. If there is no representation, then I must be my own representation for myself.

After receiving emails from various professors in my career field, most of them saying that there weren't any active opportunities or programs at that time, I was stumped on what else I could do. I really wanted to work in a university setting, but I figured that it just wasn't my time yet. I decided to focus on working during the summer break, but my motivation for pursuing other undergraduate educational and career opportunities was not yet lost on me. I knew that what my professor had said stemmed from pure ignorance, but I still felt a need to prove him, and probably others, wrong. The countless misconceptions about Black women, especially in spaces around academia, have been used to degrade self-confidence and intellectual awareness in the community for centuries. The reclamation of our own assets and advantages has been long overdue.

Once I returned to campus in the fall of 2021 for my sophomore semester, I made it a point to get more involved with the community around me. In the first month of classes, I interviewed to be a Lavender Liaison for my university's LGBTA Resource Center. I knew that I wanted to be a leader and role model for other LGBTQIA+ students at my university, and I couldn't think of a better way to do it. As a Lavender Liaison, I could really be that helping hand for the students who needed it on campus and in the Durham community. I also began volunteering at my university's Women's Center two times each week. During my time in both the LGBTA Resource Center and the Women's Center, I learned so much not only about the intersectionality of being Black, a woman, and a member of the LGBTQIA+ community but also about how those intersectional identities directly and indirectly impacted me. I took home with me each day a better understanding of what really made me who I am. I can even recall making it my number one mission to continue to attend an HBCU for grad school. I knew the importance of gaining the tools to fully embrace my own Blackness in a way that I would not have been able to at a PWI.

Despite my biology professor's words of extreme foolishness, I will always be grateful to my university for providing me with the guidance to fully step into each part of me. Since arriving on campus my freshman year in August 2020, I have put in the effort to excel in every area, whether academically, socially, or even personally. His senseless words are what motivate me to continue to do better in everything I set my mind or hand to. I know that each day, Black women are constantly being diminished and belittled due to the negative preconceptions that are made by people around them. I am taking it upon myself to break those harmful stereotypes that have been, and will only continue to be, detrimental to our collective and individual success.

REBUILDING BLACK HISTORY AS AN UNDERGRADUATE

DANIELLE GEATHERS

Spotlight Narrative

During my first undergraduate semester at MIT, I had the opportunity to take a course focused on the institution's history with slavery, which was inspired by the nonfiction work *Ebony and Ivy* by Craig Steven Wilder. As I became increasingly familiar with the MIT student experience, I benefited from the class's archival research, which oriented me to the true history of the institute. My research project focused on the first graduating class of 1868 of all white, all wealthy males—and their ties to slavery.

As a sixth-generation Floridian and a descendant of enslaved Africans in the United States, I was constantly reminded of the complicated implications of my presence at a land-grant institution founded by slave owners. Land that had been inhabited by Indigenous peoples was the foundation upon which the institution was constructed. Despite its public roots with state and federal resources courtesy of the federal Morrill Act, signed by Abraham Lincoln, the institution's culture was cultivated to be private and elite. Several students in the first class of graduates were family friends of the founder and members of the New England elite.

My research has revealed that the innovation of racial and gender inclusivity was too often undermined by the myth that diversity contradicted excellence. Programs at MIT such as Project Interphase, designed for underrepresented minorities, became race neutral. Designated seats at certain tables became undesignated. Most shockingly, the number of students who identified as descendants of enslaved persons decreased as the number of Black students rose to the present number.

Reflecting on the lack of Black women and generational African Americans at the most competitive engineering school in the country hardened my belief in the need to push for radical change within the ivory tower. But my rebellion against the constraints of the academy formally began in my predominantly white private high school as I publicly pushed back against the restrictive dress code, wrote op-eds criticizing school administrators, and founded the school's first Black student union. My activism in high school was isolating yet rewarding, and I was eager to join a "progressive" environment in the Northeast, which was very different from my experiences in Florida.

Excited to be a part of the Black community at MIT with an established history of student activism, I joined three working committees of the Black Students' Union. I was also intrigued by an engineering education that could teach me to solve complex problems, but I quickly became dissatisfied by the lack of Black students in my introductory classes. I also found that, unlike my high school experience, I couldn't escape my predominantly white environment by going to my family home once the school day was over. I worked, ate, and slept on campus and was constantly surrounded by reminders that the institution wasn't designed for me. Whether it was the financial aid policies requiring noncustodial parent income information, the women's bathroom being two floors away, or the lecture seats being too narrow for my hips, MIT did not seem like a place for me as a Black woman. Fortunately, several Black students who had gone before me faced the same issues, which drove them to create systems of their own to support Black student success and wellness. They founded organizations like the Black Students' Union, fought for designated space in the form of the BSU lounge, and embedded themselves into admissions processes. All these changes created a better environment for future generations of students like me.

While I appreciated being in a strong community of activists, I came to learn that problems in the ivory tower, and at MIT more specifically, tended to be much more nuanced than I expected. There was a new language in conversations and many more moving parts. Working groups, ad hoc committees, and strategic plans with vague language were utilized to avoid confrontation with urgent recommendations, while senior administrators, board members, and deans pointed fingers, creating massive confusion about responsibility. Despite this, I felt compelled to run for president of MIT's Undergraduate Association to prioritize equity and inclusion on campus, hoping to utilize political savvy to avoid some of the institutional delay tactics. I made this decision in my living room after being sent home because of the COVID-19 pandemic, a vulnerable position for many underrepresented students whose voices weren't heard in the rooms where decisions were made. I had a clear vision for the future of our student government, which came from an understanding of underrepresented students and our needs for an inclusive environment, flexible financial aid, and racially conscious safety policies.

My first weeks in office involved pandemic management, navigating the Trump administration's antagonistic immigration policies, and shepherding our student body through a national reckoning on race. Despite these already hefty challenges, I needed to fulfill promises to my community, a mandate involving ambitious plans, such as renaming Columbus Day as Indigenous Peoples' Day before October and distributing free menstrual products throughout campus. My presidential goals forced the development of my cooperative strategy as I learned the importance of shoulder-to-shoulder tactics.

As the first Black woman to hold my current office, I felt tremendous pressure to be the face of the racial reckoning movement that I wasn't prepared for. The cognitive dissonance of being praised for my accomplishments on MSNBC and in *Time* and *People* magazines while being unable to articulate my feelings following the murder of George Floyd triggered depression and anxiety, which forced me to lean on a support system of fellow Black student body presidents.

Our conversations expanded my perception of my role and compelled me to push the bounds of a typical student body president's duties. After weeks of brainstorming potential responses to the movement, I was inspired to design a plan for MIT to use a Black-owned bank. Utilizing the vast network of Black alumni involved in finance, I was able to revise and vet the idea with several bank executives and MIT Board of Trustee members before contacting MIT's vice president for finance. Over a year later, MIT has taken steps to increase support of Black-owned businesses in innovative ways.

While the institution is heralded for its students' intelligence, industriousness, and work ethic, MIT was, because of the color of my family's skin, made largely unavailable as an option for my grandparents and those who came before them. Now, more than 150 years after that all-white, all-male, and all-wealthy first graduating class, I am that much more aware that my position as the first Black woman president of my undergraduate institution exceeds the wildest dreams of my ancestors, particularly my late grandfather who went to an all-Black public grade school in the South for three months less than his white counterparts. Despite his limited opportunity, he encouraged me to push for change. Change takes more than just me, though. I have been blessed to be a part of a strong cohort of Black student body presidents at both HBCUs and Ivy Plus institutions over the course of my two years as president. Together, we are actively learning from the hardships and sacrifices of the giants on whose shoulders we stand as we push our universities to think differently about diversity.

WHAT I WISH SOMEONE HAD TOLD ME

The contributors to this book wrote advice to Blackademic readers under the prompt "What I wish someone had told me" when they were pursuing their undergraduate studies and graduate degrees, moving up the professional ranks, and thinking about alternatives to academia entirely. They range in length, scope, and tenor. The advice from contributors to the "Undergraduate Life" section is shared below, but you are encouraged to read advice from contributors in the other sections too because their words may resonate with you.

Find out whether your institution has a diversity and inclusion office or a similar place where you can report race-related occurrences, whether they were on campus or in a neighboring town. For me, it took two years and a strenuous capstone internship to find out I could've reported my aggressor. Second, befriend individuals who will have your back when you're in racially aggressive situations, not invalidate your experiences and feelings. Third, please seek therapy if a racially charged situation was traumatic in any way, such as causing you to relive it constantly or suffer panic attacks. Remember, these incidents can take a toll on your mental health, so take time and the necessary actions to heal your mind and soul. Last, do not blame yourself if a non-BIPOC is randomly aggressive to you; you didn't do anything wrong. Existing while being Black is nothing to be ashamed about.
   —Anisha

Kinship. I cannot overemphasize the importance of creating and actively maintaining spaces in which your experiences are centered, embraced, and understood. Entering any space that may turn hostile opens you to a wide variety of aggression, some of which you may not have the capacity to fight against. Holding a sanctuary space filled with people who share that burden is a godsend for affirmation. Having allies or coconspirators who will fight with you can be the difference between survival and failure.
   —Jewell

Negotiate your salary before you start. They will almost definitely lowball you with their first offer.

—AJ

Graduate school is not a romantic endeavor, and depending on your experience and background, it can be a very political undertaking. That is, the relationship between a Black person in the academy and faculty is political; with the university, it is political; with publishers and journals, it is political; with conferences, it is political; with everything, it is political! Also, my completion as a graduate student is political, not just in terms of the academy but also in terms of family and society. What would my family think if I am tired of the academy and of their expectations of my participation within it? What about the stigma of deciding it is not for me? Sometimes it feels like a trap or puzzle that you cannot escape once you are within.

—Anonymous

Continue to be resilient. Too much of the history of Black people has been the experience of oppression and discrimination. We have been subjected to low-class citizenship in a country we were kidnapped and brought to. Our freedom and happiness are far overdue. It is time we take back the knowledge and wisdom that was, and still continues to be, stolen from us. So much of the African and African American diaspora is rich in intelligence and culture, something that only advances our own prosperity within our communities. It is a necessity, now more than ever, to continue to prosper in the face of those who wish to disadvantage you. We, as Black people, must come together, regardless of how cliché it may sound. There is power in banding together and connecting ourselves with one another. Building strong, positive relationships with people who are like-minded and who are united through mutual experiences can only catapult our societal success for generations.

—Andraya

Part 2 **Surviving Graduate School**

After college, many adults grapple with the decision to pursue a higher level of education. The decision is an important one because of the relational, time, and financial strain that postsecondary education can have on an individual. But for some, the possibility of elevating one's career prospects far outweighs these potential costs.

Graduate school options are wide-ranging. People can pursue a master's degree to deepen their knowledge of a particular subject through an intensive learning experience. People can also pursue professional doctorates, which are internationally recognized degrees designed for working professionals to put high-level academic knowledge into practice. These include doctor of medicine (MD), juris doctor (JD), doctor of psychology (PsyD), and doctor of education (EdD) degrees. Alternatively, those who endeavor to conduct research and produce knowledge in the academic sector may pursue a doctor of philosophy (PhD) degree, the primary objective of which is to develop advanced research skills and build new knowledge that can be disseminated through publication in peer-reviewed academic journals and book monographs.

No matter the degree or program of study, one's time in graduate school can be marked as a time of great sacrifice— and that is putting it lightly. In fact, Tricia Hersey, founder of the Nap Ministry and author of the *New York Times* bestseller *Rest Is Resistance: A Manifesto*, critiques "grind culture" for equating productivity with self-worth and reducing "our divine bodies" to the level of machinery, an epiphany that stemmed from her exhaustion during graduate school in a seminary program. Graduate school expectations often include taking multiple courses at a time, perhaps three to four per term; reading copious journal articles and lengthy books in preparation for each two- to three-hour weekly seminar; writing thirty-page term papers;

participating on research teams and publishing that research in academic outlets; and working in an assistantship (for example, teaching an undergraduate course) for very modest pay. These expectations can at times become too much to bear during one's graduate school journey. And these are just the professional obligations that many students juggle alongside children and partners and caregiving, religious, and other personal responsibilities.

This grueling educational experience is compounded by the formidable barriers that Blackademics confront: navigating the educational challenges, personal hardships, and systemic barriers of anti-Blackness and anti-Black racism that are present only for Black students.

Blackademics in this section, Surviving Graduate School, share personal accounts of their graduate school experiences. Some write about recent experiences as current students, while others in faculty positions recollect incidents that happened five, ten, or even twenty years ago yet remain etched in their memory. The section opens with an essay by Eduardo Bonilla-Silva, a renowned and internationally acclaimed American sociologist. Writing from his vantage point as a full professor, Bonilla-Silva recalls the challenges and the culture of whiteness and white supremacy he faced as a graduate student—a culture that even today reminds him that accolades do not protect him from discrimination or mistreatment.

DON'T BELIEVE THE HYPE!
On the False Universalism of the American Akademy
EDUARDO BONILLA-SILVA

Lead Narrative

Public Enemy's song "Don't Believe the Hype" conveys an important truth about the nature of America. The akademy, as any other institution or organization in a racialized society, expresses and reproduces systemic racism. Its claim to universalism is ultimately false, as the academy does not address how racism shapes its very core. The academy is organizationally and culturally white. This means that Black and Brown people are made to feel at best like guests in institutions of higher learning. While some people of color deny racism and others suffer in silence, most of us do not take the abuse and disrespect we encounter by turning our cheeks. We fight the racist incidents and practices we experience, which range from the seemingly innocent microaggressions (during my first semester of grad school, my stats professor highlighted in red ink the 98 I got on my first test but did not do the same for white students) to the outrageous incidents (a professor came into my office mad as hell looking for a coat she claimed had been stolen from her office). We fight, and fight, and fight some more.

As a Black Puerto Rican, I have not been especially welcomed in academic environs from the moment I arrived at the University of Wisconsin in 1984 to pursue my PhD in sociology. I recall meetings among students of color to discuss racial issues in the Sociology Department and assess how to best make our case to the faculty that racism was central to the organizational structure and cultural life of the department. We mostly failed in our "rational" efforts at convincing our overwhelmingly white professors. For example, in the late 1980s, Chicano students on campus objected to a person the department wanted to hire as part of a university-wide targeted Chicano hire (the person was not Chicano but Latinx from South America). As we were all then members of a group called the Minority Coalition and I was the only sociology student in the organization, they asked me to speak about the matter in a departmental meeting after they made their plea. I told faculty that their disinterest in wanting to learn about who qualified as a legitimate Chicano and what constituted Chicano scholarship was subtly racist. Would they hire a person specializing in environmental sociology for a position in demography? They obviously would not because the specialty did not fit the job, much like being a "Latino" did not make the applicant in question a Chicano or a scholar with expertise on Chicano issues. When I finished, I asked whether they had any questions for me, and none did. They ignored me politely, thanked me, and let me out of the room. I learned then that a practice I label now as "inclusive exclusion" (Bonilla-Silva 2019) structures a lot of our life chances in the academy. We are in departments in HWCUs (historically white colleges and universities) (Bonilla-Silva and Peoples 2022), attend meetings, and sit in most rooms where things are discussed, but our views matter little. In many cases, decisions are made in private white settings (such as in offices, bars, homes, and so on) before official meetings occur. Interestingly, *after* such meetings, several "progressive" faculty let me know they agreed with all I had said, to which I replied, "If you agreed with me, why didn't you say *anything* when it counted?"

To be clear, race affects everyone; hence, I want to illustrate a few of the powerful ways white graduate students benefit from the racialized organization of departments. White students get incorporated quickly into research projects, interact easily with faculty, and are able to work one-on-one with white faculty. But does this happen because white students are "better" than students of color? I know for a fact that this is not the case. I took graduate classes with these students and can attest that most, despite their inflated self-esteem, were, academically speaking, just average. In fact, many of these "white stars" never shined in sociology after they finished their PhDs! The reason white students get incorporated early is because of what Ted Thornhill calls "racial comfort" (2018). White professors feel very comfortable with white students but not with us. White students can knock on white faculty office doors, call them by their first names, and even banter a bit with them. Students of color, lacking that comfort and racial connection, cannot do the same. And our white professors, like whites in general, due to their socialization in the "white habitus" (Bonilla-Silva 2003), have very limited skills to feel comfortable around us.

This subtle way in which whiteness advantages white students is the foundation for dissimilar academic trajectories. Whereas whites accumulate the academic "wages of whiteness" record-wise, scholars of color garner "weak records." But how can we develop "strong records" if we are not invited to the sociological party? How can we publish if no one tells us the ins and outs of the publication game and helps us take our first baby steps? Hate is not needed in academic settings to maintain white supremacy.

Despite the many scars grad school left on my sociological soul, I graduated in 1993. I had a very rough ride in the job market but managed to land a "good" job late in the season at the University of Michigan. Interestingly, my activism at Wisconsin did not immunize me from the insanity of believing I had finally made it. I honestly believed I had become just another professor—another "member of the club."

My colleagues were nice at the beginning and seemed to like me. But by my second or third week as a professor, the romance ended. A very senior white colleague told me I had to have my primary office in the Sociology Department (I had a joint appointment with African American studies). He added a not-so-veiled threat by letting me know that my tenure resided in sociology. The end of this monologue (it was not a dialogue) was him letting me know that the Sociology Department would likely ignore the African American studies' tenure recommendation of my case because people in the department regarded colleagues in that unit as "biased."

Initially, I assumed the problem was the individual in question (and without question, he was a real pain in the derriere) and not a collective issue. However, I quickly changed my assessment and realized that, much like in graduate school, the racial problem in my department was structural. The history, culture, and organizational ethos of sociology departments reproduce and reflect the whiteness of the colleges in which they are housed. As such, racial incidents kept happening to me as normal outcomes of the white structure and culture of my department. For instance, in my third-year review, my chair doubted that my article "Rethinking Racism: Toward a Structural Interpretation" had been accepted for publication in the *American Sociological Review* (Bonilla-Silva 1997), the top journal in the discipline. Another colleague congratulated me on the paper but told me he believed the notion of racism had no "scientific standing." And yet another colleague who thought she was "beyond race," after congratulating me for the article, stated, "I didn't know *ASR* had an affirmative action policy?"

Many more racially motivated things have happened to me in my long career. Nevertheless, I want to highlight a forbidden matter we seldom discuss publicly: how some scholars of color assist in reproducing the racial order of things in the academy. Obviously, the reproduction of the academic racial order is fundamentally accomplished by the actions or inactions of white faculty in their effort to maintain "white normativity" (Bonilla-Silva 2021). But "integration," better called spatial cohabitation, produces some dislocations and unexpected development among faculty of color. Although most of us fight and resist academic whiteness, some folks of color become accommodationist characters, always checking for the wind's direction to decide where they stand. Others are truly confused folks who dream of universalism and believe they are *above* the racial fray. Most of these folks crash hard at some point and either realize that race matters in the academy big time or become sour spirits. Yet, the absolutely worst kind of problematic scholars of color are the Brown and Black snakes. These are folks who talk radical stuff in public but keep their younger colleagues or senior "competitors" in check. (Because departments usually have few of us, some people of color position themselves as HNIC. As such, they make sure they keep those they perceive as competitors in check.)

They genuflect to whites as needed to advance their individual interests.

In my specific case, as a self-identified Afro-Latino, I know I annoy many Latinos because I insist on my Blackness and have worked primarily on Black issues in the United States. Many Latinos wish I'd take one side. They want me to be either Black or Latino. (Have they heard about Afro-Latinos and our long history in the United States? Do they understand that our particular position gives us a "triple consciousness"?) Of course, the truth is that racism affects Latino communities, so I first endured anti-Blackness in Puerto Rico and, later, from Latinos in the United States. Hence, I was not totally surprised when I was bitten by a Brown snake early in my career. The snake accused me of stepping over the line. Although the details of the accusation do not matter, as snakes have quite vivid imaginations, the individual objected to a private email I sent about a presentation one of its former students had made in the department, a presentation that was not well-received. The reptile attacked me in its office behind closed doors to avoid public knowledge of the attack. At that moment, I had two options: fight or flight. I have relived the moment a thousand times and wish I had punched the snake in the face. Instead, I cried (a version of the flight instinct). This was one of the worst things that has ever happened to me in my professional career. Thankfully, once you are bitten by a snake, you improve your skills in snake detection and develop strategies to prevent their attacks or limit the impact of their venom.

My most recent encounter was with a big Black snake. Although in general I have very good relations with African Americans, some of them resent me. They think I am not legitimately Black (not all African Americans understand the global nature of Blackness and how, as a social location and an identity, its original roots lie in Latin America and not in the United States). This snake seemed jealous of my achievements, told me that I had become president of the American Sociological Association because I ran against a white man (implying that had I run against a white woman, I would have lost), and was bothered because I did not attend its speeches in the association (had it paid attention, the snake would have realized I seldom attend *any* presentations) and by a few other truly far-out things. This time, when the snake launched the attack, I was ready and fought back! I stood my ground and answered point by point the accusations the ugly snake made. In the back-and-forth, I believe I injured the snake (who ended up emailing me asking for some information on a job matter—an email I totally ignored). Fighting back is essential when *anyone* tries to put you down. Preserving your dignity and humanity in the academy is something no one ought to compromise on, no matter what.

Although race matters everywhere we work (actually, race matters *everywhere*), I must point out that there is some variance in the academy. Some places are indeed *better* than others. This was the case at Texas A&M for me. In my seven years there, I had issues, but they were *mostly* confined to a few white colleagues without much standing. In general, most white folks there let me do *my thing*. I suspect that was in large part because my chair, Professor Rogelio Saenz (now at the University of Texas at San Antonio), created a different atmosphere. Under his leadership, the department's racial demography changed significantly (he hired four scholars of color, and at our peak, eight of twenty-five or so tenure-track faculty were people of color). This demographic reality had significant implications for the organizational and cultural life of the department. Texas A&M was not perfect or free of racism, but it was an easier place to navigate than any of the other places I have been so far.

Inquisitive minds may ponder, But if race has been so central to your career, how did you become a successful scholar? Some might even say, Come on, Eduardo, you presided over the American Sociological Association, so you have no reason to complain. (When I presided over the ASA, which should have been the apex of my career, some members of the sociological elite dropped their membership and contemplated forming an alternative "scientific" sociological organization.) But this is the wrong way of framing this matter! The question should be, If race had not been central to my trajectory, how much *more* successful would I have been in my career? I have thought about this many times and know for a fact that I would have published several more books (my first book is still unpublished because I received racialized advice from my "colleagues") and a few more articles in "top journals," would have received grant support (I have not gotten much love from the National Science Foundation, Ford, or other foundations), and would be working today in a top ten department.

But please know that I am not complaining. I am rather trying to explain things and let people know that even so-called successful scholars of color experience the sting of racism in the academy! This is so because no matter what, I am *still* a Black Puerto Rican professor who endures every now and then the racist whip from white colleagues, staff members, and even students. And, as I mentioned, although my allies are fundamentally in the Black and Brown communities, I also have been put in "my place" (race matters are about the place of people in a racialized order) by some Brown and Black snakes. Despite all my accomplishments, Malcolm X's joke still applies to me: "What does a white man call a black man with a Ph.D.? . . . A n—— with a Ph.D." (Yancy 2018).

For the academy to become truly universal, it must first accept that race matters and then begin implementing policies to deracialize (de-whiten) its affairs (Bonilla-Silva 2017). And deracializing HWCUs and their culture will also require (1) white colleagues' shifting their "I am a good person" stand and becoming anti-racist people and (2) exposing the few Black and Brown people who, for various reasons, do not defend the interest of their Black and Brown colleagues. Till then, the academy will continue to be and feel to us, "the wretched of the earth," as the a*k*ademy.

References

Bonilla-Silva, Eduardo. 1997. "Rethinking Racism: Toward a Structural Interpretation." *American Sociological Review* 62, no. 3 (January): 465–80.

———. 2003. *Racism without Racists: Color-Blind Racism and the Persistence of Racial Inequality in the US.* Lanham, MD: Rowman and Littlefield.

———. 2017. "What We Were, What We Are, and What We Should Be: The Racial Problem of American Sociology." *Social Problems* 64 (2): 179–87.

———. 2019. "Feeling Race: Theorizing the Racial Economy of Emotions." *American Sociological Review* 84 (1): 1–25.

———. 2021. "What Makes 'Systemic Racism' Systemic?" *Sociological Inquiry* 91, no. 3 (August): 513–33.

Bonilla-Silva, Eduardo, and Crystal E. Peoples. 2022. "Historically White Colleges and Universities: The Unbearable Whiteness of (Most) Colleges and Universities in America." *American Behavior Scientist* 66, no. 11 (October): 1049–504.

Thornhill, Ted. 2018. Personal conversation, October 2018.

Yancy, George. 2018. "The Ugly Truth of Being a Black Professor in America." *Chronicle of Higher Education* 64, no. 34 (May). www.chronicle.com/article /the-ugly-truth-of-being-a-black-professor-in-america/.

MICROAGGRESSIONS AT A JOB TALK
ANONYMOUS

My dissertation explored media portrayals of African American stereotypes, as well as the image of historically Black colleges and universities on reality television. I cited renowned scholars such as Donald Bogle and Patricia Hill Collins. I had presented some of my work at a graduate colloquium in my department, and it was well received. However, when I was invited for an on-campus interview and was engaging the prospective faculty during the Q and A portion of my job talk, one faculty member (a man of color) said that I had "done it all wrong!" and left the room in a huff. Another, a white man, suggested that my area of study was not important. The lone African American term faculty member in the department, a woman, was the only one who came to my defense. I was shocked, dismayed, and frozen silent. In my graduate program, we were trained to always be respectful in our responses to peer reviews and feedback, whether in the form of journal articles, conference paper submissions, research talks, and so on. *Twilight Zone* much??? I had never expected anything like what I was witnessing or even heard of other graduate students getting similar foul treatment during a job talk. I wanted to argue my point, to tell them that not only were they being disrespectful to me, but they were also utterly dismissive of an entire body of study. At the same time, I needed this position, so I couldn't clown how I wanted.

While I have since entered into the position and achieved tenure at this institution—and also forgiven these individuals for the most part—this is still a painful reflection for me. I am still quite careful to treat my colleagues with respect, and I am mindful of the stress that job candidates face and the power struggles that surround hiring. I have also stepped in when more established scholars have attempted to bully those with less power, such as graduate students or assistant professors, in conference presentations. I am forever grateful to my sistah colleague (now one of my best friends in the department) for protecting me, so I pass it on. As Black people in the academy, we have a responsibility not to overlook or excuse each other's mistakes, but it *is* our business to see to each other. Shout out to Black mentor extraordinaire Karla Scott!

THE CONSEQUENCES OF GETTING IT RIGHT

Navigating Anti-Blackness in Graduate Quantitative Methods Courses

PARIS WICKER

When you're Black in graduate school, in-class group work is a special kind of hell. In addition to the typical challenges of work accountability, exploring quantitative methods in graduate school often meant that I was either the only Black student in class or one of just a few. I dreaded in-class small group work in my statistics courses, not because of lack of preparation but because of how other students would treat me. I distinctly remember times when the professor would instruct us to gather in small groups and work through a statistics question. Everyone would turn *away* from me. Eyes averted at every turn as I searched for acknowledgment and welcome. Instead, I found rejection and avoidance. And not just once . . . but in nearly *every* class. I found myself often working alone because of this rejection.

When I explained this phenomenon to other (non-Black) graduate students and instructors, they justified the experience, claiming that "students are just choosing to work with their friends" or "that happens to everybody." But does it? So quickly were my experiences dismissed as a mere misreading of the room. This near-daily happening fueled doubt in my mind (am I making this up?) and made me think there was something wrong with me. This cognitive energy, which I could have spent on learning statistics and improving my research method skill development, was diverted into determining whether it was just a mere coincidence or whether I was facing anti-Black racism. These incidents exacerbated my already existing impostor syndrome and stereotype threat, which made me feel that I didn't belong.

One time, I was forced into a small group to work through a problem and collectively decide on the correct answer. White students in the group confidently selected one answer. I chimed in and said that I believed the correct answer to be another response. I was dismissed and ignored, though I repeatedly indicated a different answer. When the professor stopped by our group and confirmed that indeed I had selected the correct answer, it was like the air had been sucked out of the room. The other members of the group were in complete shock. One white woman spent the rest of class wondering (*aloud*, mind you) how she had possibly gotten that wrong—maybe something was wrong with the question, maybe even she was ill—every excuse except acknowledging that I, a brilliant Black woman who enjoys learning statistics, had been right all along.

Anti-Blackness in the academy means that sometimes I fear not only that I may get an answer wrong but also the consequences of getting it right. After these experiences, I felt so self-conscious in class that I would speak less and go along with the group consensus even when I knew the responses were incorrect. It seems silly in retrospect, but at the time it was an easier act of self-preservation to dim my intellectual light rather than engage in a constant battle to have classmates recognize my humanness.

Researchers Angela Harris and Carmen González (2012) have noted that those in the academy often have low expectations of Black scholars and presume them incompetent no matter their ability, and they often feel threatened when Black women act as serious intellectuals instead of a stereotype. This means that Black excellence may be met with hostility, resistance, avoidance, or isolation. It can feel like a lose-lose situation when some treat Black excellence as a zero-sum game in which my gain is someone else's (usually a white person's) loss. If you're Black, people may assume that it's just the natural order of things for you to know nothing or be academically inferior; yet, getting it right and shining your brilliance may also send others into cognitive dissonance. They may want to justify your excellence with some failure on their part (as though one cannot exist without the other).

Experiencing multiple instances of racial rejection was quite painful emotionally and detrimental to my confidence and self-esteem. It caused me to constantly question my place in quantitative and statistics courses. Anti-Blackness denies me a right that every other student has, which is to engage in a critical part of the learning process that includes making mistakes and even failure, as well as getting things right along the way, within a safe and supportive environment. I deserve a space, like everyone else does, where my ideas are heard and my intellectual capacity brings added value into any discussion or conversation. This, unfortunately, is not a given when you're Black in quantitative methods courses, but it can be cultivated. I utilized my agency to create a space for my intellect. I decided to sit in another area of the class and walk over to groups that I wanted to work with, eventually connecting with another Black woman in the course. I now know that it was not all in my head and that what happened to me was anti-Blackness in action. And although this was a disappointing manifestation of anti-Blackness in the academy, I have learned to use my agency to find spaces (though sometimes sparse) to go where I am intellectually appreciated and not merely tolerated.

Reference

Harris, Angela P., and Carmen G. González. 2012. Introduction to *Presumed Incompetent: The Intersections of Race and Class for Women in Academia*, edited by Gabriella Gutiérrez y Muhs, Yolanda Flores Niemann, Carmen G. González, and Angela P. Harris, 1–14. Logan: Utah State University Press, an imprint of University Press of Colorado.

SO Y'ALL GON' GIVE IT TO HER?
CANDIS HARRIS

During my doctoral program, I applied for an internship and was selected for a face-to-face interview. I was excited about this opportunity because it had the potential, after I graduated, to lead to a permanent position. I studied and prepared myself and felt pretty darn good going into the interview. Needless to say, the interview went fabulously well, and one of the staff shared that I had it in the bag. One of my non-Black colleagues interviewed for the position as well, but I was not intimidated: I had tons more experience than my counterpart. Sad to say, I did not get the internship, but my colleague was selected. You see, the internship had a partnership with my doctoral program, and faculty were typically called for a referral. I later found out that when the interviewers called to invite me for the position, my internship supervisor told them I would not be a good fit. I was so disappointed; their decision to hire her was completely biased, and it showed me that the faculty in my program did not respect or support my career goals. This experience made me lose confidence in myself, my program, and my trust in some of the faculty supervisors. Even after graduating from the program, I have had to build up my confidence as a professional. If they would have shown their support for me, I do not think I would have had such an internal uphill battle regarding my confidence.

Oh, by the way, that colleague who got the internship? She lasted for a few months before quitting.

DON'T ATTACK MY CITY
PRECIOUS BOONE

During my master's in social work program, I remember having a professor who had the habit of making South Central Los Angeles the butt of many of her jokes. She mentioned feeling "sorry" for any of the students who had to visit clients in that area. She once compared gang life in South Central to AIDS. I was offended. I was also shocked that I had come this far in my education to hear a professor speak so insensitively about the city where I was born and raised. For a while, I just sat quietly. What could I possibly say or do? Things progressed to the point that whenever she made jokes (and it was often), my fellow peers would turn and look to see what my reaction would be. Then it dawned on me that most of my cohort had probably never been to an inner city like South Central. The discomfort became unbearable as I knew that my mostly Anglo cohort would uphold strong stereotypes of the Black and Brown people they would encounter in the city.

I chose to address the matter with my professor. She came off very defensive, even stating that she was qualified to make these jokes because she went to the University of Southern California. She told me that if I wanted my cohort to have a better understanding of the city, I could teach a class. It felt like more of a challenge than an apology. Nevertheless, I accepted the challenge and found a guest speaker who did a terrific job of talking about the history of South Central and even quizzed us on lesser-known positive facts about the city. I was so satisfied that my classmates had a much more well-rounded view of the city. I wanted this to impact the level of hope and commitment they had when working with any clients there or any other inner city. I never had another conversation about the issue with my professor, but I also never heard another joke. I did not receive an apology, but it would not have held much weight anyway. I received the satisfaction of becoming an educator where ignorance and microaggressions reared their ugly heads. No assignment, project, or thesis was more powerful than this for me.

PRESUMED INCOMPETENT
BY A MEDICAL STUDENT
NADIA A. SAM-AGUDU

It was the early 2000s. I was a pediatric resident in Minnesota, a Black African female resident on rotation with a fellow senior resident, a white male, Dr. ABC. We were co-supervising four medical students rotating in pediatrics and alternated spending two weeks with two of the students at a time.

Among the medical students was a white male student, XYZ. For that entire rotation, XYZ interrogated every clinical decision I made, asked questions only to challenge my intelligence, and displayed disinterest when I gave student lectures. I started to doubt my own abilities. I wanted to enlist the elite schools I had attended and show him my excellent grades and academic awards. I wanted to prove to him that he had no basis to behave so disrespectfully toward me—that I had already achieved excellence in the same system he was training in.

But I did none of these things.

Just before switching to spend his two weeks with my coresident, XYZ actually said to me, "I've seen Dr. ABC and he is so awesome, like, he's sooo smart. I'm so intimidated; how can I impress him?" I will never forget the smugness on his face as he said that. I mumbled something like "Just be yourself" and walked away. Given how XYZ had behaved toward me, the faux concern about impressing my "sooo smart" coresident was a thinly veiled attempt to further denigrate me.

I could not identify any person I could trust to share this with—not in my residency program nor among my colleagues, supervisors, or department's leadership. I could see how it would turn out: complaining about something I had no concrete evidence for, and even if I had, under what policies would XYZ's behavior be addressed, if at all? I had already experienced racial microaggressions in the presence of coresidents who just stood by and said nothing. No one had discussed policies governing racial and sexist issues with me. I had completed several required online and in-person training sessions. However, as far as I can recall, there was little material on handling racial microaggressions, and none on intersectional issues involving race and gender. Sexual harassment training usually focused on employee and trainee interactions with patients and supervisors, and sexual harassment did not apply in this case.

I never told my coresident about XYZ's behavior. In fact, Dr. ABC told me later how great XYZ was during their two weeks together. "What do you think about the med students? XYZ is such an enthusiastic learner," he said. Dr. ABC was not smarter than I was; we were both excellent residents. XYZ was simply dismissive of me, no matter what I said or did. Even though I was his senior and more experienced than he was, my skin color (and perhaps my gender and having an "African" accent too) devalued all of that: I had nothing valuable to teach him, because in his worldview, I was intrinsically of little value.

Writing about this experience makes me wonder where XYZ is now and how he would be interacting with others like me today, especially if he were in a position of authority. If he could behave this way toward a senior resident as a medical student, what stops him from being even worse in leadership and with more power?

THE BLISSFUL IGNORANCE OF THE DISTINGUISHED BENEDICT

A. LAMONT WILLIAMS

During my first semester as a doctoral student, I was told that there is *no such thing as Black history*. Those words would inadvertently fuel my drive to finish my PhD and fight for our people. On that particular day, a "distinguished" white professor was a guest speaker in one of my elective courses. I was seated in the front of the class (nearest to the podium), and the man looked me straight in the eye during most of the lecture.

As the white professor began speaking, I noticed subtle hints of arrogance as he discussed his research and the work he had (seemingly) done on civil rights literature. At first, I was pleased to hear of a man with such distinguished honors and acclaim partaking in research related to telling the full story of one of the most egregious (documented) murders in American history: the murder of Emmett Till. As the professor continued, he abruptly shifted his opinion to mirror the tone of those who whitewashed the history books. He said, "What people must understand is, there is *no African American history* or *Black history*. It's all American history." I thought I knew what he meant—you know, to say that all American history includes Black history. I was completely wrong. He chuckled and continued eye contact with me, saying, "Your people don't have a history without *my* people." Silence. The Joker-esque smirk on his face created a stillness in the room as those shocking words exited his cracked lips. A singular bead of sweat traveled down my forehead, my hands began to shake, and my brow furrowed. I could tell that all eyes were on me, the only Black scholar in the room. In fact, the professor of the class (a white woman) looked straight at me, her eyes pleading with me to keep my cool and not react or cause a scene. To be frank, I couldn't tell you a single word he said after that statement, but as the only Black-ademic in that space, I knew that refuting his blatant insensitivity could quickly go awry without support. I was alone. In fact, part of me felt as if I was experiencing a microcosm of the helplessness that our ancestors must have felt: isolation and powerlessness while looking into the eyes of a smug, grinning white face and an acquiescent crowd of white bystanders. What was I to do?

I had never encountered such flagrant-yet-subtle racism. I sat there, the only Black student in a class full of white faces, confronted with the double consciousness of my existence in that space. When I walked out of class that day, I felt as if I had let my people down. I thought I should have refuted the white professor's statements, but at the same time, I felt powerless amid onlookers who seemingly didn't share my understanding of the speaker's insensitive comments.

To this day, I have never forgotten the man's words or the smug grin on his face. This interaction continually reminds me that even those who do "research" said to help our cause could potentially just be using our pain for their own prominence. Most of us understand the power that comes with sharing our experience. Unfortunately, people like the professor that day also know how to capitalize on our stories. More directly, they understand how to use our stories for personal gain while also reinforcing our powerlessness (and their whiteness ideals of superiority and savior complexes) in spaces where they control the narratives.

I do have one reason to be thankful for this experience. It was on that day that I decided I would finish my PhD and gain the tools necessary to combat people like that white professor at the highest levels. Never again will I sit idly as someone so shamelessly disrespects our cause, especially when such a person uses our griot testimonies to help his or her own advancement. People like the man in this story (you know, those who overly weaponize Dr. Martin Luther King Jr. to further their "diversity initiatives") must also learn that Black history is not a commercial entity that they can use when it is convenient for them to gain prominence and acclaim. It is up to us as Blackademics to provide the research and literature to defuse such crude weaponizations of our people's history. Many of our greatest leaders have sacrificed their lives and died for the advancement of our people. It is up to us to carry the torch, even if it means walking solo through disparate halls of ivory towers.

GRADUATE SCHOOL TRAUMA
Self-Preservation in the Ivory Tower

CAROL ANN JACKSON

Spotlight Narrative

The ivory tower seemed deceptively safe. When I was accepted into graduate school, I thought I'd entered an intellectual utopia wherein I'd be able to interrupt inequality through the study of sociology. Little did I know that when I entered graduate school in 2015, I'd be beginning one of the most abusive relationships of my life—and it started with my academic advisor.

Maybe I should have listened to my intuition after experiencing my first microaggression. It was three weeks into the first semester, and I was meeting with the critical race scholar, a white male, who would become my first faculty advisor. When I got to his office, he gestured for me to come in. He wanted to know what my goals were. I started by telling him that I wanted to utilize my degree as a resource that could be reappropriated to help under-resourced Black youth in communities—like the one I am from—but I never got to finish sharing my aspirations. A sinister and condescending laugh escaped his thin lips. The esteemed critical race scholar who was well known for his work on whiteness and institutional racism proceeded to tell me that my sole objective would be to publish or perish. At that moment, I searched his eyes for a hint of humanity. I saw none. Callous, vacant, and cold eyes stared back at me. How paradoxical—the scholar who studied racism shot down my aspirations to interrupt racial inequality. As a graduate student of color, I've come to learn that mentoring plays a pivotal role in retention and success rates. Unfortunately, this instance was one of many critical moments in which I would be under-supported and discouraged.

Over the next three years, I came to realize that the only causes my advisor cared about were growing his CV and feeding his insatiable ego. The abuses were frequent. There was the time my brother was in the ICU and we weren't sure if he would make it. My advisor demanded that I attend my thesis defense, although an alternate date had been prearranged to accommodate an emergency. I couldn't sleep the night before and prepared for my defense in the hospital waiting room. Seconds seemed like hours as I waited to hear whether my brother would live or die. During the wee hours of the morning, my family received word that he was stable. I was on an emotional roller coaster. Relief washed over me and anxiety just as soon replaced it—I had to race to campus to defend my thesis while compartmentalizing the events and emotions of life. After my defense was over, my advisor made sure to tell me that I had passed by the skin of my teeth.

Working with him became intolerable, and I eventually decided to take my first radical act of self-preservation by attempting to talk about my needs to be better supported. The two of us sat together in a classroom with the door closed. I wish I had recorded the conversation, but the words still replay in my head: "Carol Ann, you are not allowed to give me feedback. I am the advisor, you are the advisee, and you are inferior to me." Inferior? Tears rolled down my face as I repressed my pain, anger, and indignation. I chose silence as a means to protect myself. I was afraid and vulnerable, and he knew it.

Black women are often silently and systemically subject to violence; seldom are we protected. I was ignored by my department when I managed to find the courage to speak up and then ignored by the university when I escalated my issues through the ombudsman system and sought protection through the Office of Diversity and Equity.

Black women are in a precarious position, and the institution primes us to normalize toxicity and resilience on our pathways to success. There is no escaping trauma and abuse when we live in a world where violence against women of color, and particularly Black women, is embedded in the very systematic design of every institution. I know the abuse won't end when or if I finish graduate school. It may just be the beginning.

I have reached a point where I no longer consider my ability to endure adversity to be a badge of honor. It is self-betrayal. I have come to realize that I do not wish to exist in spaces where suppressing my truth or voice is necessary to be granted access. I have come to realize that it is up to me to preserve my soul and peace. The first six years of graduate school were full of panic attacks, anxiety, depression, and regular suicidal ideation. I have come to understand that I am worth more, and I will not barter my wellness for accolades or entry into gatekept spaces. I've come to realize that I do not seek to sit at a table where dignity and respect are not being served. We must be intentional with the work we do, who we do it with, and whom we do it for. As Audre Lorde says, "you cannot dismantle the master's house with the master's tools." May we utilize our gifts, our voices, our writing, and our research in the spirit of activism. May our existence inside and outside of the ivory tower be our resistance. May we find spaces that fuel our souls and preserve our peace.

YOUNG SCHOLARS LED ASTRAY
Why Advising Matters
ANONYMOUS

My experience came in my first year of grad school, where my own advisor would accuse me of plagiarism for what was just an improperly cited quotation from Karl Marx in our first semester paper, an essay about Marx in the class my advisor taught. This could have easily been a teaching moment about proper formatting for a student who was trying to demonstrate an influential idea. Instead, it's now a blemish on my permanent record.

Seemingly minor issues quickly become major ones within our dynamic. Things were mostly fine in the transition process, but after the first six weeks my (white) advisor spoke negatively about me to other faculty, both in the department and seemingly in the field at large, criticizing my work ethic, questioning my desire to improve, and gradually cutting back the time of our advising meetings upon realizing that I would not be as beneficial to their publication schedule as they had first thought. I began to wonder whether my services were solicited only because I was a Black male—the only Black male (and one of only two Black students) on an advising committee that spoke heavily on topics related to Black experiences. I began to wonder whether my advisor, who had four senior students on track to graduate, simply realized that they would prefer to take time away from students and viewed this new entry, first-year student as a burden. I can't pathologize what would make someone just drop a student, but I do know now to trust your gut. I didn't want to work with this person but was encouraged to do so for career progression from others in the field.

I earned the lowest grade of the class my first year as a graduate student, a B- in a core class, which in grad school is akin to failing. Believing things to just be a product of rough early beginnings (aka internalizing flaws that came from receiving no guidance and being overworked on my advisor's side projects that they divided among several students), I took an elective course with my advisor in my second year. I thought things would go better with lower stakes, a smaller class, and a greater focus on discussion. Most notably, I felt like I needed to "prove" myself to my advisor and others that I was a good student and scholar. I later received a C+ in that elective course, which was when I knew something was up. (I have since earned all As in my last years of coursework.) My advisor stopped inviting me to conferences, and when I would attend out of my own efforts and later departmental support, my advisor and fellow colleagues would avoid me publicly, despite our sharing panels together and similar associations. I began to notice others in the field whom I admired brush me off despite pleasant interactions in the past and was worried for my place in the academy.

I had entered graduate school to study Black families and the value of community in raising city children. I therefore proposed involving previous outreach programs I had worked for in order to study Black children in education; I had all the necessary contacts lined up and would need assistance only in gaining IRB (Institutional Review Board) approval. But I was told my plans were too lofty for a simple master's degree and was directed to join an ongoing study of white terrorist-murderers, a proposition I later found was also made toward my fellow Black advisee. This research involved intense readings of five separate racist and sexist white men's manifestos (multiple reads for accuracy) and then accumulating and coding over 5,000 newspaper articles on the topic. The constant exposure to Black death at the hands of whiteness destroyed my fast-declining mental health. After working on that project, I became not just anxious but paranoid about being an in-person instructor on a majority white campus in a nation with constant mass shootings. It became a struggle just to go on campus at times, but just like many others, I pushed through—until being told that I wouldn't be able to even register normally due to being placed on academic probation for the poor grades I had received from 2016 to 2017. In early November, just a few weeks short of assigning me a C+ in my elective, my former advisor informed me that they would be taking on some new projects and traveling for opportunities, which would mean that for the time being we would no longer work together. I was given the caveat that if I showed progress over my fourth semester, we could possibly collaborate again in my fifth after my master's.

To this day, several folks in my academic field no longer speak to me due to (what I can only imagine is) their perceptions of me as a student. Conversely, there are several folks who have talked to me behind the scenes about a trail of people who have been mistreated, neglected, and taken advantage of by my former advisor. I wrote a letter to my department in 2018 regarding my experiences and was told that either mediation or extended distance would be the best approach. My department head would step in to lead my master's committee in the meantime. Less than two years later, enough students came together with their collective horror stories to get my former advisor banned from teaching graduate students for the near future, in conjunction with a national outcry over accusations made regarding interpersonal conduct. This person still continues to work with undergraduate students weekly and at institutions beyond ours while folks are mostly wowed by their publication record and public speeches, largely unaware of how they treated those close to them. The advisor still received tenure and a promotion, despite my own letter being supposedly added to their tenure package as a warning.

I have been in therapy on and off for three years and attend church regularly. I still have nightmares about being murdered in a mass shooting. I still struggle to trust anyone at the faculty level, even the gracious folks who have stepped in to assist and advise me after my previous advisor left. The shame endured from nearly flunking out just eighteen months into graduate school sent me into depression when I went home for winter break after my third semester. I would be officially diagnosed with depression, anxiety, and attention deficit hyperactivity disorder the following spring. My entire graduate experience is defined by isolation and "figuring it out" against all adversity. This is the experience of so many grads of color, even with functional advising relationships, but it is exacerbated when those with power do everything they can to undermine those just trying to get by. Many students will have experiences like mine and receive such diagnoses, but these students are not burdens. They are great contributors who need additional—or even just a baseline level of —support.

IF I COULD BELONG
ALEXIS GRANT

I never even imagined pursuing a PhD until I met my master's thesis advisor. I was working on a two-year master's degree at an Ivy League institution from 2016 to 2018, and my public health program was one of the most diverse graduate programs across the spectrums of race, gender, and sexual orientation. Despite its diversity, I was still the only Black person in my specific program when I started and one in just a handful for the entire school. I don't think it was a coincidence that my advisor—let's call her Dr. K—was also a Black woman and the only Black professor in our department. Coming from an HBCU where I worked with multiple Black faculty, I had little awareness of the difference that just one Black colleague could make on an academic trajectory.

The entire time in my program, I wondered why I was admitted. I wondered whether the admissions committee really thought I was a competitive candidate or whether they admitted me because I added to the department's racial diversity. As some sort of recognition for my brown skin, the school "awarded" me with a donor diversity fund that paid for about HALF a class each semester rather than try to match me with a professor with 100 percent funding for a graduate student. At the end of my program, the school had the audacity to ask for a "thank you" statement to the donors. The facts were that I was the only Black woman in the department matched with the only Black woman faculty member, even though our interests weren't aligned and she didn't have funding or upcoming research opportunities for a master's student. But Dr. K and I took what was given to us and made the most of it. I felt valued as a token, at most. I felt like a fraud.

Now, I know that feeling reflected impostor syndrome, and I experienced it regularly for two years, from the beginning to the end of the program. As the semesters went on, I got involved in graduate student council and convinced myself that I had a place in graduate school, at least. Through my part-time work as a data collector, I found out that maybe I could make it in that field too. I can't say positively that I felt like I belonged where I was, but I survived.

Dr. K helped me see that Black women *do* belong in the most "elite" ivory towers like Harvard, Yale, and Brown—and that I could be one of them. She made sure I could be one of them. A year into the program, I knew I wanted to pursue research in community health interventions but was unsure about when and where to do a PhD. Dr. K encouraged me to apply and provided resources for the process. I was accepted into a program, and so all that was left was to graduate—a daunting task.

After visiting numerous professors' offices for the first year and a half of my program, I hadn't successfully developed a relationship with any of them. I had put feelers out for data I might be interested in analyzing for my thesis, but ultimately no one had followed up. I felt like a failure: my thesis was due in about three months, and I didn't have any data. Although I had done what previous years' students had told me to do—make connections with professors by going to brown bag talks, conduct informational interviews, search databases for data sets collected by professors at our university—I found myself embarrassingly behind. Dr. K stepped in, gave me a list of the data she had collected, and told me to come up with an analysis plan. I'll never forget a conversation we had where she candidly told me that I was not on track but that she would help me get there. It was that tough love that I needed. It took me several all-nighters later to do the analysis and write the thesis, but I did it. Dr. K embodied the "lift as you climb" mentality. She took responsibility for me and went above and beyond what is asked of a faculty member. She was honest with me and allowed me to learn for myself that I could belong in academia. She supported me in the ways she could. Now, I am a soon-to-be PhD, following her example but also persevering for all those who started graduate school but did not survive because they didn't have a Dr. K.

I GOT WANTS AND NEEDS

Characterizing Blackness Onstage and Offstage for Black Student Performers

LAURA D. OLIVER

My Blackness is a characterization of who I am to institutions that are seemingly invested in diversity on the surface. By this I mean that I am praised more for my presence than for my actual research. My experiences speak to a painful truth about the treatment of Black students in performance spaces at PWIs (predominantly white institutions). Simply put, many institutions are not structured to handle the wants and needs of Black students, and this oversight has hindered the rate at which some experience or achieve success. Like others, my struggles with school were due to the lack of racial and gender connections with faculty who shared my research interests. I spent a lot of time working with white professors who did not consider my positionality as a Black woman. As a performer, I was asked to play characters or develop personas that did not align with my everyday life. While this is not an unfamiliar ask in theatre and performance, my praxis has always been invested in a critique of this historical practice.

For example, I was cast in a show centered on a woman who survived a disastrous event for approximately a decade in isolation. The director didn't mention a demographic description of the character, but I concluded that she was a white woman based on key things that were highlighted in the original text about her appearance (for example, descriptions of hair). The script reflected themes often found in feminist studies: dating and marriage, loneliness, motherhood, mental health, sex, and sexuality. Eight women were cast as the main character. Five were white, including those racially passing as white. Each monologue brought attention to a search for meaning—contextually, "meaning" referred to how the character made sense of her unwelcoming environment. Additionally, we were tasked with mirroring our behaviors and actions with each other to unify the performance. To no surprise, the development of unity was most reflected in the delivery of the character's speaking style.

My first attempt to recite the lines in front of the director was shameful. I was unfamiliar with the sentence structure and some vocabulary in the text. I felt "dumb" at the end of the first rehearsal. For context, the script was giving every bit of seventeenth-century English and idioms of early Western literature. I mispronounced several words and stumbled through the flow of the monologue because I had not previously encountered this speaking style as a performer. Chile, it was a mess! I was ashamed and embarrassed when I left rehearsal and thought my status in the program was going to be questioned. I cried myself to sleep that night. The next day, I attended the rehearsal of a white woman cast member to gain understanding about the development of this character. I worked hard in the following weeks leading up to the show and excelled during the final performance. But at the end, I felt like an impostor.

On a different occasion, I was cast as a white man in a show that claimed to demystify the characterizations of gender and sexuality in a film set during the 1950s. I accepted the part because I wanted to prove to the performance community that I was a team player, but I was not happy. The director adapted three scenes to critique representation in the film; however, my character was not included. Since I was playing a white man and all, I asked when I would get the chance to make a critique that reflected my ethics and personhood as a Black woman. The director acknowledged my concerns as a scholar but did not address my intersectionality as a performer. I was upset, confused, and tired of feeling used as a performer and overlooked as a person. Whiteness has scarred me before (and it will again), so I needed to shift my energy in a direction that would benefit my career. I was determined to change the system for myself and others.

I studied works by Black performance scholars in my own time, and the next year I wrote, directed, and produced *Nappy Hairstories*, a show about Black woman identity that unapologetically centers Blackness. My radical approach to performance gained interest in my discipline because I adapted Eurocentric methods to accommodate the stories that Black performers wanted to tell. We toured the show, and I presented lectures about the theoretical outcomes regarding identity, sisterhood, and natural hair, but I was not satisfied with this limited understanding of Black performance. I felt like there was more to say about the uniqueness of Black performance methods, and I wanted to create a safe space to figure it out. I submitted a proposal for the next production season to teach a workshop, with limited supervision, for undergraduate and graduate students that focused on Black performance methods. The proposal was approved by the graduate faculty, and I taught a workshop-style seminar on Afrocentric writing, voice, and body methods. For six months, we decentered whiteness as a praxis to emphasize the influences of themes like music, dance, food, language, death, fashion, and more. We spoke and moved freely through the space, but most importantly, the participants learned about performance in ways that made sense to their everyday lives and *our community*. Every student who completed the workshop, including myself, received course credit.

I focus on storytelling as a methodological framework because it provides insight into lived experience. When I consider the possibilities that this method provides to Black performers, its structure for change is also solidified as theory. It is important for me to show others how Blackness can be positioned as a form of resistance in the ivory tower because art making is how our ancestors have survived the perils of life for centuries. This scholarship has evolved my career because I made connections to research that served me instead of to what performed well for white audiences. Trust the process.

STRANGE FRUIT, FAMILIAR TUNE

CLIFTON BOYD

Spotlight Narrative

"You should lynch him": four words I never expected to hear during my first semester at an Ivy League university, from a professor no less. This shameful attempt at humor was targeted at me during an aural skills course that I had actually enjoyed until this incident. I had a musical ear that my classmates and professor took note of, and it helped me keep the impostor syndrome at bay. Maybe I did deserve my place in the cohort; maybe I wasn't just there because I was the only Black applicant who my department thought might be able to withstand the rigor of the doctoral program.

That morning in October 2016, I was asked to sing a short but difficult melody in front of the class. To put one's voice on display like this is a standard request in aural skills courses, but that doesn't make it feel any less intimidating. Despite my nerves, I performed the exercise without issue, as had come to be expected of me several weeks into the semester. But, instead of being complimented on my performance, I became the target of violence for the professor, the sole voice of authority in the classroom. He warned my fellow classmates, "You should watch out for this guy—you should lynch him." I still remember the tense feeling that arose in my chest. How does one respond to something like this? The best I could do then was to muster a brief laugh—anything to escape the extreme discomfort. My classmates, most of whom were white, were eerily quiet, also unsure of how to respond. I wish that they had spoken up in my defense, but I also empathize with the complete shock that we all felt in this moment. What's more, we all feared challenging the authority of an esteemed, tenured white male professor—the power imbalance was palpable.

Things were never quite the same for me after that class, for both the remainder of the course and the rest of my time at the institution. Briefly, I had believed that my hypervisibility was due to my hard work and my talent. With four words, though, I was swiftly and painfully reminded that, in academia, first and foremost I am hypervisible because of my Blackness. Echoing the devastation of Black Wall Street roughly a century ago, my Black excellence was framed as a threat in need of dismantling.

In retrospect, I'm surprised by how difficult it was for me to come to terms with the violence of this interaction. The few colleagues I told about the incident were visibly horrified, yet my own emotional response was always much more subdued. For months, if not years, I put off processing the toll those four words had taken on my mental and emotional well-being. It was hard to justify taking the time to be introspective when I was plenty busy with coursework, qualifying exams, and extracurricular activities. It didn't help that the professor barely even acknowledged his reprehensible behavior: after one of my classmates approached the department chair about the situation, who in turn confronted the professor, I received a half-baked apology via email ("I'm sorry if I made you uncomfortable"). But when we saw each other in person, the topic was never broached. The professor clearly wanted to act as if this never happened—a luxury I was not afforded.

Two years later, I realized I was not satisfied with how the administration handled the incident. Was a slap on the wrist from a department chair really an appropriate response to such violent and deeply racist language? Though students of color are expected to keep their experiences of racism to themselves, I refused to let the university sweep this under the rug, as it is overly prone to do. But through this refusal, I came to realize firsthand just how woefully ill-equipped universities are to deal with the racist violence taking place on their campuses. My professor was not disciplined swiftly or thoroughly. Instead, I found myself sitting through a series of emotionally draining meetings, all of which ultimately revealed the university's unwillingness to take decisive action against racism and its perpetrators. In the end, I received a second, more formal apology that was somehow less apologetic than the first. Perhaps I could have advocated for more, but at a certain point I didn't have anything left to give.

This is how my journey in the academy began—othered, threatened, unnerved. And yet, despite academia's unwavering anti-Blackness, I've made it across the finish line and have become the first PhD in my family. As I begin the next phase of my career as a tenure-track faculty member, I'm slowly coming to terms with the fact that there will always be people who will think my success can be written off as a result of affirmative action. But if only they knew about all of the bullshit I and other Black people had to put up with to make it this far, then maybe they would be less threatened by our accomplishments and more astonished by our perseverance.

CURRICULUM PUNISHMENT IN THE IVORY
DOMINIQUE BRANSON

I had been excited about the class Post-Classical Sociological Theory since undergraduate school, but I was unable to enroll in the course due to balancing the requirements of two majors, a minor, and all the responsibilities that come along with being a student-athlete. Graduate school became my opportunity to finally take the class, but four years passed before Post-Classical Sociological Theory was offered again. In my eighth semester of graduate school, the course was made available, and I immediately reached out to the professor assigned to teach the class to express my enthusiasm about enrolling. The day before the first class, though, I was shocked and upset to find that the syllabus included not a single reading from a Black scholar or any scholar of color. *Was I being punished?* Later, I learned a new term for an old concept: "curriculum punishment." H. Richard Milner IV defines it as a form of harm experienced by students, especially students of color, when they are not exposed to racially just learning opportunities. I *was* being punished. However, years of anticipation convinced me that I would still enjoy the class. I knew that I had gaps to fill on the "socio" side of my sociolinguistics degree, and I did not want to miss the opportunity to take the class.

On the first day, after going through the syllabus, a white woman chimed in about the lack of diversity in the course materials. Grateful, I seconded her position and spoke up about also wanting more racially varied scholarship in the course. To make room in the schedule, the professor offered to update the syllabus with one Black scholar if we, the students, would sacrifice our only self-care day of the semester to go over the material. Spring break was canceled due to COVID-19, so the self-care day was our only "break" of the semester. *Was I being punished again?* It seemed he may have been retaliating for our suggestion that post-classical sociological theory ought to include Black scholarship. However, we agreed to give up our "spring break."

Disappointed, though, I soon dropped the class without speaking to the professor first. Later, I found out from my ally that after I had unenrolled from the course, the professor sent out an email to all of my classmates blaming *me* for the need to rework the student presentation schedule because I was no longer in the class. I can only speculate that he did this to ensure that everyone knew I had left on my own volition and not because of anything he had done. He did, after all, go out of his way to let them know I dropped the class without telling him first. This was all the confirmation I needed to feel confident in my decision to unenroll.

To fill the gap in my schedule, I took a course in the School of Education, Urban Schools and Social Policy, at my university. On the final day of the class, which was also the last class of my graduate career, two members of the Black Panther Party guest-lectured and shared their abundant wisdom as well as truths about academia, social justice, and racial equity. *Was this redemption?* Empowered, motivated, and inspired, I moved forward to the dissertation stage in my graduate program.

THIS IS MY STORY

BERNADETTE M. GAILLIARD

The #BlackintheIvory movement has afforded me the opportunity to reflect on my experience in higher education and meaningfully ask, *What is my story?* As I read others' stories, I think, *I don't have any stories like* THAT *to share.* But I also wonder whether I have just blocked those experiences out in order to get through life and "feel normal."

The truth is I can recall being told by white faculty members that I was "so articulate" when I gave a class or conference presentation. (*Well, what else did you expect?* I thought.) I also remember people suggesting that my research needed a control group and that I should focus on more mainstream research topics so I could get hired more easily. In fact, I ended up researching health-care professionals instead of faculty of color for my dissertation for this very reason. (Yet, for the past five years, my full-time job has entailed creating programming and influencing policy to improve the experiences of faculty, staff, and students of color.) Honestly, these instances of microaggressions and more overt forms of discrimination have been so few and far between that I *did* almost forget about them.

My story is more about the experience of being "the only." Ever since my AP and honors classes in high school, I have been the only (or one of only a few) Black people in the academic spaces I have occupied. That means for the past twentyish years, I have spent most of my professional time in institutions where I never see more than a few people who even *look* like me, let alone share a common experience of life outside academia.

As a Blackademic, being underrepresented and isolated has impacted how I navigate higher education in myriad ways. First, I have always had to search for belonging and a community where I could comfortably express my whole self without judgment. Without colleagues who looked like me or those who could fully understand my experience and serve as role models to learn from and confide in, I had to seek out other communities to support the nonacademic aspects of my life. I am grateful for the university gospel choirs, McNair programs, and student and faculty of color groups that I have belonged to over the years where I have found support systems that helped cultivate my full identity. The wonderful people I have met in these groups have shown me that I'm not alone in this journey; they've become lifelong friends and helped me develop a more complete sense of who I am outside of my professional role.

Second, being one of the few Black women in each of my academic institutions has made me feel pressured to represent all Black people in the space. I recall thinking both in graduate school and in my first faculty position that I had to excel for myself *and* so the faculty knew it was worth the investment to accept more Black people into the program or hire another Black faculty person. Specifically, in my faculty position, the school had never tenured a person of color in more than forty years of being in existence. It felt like everyone was wondering whether I had what it took to be the first. One of my colleagues outright told me, "You have to work twice as hard to be seen as half as good." I know it's a common saying among people of color, but I did not take well to hearing it as I was working my ass off every day as an assistant professor.

This leads to my third point: Being underrepresented in the academy has meant that I have (the responsibility?) to do more work. I am definitely side-eyeing the word "responsibility" because it has been a double-edged sword. In the above example, it was *my responsibility* to work twice as hard so that I could be perceived as tenurable. In graduate school, when I wanted to research race and gender issues, it was *my responsibility* to find the people on campus who could help me expand my knowledge and expertise because this area of study was not readily available in my department. As faculty, it was *my responsibility* to become the role model for students of color who wanted to do research with me or on race and identity issues because I was the only person who looked like them or who studied this topic in the department. While I do this work because it's my passion, these examples demonstrate the lack of support and acknowledgment that faculty (and students) of color get for going the extra mile and taking on the additional invisible labor to support an institution's academic mission.

Finally, what I dread most is when my experience is compared to that of the other (very few) Black faculty or students at the institution. On multiple occasions white folks have asked, "Well, Bernadette, this person says they experienced this situation. Did you?" If I can't cosign and say that I contended with the same situation, then somehow that discounts what the other person went through. But that's wrong. If I did not face discrimination in the same way that another person did, it does not mean that discrimination isn't happening. The fact that I was able to find community in some ways while another person didn't does not absolve the institution from doing more to support people of color on campus. Other Black people's experiences are just as valid as mine. What I say cannot negate their experiences, nor can theirs negate mine. Both are true and both are fact.

All in all, being the only or one of few takes its toll; there may not be clear incidents of racism, but this shit adds up. The extra labor of finding and establishing community is tiring. The constant wondering whether I'm doing enough to be seen as "good enough" is wearisome. The pressure to perform in ways that will demonstrate that people from my race or ethnic group are worthy is exhausting. The need to take that deep breath every day before leaving the house and saying, "Here we go again" is draining. The experience of not necessarily having a role model but needing to be the role model for those I encounter is overwhelming. Being unable to look around a room of colleagues and see someone who looks like me is disconcerting.

THIS is my story.

SILENT NO MORE

CHRISTINE LYNN McCLURE

Silent. That describes my early days in the academy. Now, I don't mean silent as in not talking, because I am always talking; it's what I do. This was a deeper silence, one that develops from the inside out. I am talking about a silence that causes decay, one that says if you speak you will ruin everything you worked so hard for.

As a higher education administrator and two-time graduate student at the same institution, I believed my silence was a requirement for my success. Looking back, I thought about the many times I wanted to speak up but didn't. You see, as a Black single mother who had children at the age of twenty, worked night and day just to get a college degree, and battled homelessness, domestic violence, and sexual assault, I wasn't "supposed" to be here. I beat the odds. In my mind, I wasn't going to let anything stop me from becoming successful. The problem was I never took the time to define success. After I started working in the academy and then became a graduate student, I was just happy to be there and not back where I used to be. What I found was that I gradually convinced myself that just being there would be enough and that to stay there I had to accept whatever was given to me. So, I stayed silent—in meetings and in classes when I desperately wanted to offer my perspective, opinion, or lived experience. But that voice in my head kept telling me that I would look stupid, people would judge me, and, worst of all, my perspective might ruin future opportunities. I convinced myself that just because I wasn't speaking up didn't mean I agreed with what was happening or being said; it just meant I was being strategic. My grandmother always said, "When you know better, you'll do better," and looking back, I knew better. I knew that I was really too afraid to speak up in fear of what would happen if those I spoke to didn't like what I had to say. Would it jeopardize my graduation? Would I be able to get promoted to a more senior administrative position or faculty position? I decided it was too risky at the time, but once I got to a certain level, I thought I would be able to speak up. The problem is, when you trade in your integrity for a title, you have to keep doing it.

While I can say that I did complete my doctorate and my career in academic administration flourished, I still lost. I lost the opportunity to make a difference for the other Black and minoritized women who came after me. I didn't realize that each day I was losing a little more of myself, and most importantly I lost my identity. This is where defining success for yourself is important. What I realized is I never defined success for myself, and if I had to say, at the time I believed that to be successful I had to have certain credentials, titles, and levels of accomplishment. I now can say that I have been successful, but not for anything related to my pedigree. Today, I define success very differently. I find value in building meaningful relationships and in offering my experience and expertise to benefit others and not for self-promotion. You see, if you don't know what success means to you, it's easy for others to sell you their version, and unfortunately, I bought the whole package. As my daughter Faith once said, instead of being the author of my own story, I starred in one that someone gave me.

Thankfully, during my doctoral studies, I met some badass women who were also experiencing some of the same issues, fears, and anxieties, and they helped me regain my confidence, self-respect, and voice. The first was a fellow student, a no-nonsense, exceptionally talented, and not having any of the BS Jamaican woman from New York. When I say she held nothing back, I mean *nothing*. We were assigned to the same group for a class, and we instantly became friends. The professors were lecturing, and I had NO CLUE what they were talking about. All my insecurities and negative voices started a full conversation in my head. Before I knew it, I passed her a note that read, "When we go to our breakouts I am leaving. I can't do this. It's too hard. I quit." She asked me for my telephone number and then sent me a text that said, "No one knows what they are saying. You are not alone." Then a picture of the fish from *Finding Nemo* with a caption that read "Just keep swimming" appeared on my phone. From that exchange a lifelong friendship was born.

The second woman, a Latina powerhouse, was my new advisor in my fourth year of doctoral studies. You see, my first advisor, a white man, and I never really connected, and as a result I had to figure out how to navigate the doctoral program on my own. That is how I met my new advisor. She was teaching higher education history, a class I was supposed to take early in my program. I, however, was taking it in my final year of coursework. Each week we talked about my research interests, and each week I became more drawn to her until I finally asked her if she would become my new advisor. She invited me to her monthly advising sessions, where she conducted "culturally appropriate advising." As those of the younger generation say, if you know, you know! We met to share our work, provide feedback and critique, and challenge each other to produce dope scholarly work, but our primary goal was to check in with each other. The sessions would often start with our advisor asking us how we were doing, like *really* doing. It was the safest space on campus. We could cry, vent, laugh, joke, and reflect on our lives, what was going on in the culture, and our experiences as we traversed through doctoral studies at a predominantly white institution (PWI). It allowed us to take off the masks we felt required to wear in our classes and in our professional lives.

This is where I got to know the third woman, a brilliant but reserved Latina with whom I had many classes over the years. I had a secret scholarly crush on her. Her thinking was so dope, and she was easily one of the smartest individuals in our program. If you met her, you would think she was shy because she was usually quiet, but when she spoke, you knew that she had something to say, something to offer. Once we began attending the advising sessions, we quickly grew into lifelong friends. It was that friendship that helped me find my voice. She challenged me to think more deeply about life and why I was drawn to this work in the first place. These women affectionately became known as the WOCs (women of color), and we refer to ourselves in that way to this day. They helped me find myself again and, in turn, find my voice. They helped me stay true to myself and held me accountable. Most importantly, they shared with me strategic and creative ways that I can use my voice and maintain my integrity.

One of those creative outlets has been writing about my experiences to finally give voice to and honor them. Writing about my experiences has been restorative and has given me the closure I needed to move past being that scared woman I was so many years ago. Sharing what I've been through has helped me heal and forgive myself for my self-betrayal. I finally have the courage to speak up and to be unapologetic in sharing my perspective. What I have found is a tremendous amount of support from people in places I would have never imagined. Now instead of being afraid to speak up, I am afraid not to.

I will forever cherish the WOC sessions where we talked, laughed, cried, and prayed because I know that without them, I would not be here today in this beautiful and challenging place of self-discovery and self-awareness. Because of their love and support, I won't ever dishonor myself or the sacrifice and investment these women made in my life. I will never again be silent or trade in my integrity for a title or position. I will speak truth to power, walk in my God-given authority, and provide shelter and love for others until they too can emerge and share their truth.

THE STUDENT WHO CALLED
REVERSE RACISM
BENTLEY PORTERFIELD-FINN

Being a young Black female instructor means having your competence and character explicitly called into question. In this case, a white male student accused me of practicing reverse racism in my grading. After receiving a C on an assignment, he wrote in an email,

> This makes it clear to me that you do not respect my success in life purely because of my color. My path has not been easy and just because I am white doesn't mean that I didn't work extremely hard to get where I am. For somebody who is very passionate about equal rights, you sure are quick to use demeaning reverse racism against your students. I hope that we can work this out because I really don't want to feel uncomfortable sitting in my class because my instructor looks at me as/calls me a "privileged white boy" who doesn't deserve the things that he has worked for.

It's hard to put into words how this email continues to make me feel. My heart rate increases and my chest tightens every time I reread it. When I first received this message, I wanted to crawl into a hole and never go back to that class. But that wasn't an option.

This incident happened in my first semester of graduate school—my first semester teaching undergraduate students. Let me take you back in time and provide further context.

When I was initially accepted to my graduate program in communication studies, my biggest fear was not my ability to keep up with the rigor of the classes but the impact my identity would have on my success as an instructor. As part of my graduate program, all first-year master's students taught a public speaking course to undergraduates. This meant being the primary teacher for classes with twenty-four students in each. I remember asking the director of the basic public speaking course during orientation what could be done to establish respect in the classroom—how to ensure my students would view me as an authority figure rather than a peer. He told me to dress professionally and request that students call me by my last name rather than by my first name. I knew this wouldn't be enough, but I did not push the subject much further with him.

Walking into my first day of teaching, "nervous" does not even begin to describe how I felt. Deep down, I knew I was capable, but I felt swallowed by a wave a self-doubt. Simultaneously, I was so excited—eager to meet my students and excited to facilitate thought-provoking conversations with them and challenge them. I felt proud of myself for all the work I had done leading up to that moment. As my students trickled in, all twenty-four seats were filled—with not a single Black student. I was no stranger to being the only Black person in a classroom; in my undergrad experience, I had always been hypervigilant of my tone of voice, of my body moving through predominantly white spaces. But how would this work when I was the teacher? None of my professors in undergrad looked like me, and I wondered how my identity might influence my ability to succeed in academia. How do individuals navigate conversations about identity when they themselves have been marginalized? Looking back, I think I dismissed and downplayed these fears even to myself. I took the approach that if I did not acknowledge the challenges that come with being a Black woman in academia, they wouldn't impede my ability to succeed.

Back to my first semester of teaching during my graduate program. On the first day of orientation, the director of graduate students declared, "This is the most diverse cohort of graduate students we've ever had." I understood her desire to celebrate this, but to me it felt disappointing. I was one of four BIPOC graduate students in the entire program, including master's and PhD students, and none of the faculty members were Black (one was BIPOC). The semester started toward the end of August, and in early October there was a blackface incident on campus. My student sent the email quoted at the beginning of this story in late October.

This student was already causing me stress. He asked inappropriate questions: How old was I? Did I have a boyfriend? I tried my best to dodge the questions and remain professional, but it was extremely uncomfortable. He had told me on many occasions that he was a premed student and that his grades were very important to him. When he received a B on his first speech, he tried to argue that he deserved a higher grade. But I was always sure to give very detailed and extensive feedback on speeches in case I should ever have to defend my grading decisions to a student or to my director—an example of always looking over my shoulder, prepared to defend myself should my competence be questioned.

On the day that spurred the email, my students were presenting public deliberation speeches. The speech topic of standardized testing came up, and the deliberation revealed differences of opinion among my students. Some argued that standardized tests were not accurate markers of intellect. Others claimed the tests privileged those with certain identities, who lived in more urban geographic regions, or who had the financial capital to hire tutors or pay to take tests more than once. The male student who wrote me the email was of the opinion that anyone who worked hard enough could succeed on the test and get into a good school. My eyes went visibly wide, but I did not say a word. A white female student turned to him and said, "That's easy for you to say. You're a white man." I nodded but still did not speak.

The deliberation ended, and then class ended. The male student and another white male student approached me after class, visibly upset. I should also mention that I am five feet three inches tall, and both of these students were at least five feet eleven. They both raised their voices, expressing anger that I made claims about their privilege. Remember, I'd said nothing. One of the students then said, "My life isn't easy. Minorities are the ones getting too many handouts these days." I responded, "Then may I ask why our campus, or even this class, looks the way it does?" The one who sent the email said, "You don't know my life. You don't know how hard I have had to work to get where I am." I responded, "You are right. I am not saying you are not a hard worker. I am saying if you had a different skin color, your journey might look different and you might be presented with different obstacles to success." The conversation continued along this path until students in the next class, a women and gender studies course, came into the lecture hall. Upon hearing what the two male students were saying to me, the women and gender studies students chimed in, speaking about race, identity, and privilege. When the two male students left, some individuals in the women and gender studies class apologized to me for having to deal with that. I said, "It is just hard to navigate those conversations when I am the teacher." Their mouths dropped open. They could not believe students were speaking to an instructor with such disrespect.

I had already graded the student's speech before class that day. After that conversation and his previous frustration over getting a B, I was terrified of returning his grade. I knew it would become about race. I expressed my fear to my director; he told me not to stress, that he thought everything would be OK, and that we would handle that situation if it happened.

Well, it happened. The student sent that email quoted at the beginning of this story (and that's not even the whole email). At first, I was shocked. The audacity of his language blew my mind. Reverse racism? I felt hurt as a person and like a failure as a teacher. How do you teach students about privilege when you're not white? Trying to talk about systems of oppression suddenly turned very personal.

I was absolutely crushed. On top of this, I had research papers and projects with impending deadlines. Because of my race and the need to navigate my identity in the classroom, I was under a form of emotional stress that some of my graduate colleagues will never experience. It wasn't fair. No wonder there aren't more Black academics. I escalated this issue to the head of the department, and he asked, "What would you like me to do about the situation?" Um, maybe kick him out of my class? But that wasn't an option. Colorado is also a conceal and carry state, so I had a very tangible fear that this student was going to bring a gun to class. I was terrified.

I was ready to drop out of the program. The week after the email, I expressed this to the director of graduate studies, and she said to me, "You can't leave. We need more people like you." Instead of the support and validation I needed, I was tokenized. Upon my request, the director of the basic public speaking course said he would have a discussion with the student. I thought that he, as a white man, would tell my student how unacceptable that email was. But he just asked for the student's perspective on the situation. That didn't feel like support. The student remained in my class. I continued to teach. We were both instructed to speak to each other only when necessary and to remain professional. Whatever that means. I feel like "professionalism" is a product of white supremacy.

So, essentially, the situation was unresolved. I continued going to class, still unsure how to navigate my identity in the classroom. I found a few faculty members in my department who provided validating support and made me feel seen. On the last day of class, I decided to approach the student because I still felt there had been no closure on the situation. My purpose as an instructor is to teach my students, and I could not help but think he hadn't learned from this experience. I told one of my faculty advisors I was going to do this and she told me, "OK, but be prepared to not get the response you want. He likely will not apologize, and he probably doesn't think what he did was wrong." I didn't really care what his response was going to be. I just needed to use my voice and stand up for myself.

I asked him to stay a moment after the last class. I started the conversation by telling him I wanted to speak to him as a human being, not as his instructor. I then expressed to him how that email made me feel. I even told him that it made me cry and how I considered dropping out of my program. At first, he was speechless. Then he apologized. He went on to say that he thought I was a great teacher and that he sent that email reactively without thinking. While this response in no way erases the emotional pain the situation caused me, I felt a weight lifted off my shoulder because I used my voice. I stood up for myself.

SORRY, I DON'T UNDERSTAND YOU

DIANE EZEH ARUAH

As the only Black person in my PhD cohort at a predominantly white institution, one of my greatest challenges was not having a sense of belongingness in the environment. It seemed like everywhere I went, people questioned my attire, my hair, the way I talked, where I came from, and the kind of research I did.

My name is Diane Ezeh Aruah. I was born and raised in Nigeria. In my first semester of graduate school in the United States, some of my professors and cohort members often made me repeat my words, even though I could tell they understood me correctly. On one occasion, a professor asked me to go and tell my cohort members, who were outside, that break time was over. After I shared his message with one of my peers, she turned to her friend and laughed. "Do you understand anything she's saying? I don't get her." They both laughed and stared at me once more. "What are you saying?" they asked. This time I was embarrassed, and I started to stammer. At that point, I told myself I would never speak with them again.

In the same semester, I was seated in class waiting for a professor's lecture. A classmate of mine came in and saw my new hair.

"Your hair is so beautiful, Diane," she said.

"Thank you." I was pleased and blushed.

"Is that your natural hair?"

I was taken aback by the question. "No, it's not."

"Oh! Why do you guys keep deceiving us with fake hairs?"

I was shocked and embarrassed that she could ask me that. In my home country, Nigeria, nobody has ever asked me that. It is normal there for us to wear our natural hair and also to wear wigs. I can't recall how I answered her, but since that day, I have felt a sense of resentment toward her. I even had to cut my natural hair at some point because I thought I would appear non-deceitful if I wore my natural hair instead. I had met a fellow Black colleague who was on low cut. She convinced me that wearing a low cut was the best way to feel natural.

Also, I was pregnant in my first year and was anxious about not keeping up with class activities due to fatigue. I confided in a peer whom I thought I had gotten close to. Instead of encouraging me to push harder, he began to question me about my reasons for coming to the United States to get a PhD. Was it because I really wanted a doctorate, or because I wanted my child to be a citizen? Would I be going back home to have the baby? I was completely shocked by these questions. Did he think I would travel thousands of miles to have a baby in the middle of final exams? I felt he was judging me, and that also made me withdraw completely from him. In addition to him, many cohort members and non-Black friends asked me about my motives for coming to the United States and whether I would be returning home after my education. Although some of them may have meant no harm, most of these questions made me feel like they didn't want me here.

Another experience that made me feel isolated happened in February 2020 when I attended a conference in Denver, Colorado. I was the only Black person at that conference, but that wasn't my problem. The problem was that even though I had spent time, money, and other resources registering for the conference and flying from Florida to Colorado to attend it, no one had printed out my conference badge and program. The person in charge had to use a marker and paper to design my badge, which meant that I, the only Black person in the room, was the only person wearing a shabbily written conference badge. Even during my presentation, I sensed many were on their laptops and phones. I kept speculating about what was on their mind. Could they be wondering, What in heaven's name was this Black woman thinking to attend this conference?

The worst of all these experiences was the one I had as a course instructor and a researcher. Coming from Nigeria, being Black, and being a woman, my anxiety at teaching a class in the United States for the first time was extremely high. Even though I had been a lecturer at the University of Nigeria for three years and taught more than 300 students per semester, I felt as though my students, who were mostly white, were judging whether I was knowledgeable or smart enough to teach them. I always like to introduce myself as a Nigerian in my class so that everyone can be aware of why I don't speak like them. But it seems like revealing my national identity automatically makes some students assume they know better than I do. I've had a student demand evidence of what I was teaching them. This was embarrassing to me because the information in my lecture was from the textbook and materials I had recommended for the class. In my class evaluation, I had a student complain about my accent and the Zoom background of my lectures. It was during COVID, and my husband and I were at home working with toddlers around. I thought students would be understanding if, when I was teaching, my daughter came into the room crying. I kept wondering whether that student would have made such a comment if I was a white woman. I also remember a student complaining about the poor quality of YouTube videos I showed them in class, simply because I used an Afrocentric video to illustrate the point I was making. I've also had a student message me to say my lecture on racism was too biased because white people suffer oppression too and it was wrong for me to keep assuming that it's only Black people who suffer racism in the United States. Experience has taught me to ignore these types of messages, but at the back of my mind I keep wondering whether they would react differently if I were not Black.

Finally, it was extremely difficult for me to find someone interested in my research interests; thus, I did not collaborate with people on their research projects or mine. Because my research was focused on health communication concerning African and African American populations and my college had few Africans and African Americans, I ended up writing papers on my own, which can be stressful and time-consuming. Many people I approached to work with could not relate to the problems with African and African American communities that I was excited to solve.

I would have talked about these feelings with some of my cohort and friends or maybe even authorities, but I could not. I was afraid of being perceived negatively or being denied access to things given to me. I am a Nigerian on a student visa. I did not want my name in anything that could implicate or jeopardize my status in the United States. As a young immigrant mother, I wanted to be on everyone's good side so as not to be denied anything in the future—for example, recommendation letters. Perhaps when I become a citizen and an assistant professor in a US school, I will be able to use my voice to advocate for change. In the meantime, I advise any person who has the privilege to be observant of the challenges Black people experience in the United States and develop both personal and institutional strategies to alleviate these challenges.

REMEMBRANCES OF RUNNING IN THE SNOW

Black Hidden Disability in White Eyes

NICOLE EUGENE

While at Spelman College, I embraced running to manage the occasional stress bomb of being an undergraduate student. My PhD program was a nuclear stress bomb because I was extremely uncomfortable in white spaces and because seven years had passed between earning my last graduate degree and starting this graduate program. I fell in love with running in the newly fallen snow in Ohio. Before most woke up, I would put myself in an arduous climate and persevere up a winding, hilly road, warming as I moved. Like Kiese Laymon's compulsive running in his memoir, *Heavy*, I too ran to avoid truly feeling the compounding stresses of academia. Also like him, I was eventually injured, and now I intensely feel all the things I was running from—searing isolation and institutional racism.

In the first month of the PhD program, my autoethnographic essay about my experience with narcolepsy came out in the journal *Anthropology of Consciousness*. It had been accepted months earlier with no revisions. News of the publication was included in the department's weekly announcements—and I was pulled out of the disability closet. A few graduate students congratulated me on the publication and one faculty member mentioned reading it. I was utterly unprepared for just how ill-equipped white faculty and white students were at relating to me as an African American woman with a hidden disability. Perhaps I also lacked intercultural skills for communicating with white people effectively. As fallible humans, we are all imperfect; however, in academia, some persons and some imperfections are more likely to be penalized than others.

Being in academia with a hidden disability is a tightrope act. I decided to hide my condition from my students while researching how people talk about their narcolepsy in their lives. As semesters went by, a pattern of concerning end-of-semester student evaluations emerged. The scores I received were lower than my peers, and although most details are lost to time, I do recall one form where instead of answering qualitative questions a student drew a dinosaur-like animal and wrote, "Let Jack teach the class." Eventually, I received an email from a never-a-hair-out-of-place faculty member about my being in some sort of probationary status because of student evaluations. The school wanted to kick me out. I compulsively researched the relationship between instructor identity and student evaluations. I felt under attack, although I had no idea what I was doing wrong as an instructor. A general inability to point to moments where I knew my race or disability was impacting my experience meant that I constantly felt gaslighted for thinking these factors were at play. I persevered.

One day I was invited to a meeting about the evaluations. One untenured and two tenured faculty members were present; I came armed with research about biases in student evaluations of teaching.

"We want you to succeed here."

"A faculty member will visit you and do an observation of your class."

"Try recording yourself."

"We have to take students' comments seriously. They have a right to be listened to."

"We need to see a significant improvement in your evaluations, or you will need to find another way to fund your PhD program."

I think I mentioned the research on biases, but my timid words were powerless.

"Maybe we should quantify it? We need to see a 3.9 or above as an average on most of the items at the end of this semester."

The following week, despite my reluctance, I decided to make myself vulnerable and try to be more likable and increase immediacy. I used my phone to record an example speech that revealed my narcolepsy to my students. I later watched it with my roommate, and eventually she noted, "Right there, you switch back."

"What?"

"You turn back into robot mode right there," she said, referring to when the question-and-answer portion ended and I returned to talking about the students' speech assignment. Unsure what my roommate meant, I wanted more details, yet I was unwilling to probe further. Perhaps I was already too raw from the unspecific criticism undergirding my predicament.

After sharing my story of having narcolepsy, many students offered their health stories, which gave me hope that my evaluation scores might improve this time around. Some weeks back, I had shared my precarious situation with a trusted faculty member who told me about the faculty disability services office and about someone I will call my hero. My hero went over all my emails, letters, evaluations, and medical information with me and assured me that what the program was trying to do would not succeed. I would not be kicked out of the PhD program because of low student evaluations.

One day I walked past the office of the never-a-hair-out-of-place faculty member, who abruptly waved to me and called my name. I stood at the door. This person read a part of the letter my hero sent and explained that the program would find something for me the next semester, adding, "It might not be as instructor of record. We will work something out." I remained amiable while hiding my pleasure and relief, offering a smile. My step held more pep as I continued to my destination.

That semester, the student evaluation scores were not much different; one or more students wrote "find another instructor," while useful feedback was difficult to glean. Still, wishes on both sides were granted— I spent the next few semesters as either a TA of a large lecture class or as an assistant for the speech and debate team. Ultimately, I returned to being instructor of record with the mystery of what exactly I was doing wrong still unsolved. Many faculty seemed utterly unfamiliar with Black talent and the challenges I might face performing in inhospitable spaces. Through it all I discovered beautiful new places to run to keep myself moving forward mentally and physically—to cope.

My doctor explained that my sleep was very disrupted. I would wake dozens of times, unknowingly, each night. He put me on a medication to help me sleep during my last year in the program. As I started to sleep better, I noticed subtle changes in my cognition. I wondered whether some of the mystery of the poor evaluations was connected to my untreated disrupted sleep.

These days, my evaluations as a faculty member are full of praise. I also have many anti-racist white colleagues and friends who trust and support me. The mystery of what exactly I was doing wrong lives on. Was it poor eye contact? Was it brain fog? Was I too robotic? Or was I simply too Black and too neurodivergent? And despite dealing with the pain of a recent injury, I am still quite enamored with running.

HUNG UP ON THE HANG-UPS
OF GRADUATE SCHOOL

JOHNESHA HARRIS

I came to graduate school knowing that I wanted to help students who looked like myself successfully navigate through the academic world while also excelling in their personal lives. It was my goal to create a space that centered communication and connection in a positive light for new and inquiring minds. But my own mind was new and inquiring within the academic world, and I had to adapt fast to keep up with classes, teaching, and the overall demands of being a graduate student in my department. I was used to attending school in the South because I have lived there my whole life. I was no stranger to racism, oppression, microaggressions, or any other derailment ploys. But when I decided to attend a large southern research institution with a prestigious communication studies program, the actions that I had previously seen or experienced paled in comparison to what I was faced with on that campus.

In my master's program, I quickly learned that as a Black woman you must always come prepared and stand on your beliefs to be heard in this world. Being humble is truly not in our nature because we have carried this world on our backs for as long as time. I felt how intimidated others were by my presence and presentation. I knew where I wanted to go in life and only needed directions to get there. The issue was that the people in my department couldn't help me because they were the very people I was trying to help Black students avoid. Every time I reached my hand out for help, I would get responses along the lines of, "Your ideas are not valid because they do not make sense to me," "Maybe you should try to look at the research this person is doing and follow their path," or "This is not something that we do in Interpersonal Communication; maybe you are not meant to be classified as such." It all left me confused and, in many ways, hurt. I attended school August 2019 to August 2021, and unfortunately I felt those emotions throughout the entirety of my program. I had "great ideas" but no prior knowledge of "how to do graduate school," so I ended up getting lost in the shuffle.

The real frustration came from me not understanding how most thought I needed to kiss my advisor's ass to advance or to follow in her footsteps to accomplish anything. I saw her (a white woman) put off her responsibilities of working with me for the sake of her research and daily routines, something I wish I would have spoken up about in the moment because it showed how ill-prepared she was for taking on a student like myself. At the beginning of my first semester on campus, I went to her with a research idea that she did not fully comprehend. Instead of connecting me with someone who could help, she suggested I change my focus to better accommodate the program time frame. Following her advice, I ended up putting more time into and emphasis on learning about Communication Studies as a whole and never actually took time to find something to specifically home in on for my own research. During my first semester, I felt as if I was an undecided major my junior year of undergrad; I didn't know what I wanted to but was aware that the program clock was ticking away.

A Black woman graduate student saw me the first day of orientation for our department and validated me on the spot with a simple yet powerful look. The gesture and quick conversation at lunch gave me instant comfort. She took no time in making sure I knew what opportunities were available to me outside the department and always provided wisdom when I expressed how lost I felt in it all. She saw my potential and even opened my eyes to different areas within Communication Studies, and to other departments, that might suit me and my research ideas. And it's all because she heard me. I had a lot of growing to do, but she made sure I never stopped moving, because we as Black people know what happens when we "fail." In saying all this, I know she didn't have to do any of it because she, too, was a student suffering through her own issues within the department, but she still managed to lift others up while she climbed her own mountain! And that was a true testament that the work could get done, so I made sure to keep learning and pushing. I made it to the finish line and have that official paper with my name and "MA in Communication Studies" right below it. I am in a completely different place than I imagined I would be after completing my degree. I decided to stick to what I know and utilize what I have learned to benefit me—which landed me a full-time position working with high school students on developing fundamental communication practices. This is exactly where I wanted to be when I started graduate school, but the journey it took to get here was the biggest surprise lesson that changed me in many ways.

It's hard. It's hard finding my next steps because academia holds tight to tradition. However, my experience has taught me to embrace my differences and to contiuously show why mine and other intersectional voices belong in the ongoing conversations about where academia is headed. As I continue to work on developing instructional measures for the ever changing classroom environment, I am striving to show students how not to fall prey to the number system that universities and colleges plug them into and instead help them stand out as the unique individuals they are.

THE EFFECT OF HOSTILE ENVIRONMENTS IN ACADEMIA ON A BLACK SCIENTIST

Testimony from a Lived Experience

BARNABAS

A few years after completing my PhD program, I was conducting post-doctoral research in botany as the only Black person on a team. Two people were collaborating as principal investigators (PIs) on my research project—one was white; the other was neither white nor Black. The former individual, "Chuck," was a government employee as a research scientist; the latter, "JK," was a professor.

When I started working, the PIs and their lab members were supportive, and the work environment was positive. However, things took a detour for the worse starting in 2017, about a year after I was hired. It all started when I made an interesting observation in the lab. Everyone spoke highly of me and the "discovery" I made. I thought about the phenomena I had observed and came up with several hypotheses to test them. I shared some of the possible lines of investigation with JK. I was about to initiate experiments and execute them myself, but JK immediately hired one of their compatriots, a new postdoc, to work with me. I learned about the hire only on this person's first day of work.

Sadly, as the research took off, neither the excitement nor the support lasted long. The workplace quickly turned hostile. About four months after the arrival of the new postdoc, JK insulted me in a meeting. "Nobody cares about your discovery! Other people have already made this observation." I was devastated and did not know how to react or what to do. The meeting ended shortly afterward. I was puzzled as to what may have triggered JK to behave in such a demeaning and condescending manner toward me and my work.

Following the incident, the postdoc withdrew from engaging with me. They also stopped contributing to research activities and became dismissive of me and my work. Whenever JK told me to ask the postdoc for help, the postdoc would say, "Do we have an appointment?" or "I am busy with my work!" and quickly turned their back on me. This went on for months. However, they wanted to take full credit for everything, including work they did not perform. At one point, JK told me to include the postdoc as a coauthor on an abstract submitted for a conference. The idea was that the postdoc would contribute some data, but that never happened. A week before the conference, the postdoc tried to coerce me into helping them retrieve data collected by another coauthor and transmit it to JK as their own work. I refused to cooperate but ended up in the ER due to a panic attack accompanied by signs and symptoms of harassment.

Next, Chuck became hostile toward me at a meeting where JK was present. "Why do you do all these research activities?" and "You cannot publish even a single paper!" was his abrupt reaction. I felt devalued and squeezed out among multiple hostile forces. Panic attacks became a daily occurrence. I withdrew from interactions and refocused 100 percent of my energy on the work. It was an isolating experience.

Fast-forward to the beginning of 2019, when I came up with some interesting ideas for future research. I shared the ideas with JK, who agreed to keep them confidential. However, JK shared them with another postdoc in the lab. A few days after hearing the ideas behind my back, this postdoc waited until everybody left the office and verbally assaulted me. The postdoc claimed that they did their PhD research on the topic and JK told them to talk to me about it. They aggressively pressured me to "forward all your data to me right away!" I felt violated and feared being in the office when nobody else was present. I began leaving the office early, afraid of an attack. I called a closed-door meeting in the presence of a third party. The postdoc brought anxiety medication to the meeting and admitted that they regretted their behavior. However, the situation became worse after the meeting. The postdoc disclosed issues raised during the closed-door meeting to their tight-knit friends, including the other postdoc who had been hired to work with me on the project. This opened another cycle of crisis.

Chuck now sensed something and became aggressive. He would run to my office, forcefully open the door, and demand data. I was even physically threatened as Chuck invaded my personal space and stood over my shoulder while exhibiting aggressive, nonverbal expressions. The situation became overwhelming and unbearable. Overwhelmed with a panic attack, an upset stomach, sleeplessness, a loss of appetite, and more, I ended up in the ER once again.

I reached out to one of my mentors, who suggested I seek help from the department. I also sought assistance from the postdoc union. My research, academic progress, and career were totally halted for three months as I went on medical leave. And, of course, my health was severely impacted.

When I returned to work, I met with the two PIs together for the first time in more than two years; the three of us had not been together in one room since Chuck had disrupted one of our meetings two years back. All of us acted as if everything was cool and carried out the meeting. I provided the overview of possible manuscripts, hoped for the best, and continued working. Hostile parties exhibited a bit of self-control and acted responsibly. I felt much safer. A half-million-dollar grant proposal I had conceived and written before going on sick leave was funded for two and a half years. However, when my contract was up for renewal a year later, JK decided against any extension. My employment then ended, and JK withdrew their name from my upcoming manuscripts. I felt betrayed and became consumed with hopelessness. At the time of submitting the draft of this essay, I was jobless and unsure of my future career trajectory. Staying optimistic, I had been pushing forward with manuscript preparation and staying connected with my profession. After being out of work for about 14 months, I found a job at an academic institution. I am resolute and will continue the struggle in the pursuit of knowledge in the academy.

WHAT I WISH SOMEONE HAD TOLD ME

The contributors to this book wrote advice to Blackademic readers under the prompt "What I wish someone had told me" when they were pursuing their undergraduate studies and graduate degrees, moving up the professional ranks, and thinking about alternatives to academia entirely. They range in length, scope, and tenor. The advice from contributors to the "Surviving Graduate School" section is shared below, but you are encouraged to read advice from contributors in the other sections too because their words may resonate with you.

Do unto others. To say it another way: Karma's a bitch. Also: God don't like ugly. So be a blessing to others. It can't hurt.
— Anonymous

When I started the doctoral journey, I did not realize the extent to which this process could negatively impact social and emotional well-being. The cumulative effects of hyper-competition, market-driven productivity expectations, publish *and* perish mentality, and ongoing racial stress are hard on the psyche. It's no wonder so many in the academy suffer with depression and anxiety. I wish someone would have told me early on how important it is to have a plan to proactively care for yourself. And I mean a plan for care *maintenance*, not simply getting help when things get bad or you get sick. Plan for and schedule exercise, rest, and social connection just the same as you schedule writing or reading time. Take breaks and vacation when you want them and before you *need* them. Self-care isn't just bubble baths and binging TV; it's sometimes doing the unpleasant improvement work on yourself to heal from past traumas, so go ahead and schedule that counseling appointment too. As Dr. Sará King reminds us that well-being *is* social justice (they are one and the same), prioritizing care for self and others (while calling out inequitable access to well-being) is a necessary path toward freedom.
— Paris

As a budding professional, please find yourself a mentor. I would even say find a mentor once you are in your profession. Always look for those who are in places that you want to go. If possible, find an ally or someone who looks like you. Even though my experience was negative, I learned a lot about the real world. You may be the most qualified and the best interviewed, but sometimes it is about who you know. These circumstances build your character and resilience and strengthen your compassion for those who come behind you. Take chances and volunteer for stuff you have never done. THEY do it all the time, and you will figure it out. Good luck; you got this . . . shoot, GOD got you. Be blessed. ☺

   —Candis

I now know that as an African American student, I will sometimes need to be prepared to take on the role of advocate and educator for the ones who are certified to educate me. It is pressure. It is heavy. It is not something you will necessarily get credit for, but it will do wonders for your sense of self, mental health, and confidence along the way to academic achievement. It is not your responsibility to carry the burden of educating someone's ignorance, but you can point people in the direction of how they can educate themselves. Whatever classroom you find yourself in, do not question that voice inside of you that feels discomfort. It does not matter if no harm was meant or if intentions were good. If we want the classroom to continue to be a place of change, power, intellect, and inspiration, ignorance must be called out every time.

   —Precious

I only recently heard of and have now read the book *Presumed Incompetent: The Intersections of Race and Class for Women in Academia*, edited by Gabriella Gutiérrez y Muhs, Yolanda Flores Niemann, Carmen G. González, and Angela P. Harris. This book was first published in 2012. In lieu of a well-informed colleague or supervisor confirming that the biases I experienced were real and not unique to me, a book like this would have been very helpful. What the title meant to me was validation of my experiences: *Someone else knows what it feels like; you are not the only one.* I felt both relief and profound sadness at this realization. I also felt seen and heard.

   —Nadia

I have learned that the concept of Blackness is very specific to who you are as a person. As such, do not allow anyone to place you in a "box" by forcing you to conform to their idea of how you "should be" as a Blackademic. By that, I must warn you that shade will come from both sides of the aisle, so beware and proceed accordingly. Skin does not equal kin, and some people will denigrate you for "not being Black enough," while others may say you're "being too Black." Do your research, read your books, invest in your happiness, and remember that your definition of "being Black" truly means whatever you want it to mean for yourself. Date who you want to date. Watch what you want to watch. Be who you want to be. Love who you want to love, and allow people to love you for who you are. Trust me, life is beautiful when you do so.

—Savant

You can't pour from an empty cup. Here are a few reminders to keep going:
#BlackMentalHealthMatters.
Your worth is intrinsic.
Know your worth and then add TAX!
Rest is a right.
Your professional capabilities are not a reflection of your value.
Your family and social life are pivotal parts of your existence;
    honor them.
You deserve respect.
You deserve to be protected.
A career is a means to an end.
You deserve to be happy.
Therapy works.
Unionize. There is strength in the collective.
Speak your truth even if your voice shakes.
Don't be afraid to start over.
There is a whole world outside of academia.
Stay if it feels right. Be brave enough to question if it doesn't.
Be patient with yourself; nothing in nature blooms all year round.
You made it this far; remember you are capable and competent.
Trust yourself.
—Carol Ann

The best advice I have ever received is "let them tell you no." So much of the time we give in to impostor syndrome and tell ourselves "no" to an opportunity. But if you want to do something and you think you are reasonably qualified, go for it. Even if you think you are unqualified—if it's a good fit, go for it. The worst that can happen is that you are told "no."

—Alexis

Being #BlackintheIvory means that you will learn to advise yourself. I share that with Black graduate students because it prepares them for many obstacles. Until graduate programs realize that students of color cannot perform their best in a community with little awareness about intersectional identities, we must keep teaching others how to survive sustainably. You can advocate for classes that improve your learning experience, network with faculty outside of your department or university, or take on leadership positions that give you the power to create equitable solutions for Black students. Graduate students are often unaware of hidden privileges, so I encourage you to get into the right rooms, ask questions, and listen for the opportunities that create change for everyone.

—Laura

You are not your research or your title! I first want to acknowledge all that it has taken for you to get where you are and congratulate you for all your accomplishments. So much of what we do goes unacknowledged by those around us because they don't care or don't understand. You have done great work, and I know you will continue to do great work—but know that none of it defines you. You are a whole person with people who love you and passions to pursue outside of academia, so don't forget to cultivate those relationships and those parts of yourself that truly make you the amazing person that you are. Say no to another research project and yes to that beach vacation or once-in-a-lifetime opportunity. The world will continue to spin while you refresh and rejuvenate yourself. Your students will be OK and things will still get done—no, not as well as you would do them, but that's OK. The more you choose to put yourself first, the better off everyone around you will be. Try one thing at a time, one day at a time. You got this!

—Bernadette

Always put yourself first, and always trust your gut. As Black people in the United States, we are often hyperaware of our bodies moving through spaces and conscious of how we communicate with the world around us, especially in predominantly white spaces. Academia is no different—it is a complex and sometimes lonely sphere to navigate as a Black person. Find other Black people to talk to, whether a faculty member, an administrator, or grad students in another department. Do not feel like you need to face this challenge alone. Social support from another Black person goes such a long way. It won't change racism; it just helps you feel more equipped to cope. Speaking about graduate school in particular, it's already challenging without all of the added layers of emotional labor you may be faced with. But seriously, put yourself first. Put your emotions first, even above your grades and schoolwork. Give yourself time, space, and permission to feel angry, tired, sad, frustrated, whatever it may be. Feel it and voice it. Systems do not change if we don't make people aware of how they are complicit in white supremacy.

—Bentley

I find that speaking up can help change things and bring solutions. If you have experienced any form of discrimination, macroaggression, or mistreatment in academia because you are Black, you can either report it or let the offender know the consequences of their actions. The world has normalized racism so much that some people may not be aware when they are perpetuating it. As Black people in academia, we need to keep educating young, old, and privileged people about the many ways Black people can experience discrimination, especially in academia.

Always let your voice be heard. Try to stay active and up-to-date as a Black person in academia. Attend as many conferences as you can. Join Black organizations suitable for you in your institution. Mingle with Black colleagues, both outside and inside your institution, whom you can share experiences with and learn from.

Last, be yourself. I learned to love my accent, my wigs, and my attire, and I do not care who accepts it or not. I've got no time to worry about people who do not love me. I stand tall in class, I look directly in their eyes, and I teach what I came to teach.

—Diane

Apathy can be dangerous. Many African Americans and people of various races receive apathy from white people and internalize this orientation. If anyone wants to succeed in a PWI (predominantly white institution), one must understand that being apathetic toward white culture and white people will only make learning the rules of the road more difficult. There is no need to enjoy or embrace white culture to thrive in academia, but one does need to know that only whites have the luxury to be blind to how culture creates hidden rules. It is equally important to be on guard for the superwoman syndrome, which makes Black women fear expressions of vulnerability and failure. Black women at all levels of education may fall prey to this belief, which means they are at a disadvantage when it comes to developing nurturing social relationships that can be essential when facing difficulties.

—Nicole

Never be silent in moments where your voice is needed. Trust that we are all tired of having to explain ourselves and our reasoning to outsiders. However, you must know that you will never be respected where you allow disrespect, and people have no problem disrespecting you in the name of ignorance or following the status quo. You'd best believe that somebody down the line will appreciate you capitalizing off those moments.

Also, be a community for those who look like you wherever you go. I can't say thank you enough to the Black woman who continually saved me in my master's program because she knew what it was like to be in my shoes. There were also many Blackademics who took time to hear me and provide a safe space for me. After my experience, I know to do the same for any Black or Brown person I see who needs a friend or confidant while navigating academia. You should learn and do the same.

—Johnesha

- Do not disclose information. However excited you may feel about your research ideas or insights, you may be better off keeping them to yourself. If you want to ever share your ideas and research plans, make sure those people have your back. Do not give anyone the benefit of the doubt. They are either with you or against you. Do not trust anyone with a middle-of-the-road stand when it comes to your professional or personal development. Identify people, including principal investigators, with conflicts of interest early on. Always watch over your shoulder. There may be predators looking to snatch your ideas and pass them on to their next-of-kin. Exciting developments in your research can fire back and lead to setbacks in ways you never imagined. Save insights you think are groundbreaking of sorts for later in your career.
- Cultivate relationships with multiple people as mentors for various aspects of your career.
- Be sure to be in a community of like-minded and supportive groups; it's important to maintain a sense of sanity.

- If you ever feel uncomfortable with some sort of interaction, particularly if persistent, be sure to access resource centers early. Hostility usually does not just disappear.
- Have a backup plan.
  —Barnabas

Part 3 Moving Up the Academic Ranks

Most people leave the university and enter the labor force after graduate school, putting their new knowledge into practice across professions, industries, and fields. But a small group of graduates make the decision to remain in the university as a faculty person. This decision isn't one that a person makes lightly, since the process is rather extensive.

In the United States, the most coveted entry-level university faculty job is that of tenure-track assistant professor. Tenure, simply put, is job security for life; tenured faculty can never be fired (unless under very extreme circumstances). And for many faculty, tenure is attached to them and not to an institution, which means they can work at other universities after earning tenure and retain job security. Because tenure-track positions are coveted and (relatedly) competitive and scarce, many highly qualified scholars with newly minted PhDs have to take less secure and less financially advantageous jobs in the university, including lectureships, part-time faculty positions, and adjunct positions. If a person secures a tenure-track assistant professorship, the professional pathway for that person becomes rather structured and standardized. To explain briefly: An individual works as an assistant professor for six years, during which time the individual is teaching, serving the university via committee work and professional associations, and publishing research. Then that person goes up for tenure. After an arduous yearlong evaluation process, the individual learns whether she or he earned tenure and was promoted to associate professor. If tenure is denied, the individual can no longer work at that school and has to find a new job at another university or outside of academia. If tenure is granted, the person can remain in the associate professor position for the rest of his or her career or can work to meet the requirements (as determined by the particular department and university) to be considered for promotion from associate to full professor. Attaining tenure and promotion is often the only way for faculty to move up the ranks into higher positions such as department chair, dean of a college, provost of a school, or even university president. This is especially true for faculty at universities that are research intensive (or R1). It should go without saying that anti-Blackness and anti-Black racism exacerbate the already challenging and fraught processes of applying to these positions, as well as applications for tenure and promotion.

Undoubtedly, great responsibility, power, money, institutional resources, and access are available to university faculty and administrators. One might assume that Blackademics who hold positions of power, especially those with name recognition, are somehow free from or able to maneuver around the harmful effects of anti-Black racism and anti-Blackness. But, to put it bluntly, racism is not fazed by their position or accolades. Indeed, Blackademic faculty and upper administrators contend with the same formidable forces in their professional lives that they encountered in college and graduate school.

In this section of the book, Blackademics who hold positions at colleges and universities across the United States document their confrontations with anti-Black racism while on the job market, going up for tenure, teaching college students, and serving on committees, as well as the day-to-day interactions of chatting with colleagues in department hallways and attending departmental dinners. The section opens with an essay by Cato T. Laurencin, an international thought leader in chemical, materials science, and biomedical engineering and the pioneer of a new field, regenerative engineering. Reflecting on his career of over thirty-five years, Laurencin details the lessons he learned as he worked his way up the ranks as a Black male faculty person in STEM.

DEVELOPING A PHILOSOPHICAL ARMOR
FOR ACHIEVING IN ACADEMIA

CATO T. LAURENCIN

Lead Narrative

The purpose of this short essay is to impart some knowledge, wisdom, and a bit of my philosophy to you after over thirty-five years in academia. First and foremost, while by all measures I have been eminently successful in my academic career, I must say that "the road to success is always under construction." I saw that at an actual construction site in Detroit about five years ago. It was first said by Arnold Palmer, one of the greatest golfers. As a golfer myself (a big golfer, but not a great golfer), I completely agree with him. But I also agree with the sentiment of the quote. There is advice, but there's no one road to success in academia. Gather opinions and thoughts, and put together your own philosophy of life.

A bit about me. My background lends itself to providing advice. While my bio appears in the back of the book, certain aspects may not be clear. First, I am an academic orthopaedic surgeon. I take care of patients and perform operations. I have moved up the academic ladder and have served in almost every administrative position—vice chair, chair, dean, vice president—and I now run my own institute, the Cato T. Laurencin Institute for Regenerative Engineering. At the same time, I am an engineer and have moved up the academic ladder to have a named professorship in engineering. Additionally, I have been a faculty member in the social sciences and currently am a core faculty member in Africana studies. Thus, my philosophy is universal for those in academia in that it crosses medicine, engineering, and science. I have been fortunate to have been funded federally for over twenty years by entities that include the National Institutes of Health, the National Science Foundation, the Department of Defense, and the National Aeronautics and Space Administration. I have pioneered a new field, regenerative engineering, which works around convergence (bringing disparate fields together to create new science). I first explained the new field in the *Science Translational Medicine* journal over a decade ago. It is wonderful to see how the field has progressed.

Success in academia, especially for a Black person, requires courage. Ralph Waldo Emerson said, "Whatever course you decide upon, there is always someone to tell you that you are wrong. There are always difficulties arising which tempt you to believe that your critics are right. To map out a course of action and follow it to an end requires . . . courage." As a Black person especially, your career and course of action will always be questioned and your ability to achieve always placed in doubt. As someone with an MD from Harvard Medical School (magna cum laude) and a PhD from MIT, I often marveled when someone would question whether I could be successful following a certain path.

Lil Wayne (one of my top ten rap artists) coined the phrase "Ray Charles to the bull." As Blacks striving in academics, one must generally avoid haters and doubters and those who are generally negative. Negative energy never has positive consequences. You have a choice of information you take in and process, and a key to a successful career is to filter out the negative and embrace those aspects that are positive to your career and to life.

I believe an important key is to build margin in your life. Margin can result in energy, mental calm, and security. The concept of margin originated with Richard Swenson, MD, who wrote the book *Margin*. In it he describes the equation (Margin = Power – Load). The goal is to build your power while decreasing your load. Your power, he explains, is from

1. skills and training
2. energy = emotional + physical + spiritual strength
3. positive finances
4. social supports and attitude

while your load is

1. work and obligations and commitments
2. expectations (external and internal)
3. weakness of body, mind, and spirit
4. debt and overextension
5. interpersonal conflict and fear and doubt

So, in a nutshell, margin occurs, as described by Swenson, in building your power and lessening your load.

My philosophy is that you should always focus on building your strengths, the root of your power. That is what will make you successful. Weaknesses can be hard to fix, and some weaknesses come as a by-product of your strengths. Also, some weaknesses are addressed as you build your power. Peter Drucker succinctly stated that there are three keys to success regarding personal knowledge: you must know your strengths, know how you perform, and know your values. The next level of knowledge for success is to know these categories for those working above and below you.

Regarding power, it is important to use it wisely. A key for Blacks in academia is NEVER CONFUSE ACTIVITY FOR ACCOMPLISHMENT. As an example, at my stage of my career, I turn down more opportunities than I accept. But I think I did that at all stages of my career. I weighed the importance of an activity toward my overall goals before committing. All activities that you engage in must be purposeful and address some clear higher goal. I embraced that philosophy at a young age and have benefited from it.

While on the subject of goals, it is important to create plans—and make them big. No one achieves higher than their loftiest goals. The plans should be short-term, medium-term, and long-term. But in academia, as in life, one must have resilience and adaptability. Perhaps this is the most important trait needed in academics.

One of my other jobs has been of ringside boxing doctor. I've been a doctor at a championship match with the legendary Mike Tyson. He once said, "Everybody has a plan until they get punched in the face." The quote to me explains that resiliency and adaptability are crucial for success in life.

I've made clear to my students that "tough times go away, tough people don't." I'm not quite sure who said the phrase first. It is at those times when you get punched in the face that your true measure shows. I also teach that when looking adversity in the eye, always have a victor mentality, never a victim mentality. The same circumstance can have completely different outcomes depending upon your point of view in approaching it.

Another important part of my philosophy comes from a Zimbabwe proverb: To stumble is not to fall but to walk faster. When we walk on an uneven pavement and stumble, we actually move faster. So, it is important to not be afraid to stumble. The stumbles can create the opportunities of your lives.

Finally, I want to add a personal story. My autobiography was recently published by Elsevier. It is titled *Success Is What You Leave Behind*, and in it I provide sixteen key lessons for success. The first describes my experience in administration as vice president for health affairs and dean of the Medical School at UConn. I was sitting in the academic box at the football stadium, watching the UConn Huskies play. Someone I didn't know approached me and struck up a conversation.

"Hello, I've been told that you are the head of the medical center," she stated.

"Yes," I said. "I'm the vice president for Health Affairs and the dean of the medical school."

"That's extraordinary that someone with your background would be the head of the medical center. I've always thought the head of a medical center would have to be a physician or a dentist or have some medical background," she said.

"Well, yes, I am a physician."

"No, you're not."

"Well, thanks," I said, "but *I am* a physician."

"No, I know you are not. I was told you played professional football for a number of years and now they made you head of the medical center."

"Nope, I never played football."

"Yes, you did."

"No, I'm sure I didn't. I'm pretty sure I would know. I didn't, really."

She stood up, frustrated with my answers. She turned to walk away and then turned around again. With one final incredulous look she asked, "Well, if you aren't a former professional football player running the medical center, why would they all say that you are?"

I remember recounting to myself that that was probably the only sane part of the conversation I had with the person. This is one of the everyday examples where someone chose to define me in an absurd way. It occurs throughout our lives as Black people. The fact is that there is a double absurdity to this—first, for whatever reason, that people would try to redefine who I was and my credentials, and second, that because I was a tall, strong Black man, it became immediately believable that a former professional football player was now the head of a medical center. My philosophy has been (as I explain in my autobiography) *Know who you are. Don't let others define you.* Attempts to define you—academically, morally, socially—come from all directions. Centering yourself in who you are is a key to success.

To close, I hope this bit of philosophy is helpful to you as you move through the world of academia. Remember, whatever happens, don't look backward. That's not where you are going in the end.

REMOVING THE RACIAL LADDER
IN THE IVORY TOWER

A Black Response to Racism in the Academy

MOLEFI KETE ASANTE

Spotlight Narrative

Having become a full professor at an early age, I have always believed that publication, hard work, excellent ideas, and devotion to students were the ingredients of a good mixture of what counted toward success in the academy. Of course, I have always recognized the uniqueness of my situation given the fact that I published often and with fanfare quite early in my career. Early tenure and full professorship meant that there was nothing in the academy that threatened me. I knew the place, read the contracts, followed the rules, and spoke my mind on any topic that I wanted to at any time. I challenged presidents, vice presidents, provosts, deans, and professors whenever I saw attempts to rank by race, to intimidate, and to change the rules on African American faculty and students. I reached the top tier in communication studies, having been named a National Communication Association's Distinguished Scholar, and my dance between rhetorical traditions and African cultural studies took me to the most glorious of possibilities in the academy: as an ardent seeker of cultural revolution to overthrow the racial ladder. By the time I was thirty years old, I was a full professor at State University of New York at Buffalo.

As chair of the Department of Communication at Buffalo, I administered a department that was rife with factionalism between two major professors, each occupying different methodological and theoretical interests. I later came to understand, thanks to a private letter to me in 2020, that although I was eventually selected as the chair of the department, my appointment had not been guaranteed, because a few people on the faculty objected to a Black person taking leadership of the department. David Bradley, one of the youngest in the all-white program, got two other young rebels to appeal to the university's academic and diversity leadership about my not being on the list of finalists, although I was considered the best and most knowledgeable person interviewed. As Bradley, now long retired, explained to me, it was clear that if the young white professors had not spoken up and had not decried the discrimination that they saw, I would not have been one of the finalists. Fate is a tricky companion, because in all the decades up until I saw the letter that Bradley and his compatriots wrote to the university on my behalf, I had felt there was no opposition to my selection. Indeed, in the end, I understood that most of the faculty members *did* vote for me to be chair and the tenured faculty approved my appointment as full professor. Having someone on the faculty to stand for right, truth, and correctness is a prerequisite for strong statements of diversity.

I came early to the recognition of the unequal and uneven paths that African people have had to take in the academy. Whites were often and still are granted tenure with far fewer contributions than African Americans. The adage of our parents that we had to be twice as good as a white person to demand equality did not make any sense to me, and so I became someone who challenged cases for other Black and Brown scholars and, in one case, a Chinese scholar being denied promotion, although technically this individual was more qualified by hard facts than the scholar's white peers. These experiences and observations further enshrined in my thinking the idea that race was only a part of the problem. It was true that race was a social construct, but on the other hand, it was also based on a false cultural construct. The imaginary racial ladder was just as bad as the illusion of race; both victimized the society with illogic, irrationality, and violence. I vowed to steadily take on the dismantling of the illusion that whites were more intelligent, stronger, better, and more ethical than other people. Human capabilities are equally distributed by nature among all cultures, and the lie of white superiority as the identity of the Western moment in human history must be erased from our imagination. It is this mechanical structure that has made the university troubling, hard to navigate, and downright dangerous for many African professors.

Hiring committees had to answer departments' questions about our qualifications, credentials, and capabilities, despite our degrees from the same universities as our white peers. White faculty members and administrators often claimed they could not find "qualified" Black professors for positions in the universities.

This is not a tidy arrangement; in fact, it is brutally reprehensible and can be resolved only in some future constitutional convention when society has arrived at sufficient democratic consciousness to overcome the imaginary racial ladder invented to maintain hierarchy. Yet here we are,

African American faculty members teaching in institutions that, for the most part, were designed to uphold our inferiority and European Americans' superior place in society. We have always dared to challenge this irrational idea and consequently have had to endure, through decades of trial and error, various forays into demonstrations, meditations, curses, and medications.

THANK YOU FOR YOUR BLACKNESS
An Honest Offer Letter
CHARISSE L'PREE

Welcome to our department! We are so excited to have you join the faculty and our family. You may notice that we don't have much racial diversity, but we are actively working on it. Please let us know how we can help you thrive. But don't ask for too much and don't ask for more than what we do for non-marginalized faculty; otherwise, you will be seen as difficult. We are very proud of simply hiring you; please don't remind us how that was literally the least we could do.

We understand that you identify with multiple racial groups, but we need you to be Black. We will check the Black box for you and disregard your other categories—unless you're Latino; that works for our diversity numbers. Are you Latino? No? Never mind.

In your first months, you may be told by senior faculty that you weren't hired because you were smart, that there were other reasons. Or you may be asked when you will be leaving, because it's clear you aren't happy here. Please disregard these people. They are, after all, part of the old guard, and we are all just waiting for them to retire, but we celebrate them as essential faculty members despite their continued problematic statements regarding race . . . and gender . . . and class. Everyone has a story about these people, but nothing changes. That's what makes us a family!

We hired you as an essential addition to our research faculty, but 90 percent of your overall teaching load will be required undergraduate theory courses to production students. Ultimately, three-fourths of your classes will meet our program's diversity requirements, a unique lift given that our students are predominantly white and upper-class. Technically, "diversity" is a subarea of the faculty expertise, but there are no other Black faculty doing this work. Did we mention that we need you to be Black?

Along with your positionality—we are conversant with the key terms— these courses will inevitably pull down your teaching evaluations, especially in comparison to many of our faculty who are older, whiter, and male-r and who do not teach diversity courses. You may be above the department average on preparedness and you may win the Award for

Teaching Excellence from the graduating senior class, but we will ignore that information.

You are also expected to produce high-quality research. We have only a handful of research faculty who seem to be doing fine, so we will assume that you can publish in top-tier journals while teaching five of our most emotionally draining classes per year. We will happily reimburse your participant fees and travel expenses, as well as provide a professional master's student outside of your area to assist for three months at a time. If you need anything else, please let us know so that we can nod sympathetically.

As our only Black PhD on the faculty, you will be asked to speak on one diversity panel after another. You may even be asked to lead some, but you will be micromanaged—effectively becoming a mouthpiece for the less-minoritized chair of the diversity committee—even though your teaching, research, and lived experiences make you qualified to lead these panels in your sleep. We thank you for your Blackness!

You will also be expected to provide free consultation services to less diversity-minded colleagues. You can talk about your other identities, but they will need you to talk on behalf of all Black people, ironically reinforcing stereotypes for this group while also being an exception. Rest assured, it will absolutely take time away from your teaching and your research, but we know you're excited to save us from ourselves. Few of these people will write tenure letters on your behalf, but many will convey your lack of commitment to the department if you do not accommodate their every request.

We know you are concerned about tenure, but almost everyone gets tenure—except for the other young woman who did not get tenure the year you started and several junior faculty of color in your department who all left before tenure. Actually, no Black woman has been promoted from assistant to associate professor in our fifty-five-year history, but we keep that fun fact out of the promotional materials.

Don't worry, though. You are an amazing scholar, and you will get a unanimous vote from external reviewers on your tenure case. But you won't celebrate because it will be undermined by a pity vote from our tenure committee. In the opening paragraph, you (and the Board of Trustees) will be informed that several members of the committee did not think you met the bar for teaching excellence but voted for your case anyway.

Your letter will feature NO undergraduate quotes despite teaching almost entirely undergraduate classes. It will present one non-anonymized quote from a PhD student who disparages you personally yet has never sat in your classroom. It will deploy a metric that was eliminated from evals the year before and for which you cited research demonstrating its race and gender biases. Your letter will make you feel devalued, but everyone will tell you to be grateful and move on.

You will be thankful for the security and frustrated with the ongoing lack of respect. You will become sick of our lip service to diversity while we are unable to see your whole diverse self. You will want to leave, but we will ensure that you are not a competitive candidate because you have neither the time nor the cognitive energy to be the best academic you can be.

Welcome! We are excited to have you as part of our family!

HEY, YOU'RE BLACK
What Do We Do? We Don't Know What to Do
ANONYMOUS

Even now, more than fifteen years into my career in Catholic higher education, there are so many things—shadows of my childhood growing up a Black male in predominantly white spaces—that are familiar yet foreign to me. I have learned to live with, and even find my voice within, this steady undercurrent of "alien-ness," but my early career as a *Blackademic* in Catholic higher education was a strange and intimidating space for me.

In 2005, during the early months of my first one-year instructor contract at this Catholic college, students wrote the N-word on the walls of a residence hall and used a black sock and rope to fashion a hanging in effigy. The all-white administration was paralyzed, not even informing faculty and staff of this heinous spectacle of anti-Black racism. I learned the details two days later from my white students in my African American history class.

Imagine the scene! I, the only Black male faculty member at the institution, was lecturing about lynching, and my white students were telling me about this hanging in effigy that they bore witness to in their dorm. To their credit, my students were outraged and spoke to me with empathy and concern. I am sure my face registered all kinds of horror and disgust, and I remember having a hard time finishing the class. So much of me wanted to run to my car and never return to this place. As I continued teaching, I remember the rage building up in me that I had to hear about this crime from students. My fury at administrators grew as I realized that they had not reached out to the faculty in general or to me specifically. Surely, if this school wanted to hire me on a tenure track, they would have shown enough concern to send me an email preparing me for what I would encounter that day in class. The absence of notification read to me like an absence of care for my physical and emotional state, and I was determined to address this affront.

Shocked and horrified, I went to the academic dean to voice my outrage. The dean listened and told me he would get back to me. What I see now as his paralysis felt at the time like a full dismissal of my well-being, and again I considered leaving and never returning to this place I was beginning to hate.

I did stay that day, and within hours I was called back to the dean's office. When I arrived, I found half of the president's cabinet seated in a semicircle with an open chair in the middle for me. Instantly, I believed I was going to be reprimanded for my outrage. I conjured up so many of the "angry Black man" stereotypes in my head and assumed this was what the cabinet members pictured when they saw me entering the room.

The vice president for Mission Integration began the meeting by acknowledging that I had raised an issue with the academic dean and asking me to rearticulate to the entire group assembled there my concerns about the institution's lack of response. Poised to leave the office immediately and never return if I did not like what transpired, I repeated my complaint. I pointed fingers, focused on the lack of institutional response, and highlighted the fact that no one informed faculty and staff of the hate crime. I told these administrators that I did not feel safe and *was* not safe at a place where such heinous white supremacy was met with such disregard and inaction. As I finished my account, I expected someone to tell me I was overreacting.

Instead, the vice president of Mission Integration asked me, "What do we do? We don't know what to do."

It was in that moment that I began to see the paralysis. Individually and collectively, these white administrators had never confronted an incident like this before and had never had to consider the impact of such crimes. My presence on campus and in that office MADE them accountable—but they had no experience and were unequipped to respond.

As a young Blackademic eager to make my mark and change the world, I dove into this uncompensated work of training and equipping white administrators and the predominantly white institution to address white supremacy. My many tasks and roles at this institution have included coordinating all diversity education in the curriculum and serving as the de facto academic chief diversity officer. While this work has been fulfilling, and I know I have made a difference, as I look back I see how so many white administrators have advanced their careers on the back of my anti-racism work.

Standing now at a crossroads in my career, I feel both enriched and exploited. I doubt I am alone in these feelings, and I imagine other Blackademics have similar experiences. Reflecting on my time in the academy,

I see clearly that my #BlackintheIvory career began with, and has largely remained, the experience of being the only Black person (and often the only BIPOC) in the room telling white people who make at least double my salary what to do with every crime of anti-Black racism.

I BELIEVE I'LL RUN ON

E. PATRICK JOHNSON

Spotlight Narrative

In the fall of 1993, as I was finishing my dissertation, Amherst College in Massachusetts, where I later became a faculty member, gave me a Five College Minority Dissertation Fellowship. My days at Amherst were the best of times and the worst of times. Amherst, where pedigree, region, and class make or break you, brought out all the various aspects of my identity: Blackness, queerness, maleness, lower class-ness, southernness, and so on. Nonetheless, when I arrived there, I thought I was in Oz. Louisiana State University, where I had gone to earn my PhD, had been a living hell: The first luncheon the graduate students in my department invited me to was in the "Plantation Room," the "upscale" cafeteria in the student union. For several weeks, the student newspaper, the *Daily Reveille*, featured letters to the editor whose titles ranged from "Reader Fears Black Power" to "Homosexuality Has Raped Our Nation; Jesus Is the Answer" to "Women's Battle for Equal Rights Already Won." Indeed, the signs of Louisiana's racist past were embroidered all over the campus of LSU. Amherst College seemed an idyllic place to recover. The English Department had its own half-million-dollar endowment, long-distance phone calls and postage were limitless, and gone were the days of running copies on a mimeograph. The "fairest" college, as Amherst is called, also provided subsidized housing for its faculty and a budget to "entertain" students in their homes.

Of almost 160 professors, I was one of only seven African American faculty at Amherst. Moreover, I was one of only four faculty in my department (one was a Black woman) who had attended public institutions of higher learning; most of my English Department colleagues had attended Harvard, Yale, or Princeton. I was the only southerner. Most students were second-, third-, and sometimes fourth-generation college students whose parents and grandparents had attended Amherst. While the student body was the most racially diverse among the consortium that made up the Five Colleges, 65 percent needed no financial aid despite paying $35,000 a year in tuition.

Being surrounded by all of that wealth was foreign to me. But the abundance of wealth and resources could not hide the fact that notwithstanding its professed liberalism, Amherst was a country club of "good old boys" with no interest in allowing undesirables (such as myself, a Black southern working-class queer) to join. As one Black administrator warned me when I arrived on campus, "First they seduce you. Then they feed you. And then they eat you." Eventually, when I was a candidate for a tenure-track position in the department, I understood what she meant.

When I was a dissertation fellow and then a lecturer, the members of the department tolerated my "nontraditional" pedagogy (teaching literature through performance); "quaint" southern ways (cooking for students); and "unsophisticated research" on performance studies and Black gay vernacular. They figured some temporary exoticism at the college could be exciting. But they could never allow practices so far afield as these or a person like me to become a permanent part of the fabric of the fairest college. For instance, when the college authorized the English Department to conduct a search for a tenure-track faculty member to teach African American literature, I was encouraged to apply and was given a courtesy interview. Twice the department offered the position to other candidates. Both candidates came to campus and left screaming. Rather than scrap the search, the department reluctantly offered me—its last resort—the job. It was the beginning of a torturous journey that would take its toll on my psychological, emotional, and professional well-being. Some mornings the thought of walking through the doors of Johnson Chapel, where the department was housed, paralyzed me. I never knew what form of racism, classism, or homophobia I was going to experience on any given day. One morning, a senior white colleague groped me in the department office, believing that he had been given such authority over my body because the campus LGBTQ student group had written "Hug a Queer Today" on the sidewalk. After hearing me sing for the Martin Luther King Jr. worship service on campus, another senior colleague, who was married to the dean of the faculty, relayed that the dean was quite impressed with my voice. He added that because the dean's mother was an opera singer, she knew a good voice when she heard one. He ended the conversation with, "So the dean thought your voice was quite remarkable—untrained—but good." This same dean would later try to console me after the English Department voted to reappoint me "with an appreciation for the risk" it would be taking by doing so: "I want you to know that the president and I will do everything in our power to make sure you're a strong candidate for tenure—even if it means getting you some remedial writing courses. I'll set aside the money."

To muster the courage to go to campus, I sat in the middle of my living room floor and sang Negro spirituals trying to find some comfort, something to shield me from my colleagues' voices, which had become cancerous to my body. I believe faculty and administration at Amherst tried to stall my growth as a teacher and as a scholar by constantly saying I was not good enough to be among them.

After my third-year review in the tenure track, I discovered there was "no place like home" and took a leave of absence from Amherst after receiving a postdoctoral fellowship at the University of North Carolina at Chapel Hill, my undergraduate alma mater. The move "home" saved my life.

Two years later, in 2000, I accepted a position in the Department of Performance Studies at Northwestern University. It was a dream come true. All my professors from the University of North Carolina at Chapel Hill and Louisiana State University who had mentored me had graduated from performance studies at Northwestern, including my dissertation advisor. I was also excited about teaching graduate students for the first time. At Northwestern, I can finally say that I have arrived "home." Surrounded by supportive colleagues, I've been able to "run on" to obtain tenure, be promoted to full professor, and now serve as dean of the School of Communication. The voices of my mother, grandmother, and other Black mother figures in my life telling me to "run on" helped me keep my eyes on the prize. Like Dorothy, I had to discover that "home" is what you carry inside you.

Although this, my cautionary tale, might speckle the yellow brick road to the ivory tower with a little blood and shit here and there, I nonetheless encourage those who are not yet hooded with their PhD, not yet tenured, not yet mangled by the academic grinder, to "run on and see what the end gonna be." For while there is racism, sexism, homophobia, classism, regionalism, and pedigree-ism along the way, we must remember the words of "Lift Every Voice and Sing," aka the "Black National Anthem":

Stony the road we trod,
Bitter the chastening rod,
Felt in the days when hope unborn had died;
Yet with a steady beat,

Have not our weary feet
Come to the place for which our fathers sighed?
We have come over a way that with tears has been watered,
We have come, treading our path through the blood of the
    slaughtered,
Out from the gloomy past,
Till now we stand at last
Where the white gleam of our bright star is cast.

As a Black gay southern feminist revolutionary, my presence in the academy is bolstered by a legacy of poor queer little colored boys who challenged what it means to be a "professor" despite tripping on and being hit by the yellow bricks on that stony road. The academy is full of folk who uphold the virtues of the most pernicious forms of sexism, racism, classism, and homophobia. While I'm not so naive as to think I'll soon see the end of this reign of terror, I am fierce enough to know that the "schooling" I received in the projects, for which I owe my PhD in how to "read" and write, is the only weapon this little colored boy needs to "run on."

THE JOURNEY OF DESTINY FOR AN AFRICAN AMERICAN MALE IN THE ACADEMY

HERMAN O. KELLY JR.

I am an African American male teaching at a major university in the South. I interviewed several years ago for an adjunct position in the Religion Department at Louisiana State University. I am a graduate of Morehouse College, Springfield College, Boston University School of Theology, and Memphis Theological Seminary. I was also a King Scholar and a Bethune Scholar at Boston University School of Theology and the president of the Association of Black Seminarians at that school, an organization that helped us have community at the university.

This introduction indicates my qualifications for the adjunct position. Yet I was interviewed by twelve white faculty members in a circle. This was an indication of a toxic and racist environment at its best. I was hired, but no one to this date had gone through such an experience. It was traumatic, but because of my familiarity with racism as a student in high school and in other situations, I moved through this space with confidence. On the first day of my employment as an adjunct in the Religion Department, the secretary was surprised by my résumé. She said, "You have more letters behind your name than most people in this department."

What a toxic statement. For her, my face did not match the résumé. That is, the résumé she reviewed was not supposed to be that of an educated African American male.

My legacy was touched by excellence and commitment from my maternal uncle, who served as a missionary in South China. Dr. Thomas Harris inspired me to attend Morehouse College in Atlanta, a place that helped me join the company of other African American men devoted to making a difference in the space they occupied. My advice as you take this journey is centered on being true to yourself and the calling to higher education. Present a positive image to your students and never be afraid to tell your story. Our stories give our students an indication of our journey and the importance of the trek.

TO BE BLACK, A WOMAN, AND PRE-TENURE
A Narrative of Faculty Devaluation and Exclusion
ANONYMOUS

According to the US Department of Education, as of 2019 Black women represent no more than 4 percent of full-time tenure-track faculty in the United States. It is fair to say that we, Black women, are indeed the "unicorns" of the academic system; we are special, possessing the intellect, ingenuity, fortitude, and beauty of the women before us. Yet, in the eyes of many within the academic system, we are simply seen as an anomaly, token, or fixture. What I came to learn is that when you are viewed as a "fixture" within the academic system, you are treated accordingly; your opinions are ignored and minimized, your accomplishments are diminished, and you are, overall, treated as if you do not belong. These experiences, which are commonplace for underrepresented minority faculty, emerged with a vengeance throughout my first year as a faculty member, thereby reifying the challenges associated with being Black, a woman, and pre-tenure within the academy.

As the unicorn I knew that I was, I started the year with great enthusiasm about how I would make meaningful contributions to my institution through my teaching, mentoring, and research on minority mental health. The institution was a research-intensive and minority serving school, a place where I believed my research program and culturally informed pedagogy could be further actualized and supported. However, my excitement was quickly thwarted when I arrived on my first day only to be ushered into a dilapidated "temporary" office space, equipped with a green plastic armchair that was in no way suited for long hours in the office; a dated desktop computer, which, by the looks of it, had not been used in years; and a crumpled academic poster in the corner to match. I left that day feeling disenchanted and confused—sentiments that only intensified when I learned that other newly hired non-Black faculty were settling into their permanent offices. These spaces were not lavish by any means but were at least well-kept, clean, and equipped with a workable computer, desk, and chair.

Months passed, and what was once considered my "temporary" office space became more permanent. With great frustration, I questioned myself and my colleagues. I asked my department chair about my office space and equipment to gain understanding as to why I was lacking the things necessary to do my job; I asked my peers about their onboarding process to explore whether I was receiving differential treatment; and I asked my mentor about the hiring process in order to gain insight as to why I was ushered into a department that elected to devalue and exclude me. My department chair met me with excuses and little action, stating, "Well . . . we have *never* experienced anything like *this* before." I thought, *Right! You have never hired a Black woman tenure-track faculty member!* Then, my peers and mentor confirmed what I already knew to be true: *To be Black, a woman, and pre-tenure was one sure way to ensure exclusion and devaluation in the academy.*

I knew this. During my postdoctoral fellowship, I had read over 100 interviews with faculty of color about their less-than-pleasant (a major understatement) experiences in the academy. So, I really knew this! But, for some reason, I never imagined these experiences happening to me. I was a unicorn, right?

The reality of it all was that these things were happening! I was being mistreated and gaslit at every corner, but I felt as if there was no recourse. If I spoke up, I risked being labeled the "angry Black woman." Or if I disclosed the level of mistreatment I had experienced, it could lead others to consider me as less than collegial, thereby putting me at risk for a negative annual review. I was at a crossroads with a decision to make—sit back and allow myself to be mistreated, or take action.

I decided to act. I, once again, confronted my department chair, calling the chair to the carpet on the mistreatment I had received; I made the necessary phone calls to have my office renovated and materials delivered; and I worked (really worked!), publishing several peer-reviewed articles, securing a federal grant, and mentoring multiple students in our department. Through my hard work and accomplishments (truly a representation of my "unicorn-ness"), I thought I could solve the problem and thus show my colleagues that I was worthy and I did belong. But I quickly came to realize that this was an ineffective strategy in an academic system that devalues faculty like me, and in sum, to be Black, a woman, and pre-tenure can be challenging. For me it was (and still is).

CROSSING OVER
To the Other Side
MARK BROOMFIELD

> *The system is not set up for you to fail; it's set up for you to quit.*
> —*Nathan Lee Graham*

I returned to my undergraduate alma mater to teach after receiving notification of a dance job opportunity from my mentor. It was the spring of 2012, and I was finishing up a postdoctoral fellowship at a southern university. There was no guarantee I would get the position. I could only hope my PhD and MFA credentials, along with my experience in teaching, research, and performance, would edge me out from competitors.

I interviewed and landed the visiting professor position.

I was on a high; relief and excitement filled me. I would be returning to my alma mater as an artist and scholar, after years of professional accomplishments and itinerant work, to contribute to the department I had graduated from almost two decades earlier.

The high didn't last long.

After my dance mentor and I met regularly about the curriculum and the program, it became clear that my visiting professor status was conditional. I would move after the one-year appointment—so it was assumed. Things began to change once the provost nominated me for, and I submitted my application to, a statewide program advancing faculty diversity in higher education. In December, the news came that I'd won. The award stipulated my appointment and promotion to a tenure-track position as an assistant professor. E.L.A.T.I.O.N. My itinerant life, for now, halted.

Eventually I observed that my enthusiasm for growth in the dance program was not a shared value. Soon exclusionary behavior became standard practice. Even with an official title, I enjoyed representational power only. For advertising purposes, I visibly represented change and progress, but behind the scenes I was excluded from program decision-making. An entire academic year would be planned without my inclusion and then announced by email to the whole department over the summer. The email gave the impression of my involvement. This happened yearly.

What saddened me the most is that my mentor continued to engage in the exclusionary practices even as I shared the impact it had on me. The behavior went unchanged. The Jekyll and Hyde personalities created a distressing environment. One championed my career, prior to returning. The other actively resisted my presence and contributions as a colleague. When I dared to speak my truth, fighting for equal treatment as a colleague, attacks, offensive behavior, and microaggressions from my mentor became relentless. As director of the dance program, my mentor made an all-out effort to constrain my contributions and limit my growth. I introduced a new course to the curriculum that students had expressed interest in. It failed. Without support, not one student registered—a first in the history of the department. Knowing the importance of documenting events (*keep your receipts!*), I shared with the administration the exclusionary behavior I endured. No intervention.

Another summer came with a mass email sent to the entire department. I was DONE—*you hear me.* This decisive act of exclusion, after years of enduring this behavior, had to come to an end. I consulted with administrators outside my institution. They determined that the examples of exclusion were actionable. As a result, I filed a complaint. After the institution's investigation, undertaken by all-white members, my complaint was dismissed. No accountability.

After the investigation, I experienced heightened racial terrorization and retaliation based on what I describe as the four I's of whiteness: innocence, ignorance, illiteracy, and indifference. The white racial performance of the four I's kept my Black body in white space on red alert. Professionalism, aka white racial performance, maintained smiling faces throughout frequent encounters. White racial terror asserted itself through invisibility. The weaponization of emails—online bullying—became a wholesale engagement to intimidate me into submission and eliminate my voice and presence from the program. The invisibility hid the most abhorrent online behavior and continued with the onslaught of psychological terror in my daily adverse working conditions.

When you work in an art form expressed in a body-based practice, as I do, escaping the inflicted trauma sustained in my body is difficult to do. I felt like a beach ball, used playfully, smacked, dunked, and battered by the riptide currents, then left deflated and lifeless on the sun-kissed sand, and in the words of Langston Hughes (2020), dried-up like a raisin. Exhaustion and depression, sleepless nights, comfort food, and weight gain followed. Hypervigilance and hyperawareness of my body in white space led to my body becoming sensitized to the unrelenting attacks. In short, I was experiencing what can be best described as post-traumatic stress disorder. White racial terrorization insisted on compelling me to "know your place." Truth is, white supremacy and the terror it inflicts does not respect boundaries to make everyone serviceable to it.

Silencing functions like invisibility. Inspired by the life and writings of Audre Lorde, I moved from silence to voice while a pervasive undertow undermined my presence. Crossing over—to the other side of tenure—began with a clarity and resolve about my voice, my story, my journey, and a belief that my life matters. This required integrity borne of *my ancestors*, a commitment to excellence, and building an external support network outside my department and the institution.

Now, as a "university citizen," I direct a new interdisciplinary program in a new department, offering students open access, opportunity, and a voice to create democratic futures for all at the same institution that tried to silence my own voice. But my journey to tenure and promotion makes me think about the recent revelations by the Duke and Duchess of Sussex that made clear to me how racism destroys relationships to maintain white supremacy. The willingness of British royalty to disown family reminds me of my treatment as a Black alumnus invited back to teach at my alma mater.

Reference

Langston Hughes. 2020. "Harlem." In *African American Poetry: 250 Years of Struggle and Song*, edited by Kevin Young, 200–211. New York: Library of America.

INTERSECTIONALITY

The Tightrope of Career Success in the Medical Ivory Tower

TAMORAH LEWIS

As a Black female physician-scientist, I have experienced everything from isolation to tokenism in academic medicine. It is an odd mix of being hypervisible as "the only" and feeling as though I must prove again and again my competence to be acknowledged and seen as a "worthy" peer. As I climbed the faculty ranks and held increasing hospital leadership roles, other faces around the table rarely ever looked like mine. As "the only" in the room, I felt tasked with representing entire faculty demographics, made harder by having to discuss nuances of intersectional disadvantage. This experience caused waxing and waning exhaustion and varying abilities to be truly cognitively and emotionally present. Sometimes I ponder how my experience would be different if my mind was not occupied with stereotype threat and the need for affect and language modification (that is, code-switching) to keep colleagues maximally comfortable.

I worry that, increasingly, I am viewed as "the exception to the (unwritten) rule." This unwritten rule is that minoritized women do not belong in leadership in academic medicine, but a few will be let in—the "unicorns." The truth is that many, many minoritized female faculty are amazing and smart and would make excellent leaders. But they are not sponsored into opportunities and are not tagged for success the way many white males are. I have seen firsthand that when one places her hat in the ring, she is often treated as if she is "not ready," even when her skills and accomplishments are equal to or exceed those of her peers. These occasions cause multitudes of pain—for the person who experiences the event and for those faculty who watch it play out and absolutely can see themselves in the victim.

One of the hardest parts of being #BlackintheIvory is the tightrope. I have learned to engage in just enough anti-racist work on campus to keep my integrity and make change for my patients but not so much that I get labeled as troublesome. When I engage in advocacy work, it takes so much mental energy to plan what I will say with just the right words and tone to not alienate my majority white colleagues. Telling truth to power is a very difficult task, and the danger is magnified when the truths you tell have the potential to invoke hard self-reflection in others. Even as I have become bolder in my truth-telling, I still experience fear and anxiety about backlash from majority white gatekeepers who would rather see topics of racism in medicine remain taboo and undiscussed.

IT BE OUR OWN SOMETIMES

What Is Institutional Misogynoir When One of the Main Perpetrators Is a Black Woman Herself?

ANONYMOUS

Incident recap: My department chair forgot to assign a TA to my upper-level undergraduate elective course, which was a new course prep for me. The chair had told me that I would receive a TA for the course, and all faculty members who had previously taught this course had a TA, so I naturally expected one—and had structured the course accordingly. I initially contacted my department chair about this oversight in January, upon hearing other junior faculty discuss their TAs and realizing I hadn't heard anything about mine. The chair first asked if I knew any available students (I was a first-year faculty member who onboarded during a once-in-a-century pandemic . . . so, no?). The chair ultimately responded, "Our students are fully tapped out at the moment." Hearing nothing else for several weeks, I naturally assumed I would have no TA that semester.

Midsemester, I emailed the department chair a request for redress for unexpectedly—and untraditionally—teaching this class without instructional support. I repeated the facts of the situation; I spelled out expected resources; I explained how it was affecting me; I stated a need for a course buyout; I asked for oversight and assurance that this situation would not occur again; I requested priority for the next semester's TA assignment; and I stated a need for a note on my record for the error so that the semester would be weighted less than others when it came time for reappointment and tenure. I then expressed how I was honored to be a faculty member in the department but also disappointed and devastated by this situation. To my chair's credit, they at least found two graduate students who were TAs in other courses and were able to split their time between my class and their originally assigned classes within that week—but it still bothers me that the chair took several weeks to accomplish this, if their original claim that they were working on finding a TA were true. (Contextual clues suggest otherwise.)

In comes the associate dean: During the students' finals week, one of the associate deans called me for a virtual meeting to "check in." I was initially grateful to have this space with the one senior in my entire school who looked like me, but it quickly went south once I explained the incident pertaining to my midsemester email. She told me that I was "overreacting," "blowing things out of proportion," and "asking for too much." She continued to say, "Besides, your email contains inaccuracies; we are not obligated to provide you a TA and it's not in your contract. And you say here [referring to my email] that you want to be an excellent research faculty. Well, we have a teaching expectation here. And I found your tone to be combative." I replied, "I apologize. I didn't mean to be rude." She said, "I didn't say your tone was rude. I said it was combative."

Upon confirming that I would not receive recompense for my lost time, she was appalled when I mentioned that I would never exceed 20 percent per class (per my contractual responsibilities) ever again, because as "we both know, assistant professors of color, especially, fail to achieve tenure because they either spend too much time in service or too much time teaching." When I requested written information about course scheduling and TA allocation determination and procedures in the school, she stated that such information in writing was unnecessary because the organizational culture operated on "word is bond." I eventually asked whether I was not allowed to self-advocate (should I not have said anything?), to which she said, "It's not that you can't self-advocate; it's how you say it."

I was so frustrated that neither she nor the school could see the bigger issue, so much so that I started to cry during our virtual meeting. She proceeded to tell me that "the tenure track is hard" and trivialized my incident by saying, "The first year is hard anyway, [so the TA assignments aren't] going to affect you that much." I felt embarrassed that I was crying. I had no tissue near me. At that point, I couldn't move; I couldn't ask to excuse myself; I couldn't turn off my camera. It was horrible. Even today, my chest tightens whenever I receive correspondences from her or see that she is handling resource requests for junior faculty or whenever she speaks about creating an equitable environment.

Effects on academic career: I could not move research forward during the first several weeks that I had no TA. During that semester, I declined a renowned senior professor's opportunity to join a major federal grant because I had no time to contribute. I could not complete a working paper to the level that I (and the granting research center, apparently) originally anticipated. I failed to complete two R&Rs (revise and resubmit) in a timely manner. I spent my summer gathering information about university resources and suggested strategies from several faculty outside my school as well as outside my institution. This time could have gone toward my research. But if I neglected self-protection and contingency planning, then I would not survive my current institution (or the professorship at large).

Remaining questions: I have never been so confused, frustrated, and angry. I am even more perplexed that this associate dean, who is a Black woman herself, is exuding internalized misogynoir, a form of oppression where Black women (sub)consciously project or uphold the very misogynoir attitudes to each other. I "overreacted" to what was effectively an adverse welcome to the institution, school, and department (gaslighting). I was "combative," practiced insufficient restraint, and caused unnecessary issues (tone policing). "The tenure track is hard," so I must deal and quietly absorb the *isms* I experience along the way (be a "Strong Black Woman"). I was only a first-year, so what do I know anyway? Ironically, I was the one ultimately reprimanded for speaking up. I felt like my mistreatment was dismissed—in fact, flipped, even—to cover my chair's mistake.

I knew that institutional racism, sexism, misogynoir, and even elitism is to be expected at R1 PWIs (predominantly white institutions). However, I was stunned to experience it from a Black woman—more so, one in administrative leadership meant to specially steward diversity, equity, and inclusion. I might not remain in academia if I must internalize misogynoir to ascend the ranks. My biggest fear as a Black woman is having an attitude of misogynoir perpetuated against me by someone who looks like me. This is when it most pains.

THANK GOODNESS WE DID
ANONYMOUS

Yes to tenure, no to promotion. That was the verdict from my all-white colleagues who voted. At the last minute, I had checked the boxes on the promotion-tenure application stating that I wanted my tenure and promotion to be considered separately. Thank goodness I did. The School of Communication director, whom I trusted then and now, told me later that the verdict would have been no to tenure and promotion if I had checked the boxes to have them considered together. So I planned to drop my promotion bid to avoid further embarrassment and apply for tenure only. If my colleagues in the School of Communication didn't think I was good enough to become an associate professor, why would my colleagues in the College of Arts, Humanities, and Social Sciences or the dean or the provost recognize my value?

I went to my white mentor for advice—a mentor whom the diversity office appointed so that she could list me as "service" on her application for full professor. She suggested that I abandon my promotion application to avoid upsetting my colleagues. I ignored her suggestion. That's because my boss called my husband and a former colleague I respected to get them to help me change my mind. Thank goodness she did. My boss, the college committee, and the provost all supported my separate promotion application. After an eight-month process during which I was asked to rewrite some documents on deadline, I earned my promotion. Enter another white woman, a self-appointed mentor. "Don't talk about your promotion publicly," she said. "Don't post it on social media. Doing so will damage your relationship with your colleagues," she said. "Your relationship with them is the most important thing." I ignored her suggestion, too. In the end, I wrote a social media post that fall noting that it was my first day of class as a tenured associate professor. Thank goodness I did.

THE PATHS TO NOT-TENURE
ARE LITTERED WITH LANDMINES
AND BURNED-OUT CARS

DONALD EARL COLLINS

Spotlight Narrative

In my various careers in academia, in the nonprofit world, and as a writer, I have suffered too many racist incidents and microaggressions to reasonably count. The years of isolation and marginalization, the belittling of my work, the denials of racism and promotion, even the occasional theft of my words—it all "make me wanna holler," to quote Marvin Gaye's "Inner City Blues." So far, I have not had a nervous breakdown, which has happened to some of my friends over the past thirty years.

One particular episode encapsulates my experiences with anti-Black racism and its intersections with other isms in higher education. I interviewed for a job at Seton Hall University in 2019. The school was looking for a new director for its Africana studies program—this after Black and Latinx students had staged a forty-four-day sit-in to get the university to expand its commitment to racial inclusivity and anti-racism. Seton Hall had advertised the position in the *Chronicle of Higher Education*. To me, that meant its candidate search was a national one. That, and my years of teaching on the connections between social justice and African American identity issues, prompted me to apply.

When the search committee invited me to campus, I told the committee I would need my travel and lodging arrangements covered in advance. The committee chair seemed accommodating at first. But somehow the committee had failed to book a room for me at the chosen hotel. As someone who has sometimes waited months for reimbursement or even eaten the costs of such visits in the past, my rule has been to have the institution cover these travel and lodging bills.

The search committee chair showed up to cover the hotel stay. "This is why job candidates should pay for their travel," she said to me, miffed that I didn't pay up front, despite our previous agreement. On the way to dinner that evening, she continued on about the sanctity of the process and how "it's just more convenient when the candidate pays for these expenses" and waits for reimbursement.

I have heard all of this before. But what I have never heard is a search committee chair acknowledge that when one conducts a national job search, it is the height of hypocrisy to expect job candidates to cover their expenses up front. It is elitist and discriminatory and privileges white job candidates above all others, as Black and Brown candidates typically have more debt and less discretionary income.

The next day was my job talk. During the Q and A session, a search committee member—an older white man—asked me, "What will you do to reach those people on campus who don't just have concerns" about my work and the work of the program "but are in opposition to your work" and the program's very existence?

"Ultimately, I don't believe it's my job to reach folks who stand in opposition to equality, to my insistence that I am equally human. Why would I want to spend time and energy trying to reach those people? We've tried that already with respectability politics, with assimilation. It hasn't worked," I said. In my head, I thought, *Do you really think it's my job to convince white people like you that my work, my classes, and my students have merit? Are you kidding me?!*

The search committee did not offer me the job, and I would have said no even if it had. The unthinking elitism of the chair and the commitment of other committee members to a campus of whiteness were the main factors. The dour mood of the two Black professors I met (the search committee likely used them as props for my benefit) made me feel sorry for them, but it did not change my resolve. "It's not my calling to save white people from themselves," I said to my partner after telling her about the interview.

I have applied for more than 3,500 jobs since completing my history doctorate at Carnegie Mellon in 1997, and I have held more than a dozen contingent positions over the years. I learned long ago that meritocracy was a lie of a myth, a lie that can kill, a myth that can render one insane. The everyday racism of highly educated white people is cloaked with denials and objectivity and layered with elitism and narcissism. The expectation that Black and Brown others give their labor and time for free or at an emotional cost is too high to live with. Like so many American institutions, academia is too racist and elitist to change. Tokenism isn't enough. Being the "first Black to . . ." isn't enough. It would be better to dismantle academia and start from scratch because there is no reform that would ever make higher education anti-racist and inclusive enough.

#JusticeforBlackWomenFacultyandStaff

LUCY ANNE HURSTON

Justice. Accountability. Ethical behavior. We expect these tenets to be sacrosanct: a foundation that frames and uplifts the culture of higher education to provide a vibrant and safe place for students and faculty to excel beyond their wildest dreams. Unfortunately, higher education has been built on a structure of racism, ableism, and oppression. Within the microcosm of higher education, systemic racism operates brazenly when barriers to advancement exist for racial minorities and when unequal opportunities for success are not acknowledged. The ivory tower does not provide a smooth climb to the top for those who are minorities based on race, gender, ability, age, and so on.

Equality, ethics, and equity should be our goals, yet we often fall short, sometimes openly and blatantly without considering the consequences for our words and actions. Let's imagine that, during a governance meeting open to the entire college community, discriminatory barriers are in stark relief, since there is an openly hostile environment to Black faculty and staff. Imagine you are a Black woman who has worked in the college for over twenty years. You are a highly respected member of the community. You care deeply about your students, your work, and your institution. Now imagine that discriminatory actions occur and oppressive words are spoken repeatedly, month after month. To your embarrassment, many members of your beloved community attend these meetings and see you being singled out and overlooked. Now your relationships with your colleagues are starting to change. You hold on as long as you can, but finally it becomes too much.

This was the scenario I faced. Despite months of trying to find a solution to the problem, nothing changed. I decided that it was time to amplify this situation, since I knew that I wasn't the only one facing these barriers. As a result, I filed a formal complaint with the college's equal employment opportunity (EEO) officer. An investigation was conducted, and the accused was found to have violated college and systemwide policies on discriminatory practices. However, the accused occupied a position of power within the institution, serving as the union representative for the same union that was supposed to protect me from this kind of treatment. The union representative was white and male.

After the investigation was completed, there was a questionable delay before the eventual release of the investigatory report. How much time? A full 234 days! The investigatory report, when finally issued, concluded that there had been a history of culture and climate issues with racial undertones. The report went on to find that there was conduct that was designed to discredit and embarrass Black female faculty. Our concerns were validated, but no one other than the authors of the investigation were aware of the findings. No reports were shared with anyone. The offending person remained in his position for the remainder of the academic year in a position of power. His behavior persisted despite the findings, as he continued to threaten, belittle, and bully Black women on campus.

Amazingly, just a few days after the academic year ended, the perpetrator was permitted to retire without any accountability. He did not have to answer for the explicit violations of policies protecting against discrimination and harassment. For the victims, there is no closure at all. According to the EEO office's procedures, ninety days after a complaint is filed, all parties must issue a formal and final report. Despite these rules, the administration of the college and the EEO officer held back their findings. After the required ninety-day limit had passed, I requested a copy of the findings. Radio silence. Then I wrote the investigators requesting an explanation for the delay and received no response. Becoming increasingly frustrated, I then wrote to and called the EEO leadership team for support. Their help was not forthcoming. I asked for a meeting with the EEO leadership team to discuss steps as we advanced with this complaint and still received no response. Even after several attempts to get the EEO officer to respond to inquiries about the status of the case's outcome, I got nothing but silence. As a result, I also filed formal complaints with state and federal agencies (the Commission on Human Rights and Opportunities and the Equal Employment Opportunity Commission), and those complaints are now under investigation. Additionally, I retained counsel.

It has become my job to make it known: Black Women Are Tired!! We are tired of the humiliation and brutality we endured in this case and, even more egregious, the lack of response. Black women daily face situations that can hinder or derail careers, promotion, and tenure. Though these behaviors have become entrenched in our campus cultures, they cannot continue. Such treatment comes at the detriment of everyone, from students who look up to teachers as role models to faculty who feel valued and supported. When we don't recognize our shortcomings as an educational organization, we cannot succeed.

The brutality of Black women in higher education must stop. The first step is to shine a spotlight on this issue, which is not an isolated one. Those who uphold the status quo would have us believe we are all individual cases. On the contrary, I have heard from Black women faculty in numerous institutions since I exposed my situation, and their stories mirror mine.

The toxic environment on campus and in professional meetings took a toll on me. This situation impacted my mental and physical health and eventually caused me to retire before I was ready to leave the classroom. The milieu at the college resulted in the only possible outcome: constructive discharge. The culture and environment remained toxic, making it too difficult and dangerous for me to continue working there. These forces hastened the end of my almost twenty-five-year career at that college. Some of my colleagues were shocked and voiced concerns, which led me to wonder: What level of fear keeps others from voicing their concerns about the treatment of colleagues? The colleagues who did nothing disappointed me the most and are the reason behaviors like this persist. Doing nothing is doing something. But doing nothing and letting a vile situation continue is compliance and acceptance.

Following this incident, several talented faculty and staff of color and I left the college or are planning to leave, seeking a more hospitable place to continue our careers. Yet, this exodus of professionals of color maintains current power structures. When students don't see teachers who look like them at the front of the classroom, we send messages about who is in power. "The nation's college students benefit from learning from diverse faculty," note African American education experts Leslie T. Fenwick and H. Patrick Swygert (2015) in the *Washington Post*. "Such interaction teaches students that all people can serve as models of intellectual authority and can provide students a visceral antidote to the myth of Black intellectual inferiority." It is key that we show our students that they can achieve excellence in their lives.

Furthermore, what does current academic culture imply regarding the value of Black faculty in our ivory towers? Where is our protection? How far is the status quo willing to go to protect historical foundations of access? Is it intentional on the part of the status quo to make an inhospitable environment for Black faculty and to run them off? Not so fast! Justice.

Accountability. Ethical behavior. These are essential building blocks for our institutions because we cannot complete our mission to provide a safe place to learn and grow within academia without them.

#JusticeforBlackWomenFacultyandStaff

Reference

Fenwick, Leslie T., and H. Patrick Swygert. 2015. "Where Are All the Black College Faculty?" *Washington Post*, November 12, 2015. www.washingtonpost.com/news/answer-sheet/wp/2015/11/12/its-2015-where-are-all-the-black-college-faculty/.

FOOL ME ONCE, SHAME ON YOU
Fool Me Twice, Shame on Me
TUESDAY L. COOPER

> *If you are silent about your pain, they'll kill you and say you enjoyed it.*
> —Zora Neale Hurston, Their Eyes Were Watching God

Due to changes, I was one of two women in an academic director level position who was transitioned to a tenure-track faculty position. The other was a white woman, and few questions were asked about her transition. A junior faculty member (the department chair) decided that I, the Black woman, was not qualified to teach in her department and filed a complaint with the union. I had taught before when the department needed emergency coverage for a course midsemester. At that time, she had thought I was qualified. When coverage was needed at the last minute for a fully enrolled course, I was qualified. But according to her, I was not qualified to teach in the department full-time as there were more qualified adjunct faculty (white men) who would be a better fit and would not "disrupt" the flow of the department. She was a newly minted PhD who had taught for ten years. I have a law degree, a doctorate, and twenty-five years of teaching in the field. The state system investigated her claim against me.

The investigation revealed that three white women, including the department chair mentioned above and two others outside of my academic department (all of whom I supervised when I was an administrator), stated that I had bullied and intimidated them by making them cry, telling them to keep their "mouth shut," and forcing them to put me on the teaching schedule. In each instance, their word was their evidence. When the investigation concluded (it was determined to be unsubstantiated and filed without merit), I was asked if I would agree to attend supervisory training and mediation. I was told that it would be "something" that the system could give the union to show that I was "agreeable" and collegial. Both my supervisor at the time (another Black woman) and I said, "No, thank you." Subsequently, two white men, from other academic departments, who supported the three white women proceeded to find other ways to sully my name and reputation. One filed a false complaint with the state's ethics commission claiming that I was using my administrative position for economic gain (a charge it was required to investigate regardless of the motive or veracity of the filing). The second white man sent a college-wide email in support of the three white women, questioning my credentials, qualifications, and integrity. He then discussed the email and my "unique personnel situation" at an open faculty governance meeting.

During the same time, another Black woman on faculty experienced bullying by the same folks. It was so bad that she left her position at the college. She, another Black woman administrator, and I were frequently referred to as "those three little Black girls" by some of the white men and women on campus.

The stress that I felt during this time was almost unbearable. I gained weight, my hair fell out, and I was disengaged with my job and my family. I felt silenced because I didn't respond to the public defaming and humiliation. At the time, I felt that I shouldn't because I knew that my colleagues were wrong and that I was qualified to be transitioned into the faculty position. I was more qualified than the department chair and the white woman who had been transitioned to faculty six months prior.

If they had only looked at my experience, they would have seen that I had a twenty-five-year history of teaching in the field, along with course and curriculum development. But they didn't look because they didn't care. I was just one of the "three little Black girls" who didn't deserve to be on the same level as they were. How dare I think that I was as qualified as they were?

I was embarrassed and felt ashamed because at my age and level of experience, I should have known that I could fall prey to racism. I had foolishly allowed myself to think that if I had played by the rules, I would be left alone and treated like everyone else.

Some of my white colleagues have whispered to me in the hallways or typed in the chat during a virtual meeting, "I'm sorry for what they did to you" and "I am not strong enough to fight, but know that I am on your side." Some of them were women whom I supported openly when they were being bullied by some of the white men on campus. It made me feel like we weren't really colleagues after all.

My Black woman colleague whom I mentioned earlier filed a racial discrimination complaint against the college after she left, and I served as a witness. I couldn't be silent anymore. So far, it hasn't affected my academic or professional career. I have rank, but I am not tenured; it's a "wait and see" game. I feel like I'm falling into the same trap, though. I'm playing by the rules for now in hopes that in a few years my qualifications, achievements, and efforts will earn me tenure. Am I setting myself up to be fooled yet again?

I'm taking a risk just by writing this and allowing it to be published. We all are. The possible backlash for those of us who are vulnerable, without tenure, is tangible. However, we have to have the courage to change the narrative. Otherwise, folks will say that they never knew what we experienced. They may even say that they didn't know that their very overt acts were racist. Putting my name on this essay and claiming it as my narrative is so necessary. These experiences have taught me that remaining silent and allowing our souls to be killed because we don't want to bring attention to ourselves and our plight do not make us martyrs. Rather, when we don't speak up, we aid the perpetrators of the racist acts in committing further acts of racism against others. And we further kill our souls, on their behalf, at our own expense.

NOT EVERYONE WHO WANTS A BLACK FACULTY MEMBER WANTS A BLACK FACULTY MEMBER

MICHAEL IRVIN ARRINGTON

I replay a customary internal monologue as the search committee begins our first meeting. *You are the newest member of this faculty*, I remind myself. *You are the only Black member in the department—the only one ever, as far as you know—and you go up for tenure in a year. Be careful what you say—and how you say it.*

As we draft the position announcement, one colleague suggests that we include a diversity statement, something beyond the university boiler-plate. We want more diversity, she contends, so that the new faculty hire matches the demographics of the student population. "We want all our students to see themselves as future scholars."

"But not one of those critical scholars," adds a member of the department's old guard.

Ay, there's the rub.

The suggestion brings the meeting to a halt—in my mind, anyway. While colleagues caution against hiring a critical scholar, the conversation transports me back to my senior year at a southeastern university. "You have to be careful," my advisor began as he sat a couple of feet from me; his small office—or was it merely cluttered?—necessitated our physical closeness. At first, the conversation was indistinguishable from so many others before it. At least once every semester, I had met with my advisor in his office. During my freshman and sophomore years, we convened to discuss my program of study. Later, after I expressed an interest in an academic career, the conversations turned to research, graduate study, and the current state of the professoriate. Every conversation increased my excitement about my academic future . . . until this one. The chair had learned that I had selected a topic for my undergraduate honors thesis: a comparative rhetorical analysis of speeches from two prominent African American political and religious figures. In response, he felt the need to warn me. Leaning forward, he lowered his voice to nearly a whisper: "You don't want to get a reputation as a person who studies only Black topics. If that happens, people won't take you seriously."

As I left the office at the end of our meeting, I wondered whether my advisor noticed my silent response to his advice. Throughout my undergraduate years in the Deep South, silence had become my default response in such situations. I thought it wisest to gather as much information as possible from my professors and peers instead of spontaneously offering my opinions to people who held more experience and power than I did.

My thoughts return to the present, where I possess more agency than I did as a college senior. I am on the search committee for a new tenure-track assistant professor. My internal monologue adopts a different tone. I have a voice. And I will not keep silent. This, I persuade myself, is the time to act on the knowledge I have gained over the intervening years.

I urge my peers to consider our field. At our national and regional conferences, many (if not most) of the top Black scholars employ critical methodologies that investigate the strengths and shortcomings of traditional social sciences—shortcomings that we ignore at our own peril. "But what about you?" asks a peer who, I assume, has not read half of my publications. At this moment, I wonder how closely my colleague read my CV when I applied here—or when I submitted my annual review materials—or whether my CV ever has mattered. I wonder whether my CV will matter to the tenure and promotion committee next year.

And then I explode, the repressed frustrations of decades of silence bursting forth. It is hypocritical, I contend, to court minority bodies without valuing their voices, critical or otherwise. Eventually, the committee approves a position announcement that avoids the word "critical," instead describing our search for "an empiricist with expertise in quantitative, qualitative, or mixed methodologies."

Over the next few days, my colleagues email me, contending that they are not racist. Some will note that other colleagues took offense to my use of the word "hypocritical." They will tell me that they value me, that they are glad I am here—and not (just?) because I am Black.

COMMUNITY AND COMMISERATION
ROSAMOND S. KING

I was expecting a routine department meeting, with some colleagues eating lunch and others grading quizzes while we addressed necessary but noncontroversial administrative matters.

Then our department chair added an issue to the agenda: she proposed that the department issue a formal statement condemning the violently sexist language a professor in another department had posted on his off-campus blog. For context, this was in October 2018, when Brett Kavanaugh's confirmation as a Supreme Court justice—and his alleged sexual assaults—were a top news story.

Here's the thing: in the months prior, there had also been several widely publicized cases of police murdering Black people—including Chinedu Okobi, who died after being beaten and tased by California police just a few days before our meeting. And in the years prior, our local police department had gone undercover to investigate Muslim students *on our own campus.* Never had anyone expressed outrage within a department meeting or suggested that we make a public statement to denounce such behavior and policies.

As soon as the chair finished presenting her resolution, people—mostly white women within the department—enthusiastically supported the proposal and excitedly made suggestions for the language we should use. It seemed a foregone conclusion that the vote would quickly and easily pass.

Until I spoke up. I shared the context I brought to the conversation. I didn't speak against the resolution, but I ended by asking two questions: "In my more than ten years in this department, we have never made a similar declaration. Not when any number of horrible things have happened in the world. And not even when the police targeted our own students. So why this issue, and why now?"

For a single moment, there was complete silence, the kind of silence that feels like people are remembering that you're present and you're Black. The silence during which you can feel white people recognizing, again, that you are *not one of them* in any of the ways that truly matter— the silence and the looks that remind you (if you'd ever forgotten) what a shame and inconvenience your Blackness is for them.

After that moment, my colleagues fell over themselves to explain why this issue was different, was worse, merited more attention. "Because the students are upset and afraid," said one, to which I responded that students were upset by undercover police on campus and Black students were sometimes afraid walking down the street. Their counterarguments kept coming. "Because it's so egregious," someone said, and at that point I stopped responding. They couldn't see police entrapment and state-sanctioned murder as egregious. They couldn't see or hear our mostly Black and Brown students—and they couldn't conceive that lives or experiences or feelings that don't resemble their own mattered.

One colleague turned to me and said, "*Anyone* who feels outraged by *anything* can make a resolution *anytime.*" Her comment seemed to restore their collective sense of fairness while putting the onus on me to—what? Propose a series of statements condemning institutional racism, police murder, state violence, white supremacy . . . ?

My energy drained away. I was upset and disappointed less for myself than for my students, *our* students—the students many of these professors claim to love, whose lives and experiences they could dismiss so easily. I don't remember what else was on the agenda. I remember abstaining from the vote and retreating into the solidity of my own body and mind. I wrote a poem during the rest of the meeting and jotted down notes that resulted in my "Welcome to rage" project. The poem indicts my colleagues for rushing to protect white womanhood while Black people die around them. The project is both more direct and more empathetic. If you are a Black person living in the United States, you have a deep familiarity with rage—against injustice, fear, willful white blindness—that is as old as your time in this country. But for many white people, rage—at the prospect of a rapist on the Supreme Court, the destruction of the climate, or even police murder—is a new, recent feeling. So the project welcomes those folks to rage. The cards follow that welcome by stating that we'll "see you in the streets," encouraging people to move beyond rage to take the action required to change the sources of that rage.

When revising this essay, I asked to see the minutes of that 2018 department meeting—and none of my objections appear there. With all dissent erased, there's an even greater probability that most of my white colleagues would probably still describe what happened that day as a routine department meeting. The sad reality is that they're right.

That resolution made my colleagues feel better. But I doubt it did more than that. Remembering the incident, my chest still gets tight, but looking at my art, I relax, and I feel satisfied. My colleagues may not have heard me, but plenty of other people have. The poem is in my collection *All the Rage*, and I've given out over a thousand small business-style cards that read, *Dear Friend, Welcome to rage. See you in the streets!* I suggest to people they keep one and give a few away. (If you'd like to receive a few cards, contact me through my website www.rosamondsking.black.) I spoke up, and in the face of illogic I protected and vindicated myself— and turned the experience into community, commiseration, and humor.

(after depart meant

Blind-colored glasses and the damocles is in
Visible. No threat against an Abattoir dweller enrages
Elsewhere. Even the shock of death lasts only
One news cycle. Rinse and repeat. But
Care covers women Elsewhere
Like a dropped cloth Like a tablecloth
Protecting precious   The straight, pressed
From blood spatter   Foundation of every wholesome

Blind-colored classes and
The damocles is in\visible over
The Abattoir
Over Elsewhere too

AUDACITY AND ANGST

The Emotional Trauma of Audacious Encounters

KERRI-ANN M. SMITH

Trauma is the angst you feel after you've walked away from an argument realizing that you missed an opportunity to give the ultimate rebuttal. In that moment, you remember all the clever comebacks, the sharpest shade, and the most brutal blows. Alas, you didn't say what you could have—no, should have—said, and in a professional setting your proverbial clapback was not even a snap. That was me after an untimely and unwelcomed encounter with a colleague.

I arrived early to administer the final exam. Several of my Composition 101 students had also arrived early, and we realized we were sharing the room with another class. The professor for the other section had not yet shown up and some of my own students were running late, so to ease the tension of my students already in the room who would be taking the exam, I took some time to engage them in conversation. I stood in front of them, offering reassurance, good vibes, and lots of positive affirmations. In my hand was a stack of blue examination booklets. My awareness of the hypervisibility of being one of only a few Black women in my department compels me to always wear "professional" attire, so I had opted to wear heather-gray slacks; a ruffled, short-sleeved blue blouse; and wedge heels that morning. I was in the middle of a sentence when a white male of medium build and advanced age, wearing a checkered button-down and carrying a briefcase, barreled into the lecture hall, huffing (perhaps from walking across campus). I had purposely seated my students on the side opposite the lectern, and he walked directly to it with presumed authority over the room.

"You! Sit down!" he said, as he pointed at me, dismissively.

I looked around to see who "you" could be, and my students, equally annoyed, gave me the confirming, "It's you. You are you!" look. I continued talking to my students, and when he finally got to the podium, he used the microphone to repeat his directive.

"You! Let's go! It's time to begin the exam."

Again, I ignored him, assuring my students that I was fine and would handle this. I asked them to begin the exam, and I noticed, through my peripheral vision, that he was charging over to my side of the room. I did not hear all of his initial statements; I already knew what to expect: "I didn't realize you were the professor! You look so young!" And he didn't disappoint.

Even as I recall this incident, the emotions are palpable—the feeling of demoralization that arose and how I defaulted to my safe inner space (thinking of the prologue of *Invisible Man*, where the narrator beats a man nearly to death for calling him a name). Upon realizing I was a colleague, he switched to small talk—the injurious denial of his wrong and a superficial compliment that masked his audacity in ignorance, marked by the conventional "I didn't know"—as if students, particularly our Black students, aren't entitled to respect.

Some faculty have the privilege of distancing themselves from students' identities to the point of being unable to recognize who is not one of their students. He had the privilege of keeping them at arm's length, while a Black woman, whose career centers on representation for our students, was perceived neither as a faculty colleague nor as someone worthy of his respect or even of a mere apology for the disrespect he rendered upon walking into a room he thought he had owned.

He continued in the conversation, bragging about his own children. I noted the unequal and presumptuous comparison while thinking of all the things I truly wanted to say but could not. He offered up that his daughter, now a college lecturer, is also young. Therefore, his excuse that I looked so young didn't hold weight, for in his own attempt to pacify what I felt was an emotionally violent situation, he confirmed his familiarity with young professors. I stood there in all my doctoral glory, the young and gifted Black tenure-track assistant professor, listening to him, a long-term adjunct faculty member whom I had never met (although we worked in the same department), while biting my tongue to the point where I wished it would fall off. When he finally walked away, quietly, never having apologized as loudly as he had chided me, the myriad things I "should have said" consumed my thoughts. I should have called out his blatant racism. I should have pointed out that his excuse was a farce. I should have thrown my credentials in his face. I should have shown my students that I was "'bout that life." I should have demanded he "keep that same energy" and apologize so he could feel a slight touch of the humiliation to which I was subjected. Why did I censor myself?

So many times I've had pithy comebacks, but I've bitten my tongue in the name of perfectionism and professionalism as a Black woman on my campus of predominantly white faculty members. I held back on that spring day. I wanted my students to respect us both. I wanted them to do well on their exam. I wanted to decrease distraction. I wanted to validate their feelings, but I also wanted to remain collegial. I wasn't yet tenured, and while he had no bearing on my tenure, I did not want to explode and create a scene. But why? He had already created a scene. He had already "chosen violence." Why did I have to restrain myself while annihilating him mentally and holding the burden of the emotional trauma? I outranked him and he had no power or influence over my position, and yet I allowed him to walk away.

I begrudgingly glanced at him as he stood at the podium. He had gone on with his life, scanning his side of the room, making sure his students weren't cheating, joking with some, helping others, and reading whatever he had brought along as he invigilated the exam. But I was emotionally paralyzed in this large lecture hall, facing my students. Perhaps if told today that he did this harm, he would deny it and so would our colleagues, since I later found out he was endeared in our department—an "innocuous" and "nice" guy, they said. For him, this was perhaps a casual, forgettable encounter, but for me, it left an indelible, injurious scar.

EVEN WHEN WE WIN, WE LOSE
ANONYMOUS

When I published my first book, I decided to submit it for multiple awards, including one from a relevant division of my national association. Unfortunately, the eligibility window ended around the same time as the expected release of my book, and my editor had cautioned me against relying on the scheduled release date. I contacted the awards committee chair for advice on how I should proceed; she advised me to wait until the next year to nominate my book for the award. I then noted a months-long gap in the eligibility window that, if replicated the next year, would render my book ineligible. However, she assured me that she would make sure that that wasn't the case. I kept the email "receipts" of this conversation.

A year later, when the call for nominations came out, I noticed that my book did indeed fall outside of the eligibility window. I contacted the then-current division chair, explained the prior year's eligibility gap issue, and noted that the previous chair had assured me that my book would be eligible for the current awards cycle. In my email exchanges with her, I became dismayed when she accused me of requesting favorable treatment because of a presumptive interpersonal relationship with the past chair, with whom I had never worked in any capacity, conversed with outside of the previous year's conversation, or met in person. When I produced the "receipts" of our conversation, I was told that the awards committee would have to vote on revising the eligibility window; this information was accompanied by the snide remark that if the window were to be expanded, it would be done so for everyone, not just me (something I never said or implied was expected). The committee elected to expand the eligibility window. Months later, the division chair sent me a terse email informing me that my book had won in a unanimous vote. Nevertheless, I never heard from anyone again about the award, and no one inquired as to whether I would be available to attend the ceremony in which it was formally conferred. Years later, I have yet to receive my plaque; indeed, that email is the only evidence I have that my book won the award. I have always suspected that, given the circumstances surrounding my winning, there was some conflict within the division over it, and it was likely decided that it was best that it be kept as quiet as possible. In contrast to this experience, the next year, my book won another award from a different, more racially diverse division of the national association. I was immediately asked to attend that ceremony and received a plaque, as well as an unironic "congratulations" from the other division's previous division chair.

The story doesn't end there. It is quite an achievement to receive a book award—doubly so two—and it would seem that one's home department might also see it that way. For me, this was not to be the case, and it was the issue that prompted me to finally decide to leave what had, by then, become a toxic workplace. I listed my two book awards on my CV, the national association had announced the second one on its listserv, and my college's dean's office had recognized the award at an end-of-the-year reception. Over the years, my department chair had issued public congratulatory announcements when my colleagues garnered notable—but often lesser—accomplishments (for example, awards for published essays); nevertheless, aside from a few individual congratulatory gestures, I never received any kind of departmental recognition, either for the book or for the awards it garnered. Indeed, my department gives out a "faculty of the year" award at the end of each academic year. There is no money attached to it; the winner gets a certificate during the final faculty meeting. It is, however, an important recognition of one's accomplishments. More specifically, it is an acknowledgment that one's scholarship is seen as important and that the individual is a respected and valued member of the department. Eligibility is contingent on annual merit evaluations, and it is very difficult to receive an "outstanding" evaluation without a published book. Because faculty in my department received credit for publications for three years, I was eligible for the award three times. I had seen colleagues with less prestigious accomplishments receive the award in the past yet had a feeling that, in spite of my book, awards, and two small external grants, I would be overlooked. I had been passed over for it the first two times; the second time, I received the highest rating in both research and teaching—a rarity—and yet the award had gone to a junior faculty member. This final time, my expectation was borne out when a colleague won the award, based on an accomplishment that was, by any objective standard, far less notable than mine.

Two months later, as I was resigning and cited this type of marginalization as a reason, I was told that the award recipient had made it known in advance that she expected it to be given to her. The executive committee had decided that, because she outranked me as senior faculty, she would get it. I am an associate professor, but I declined to point out that a junior faculty member had received it the year before or that this was not the first time that hierarchy (the exact, loaded term used) had been invoked as an excuse for favoritism toward a white colleague. I just left.

One of the more infuriating aspects of this story is that the former division chair was a signee of a solidarity statement with BIPOC in the aftermath of an "inclusion versus merit" controversy that erupted with one of our discipline's premier journals. Later, my former department issued a public statement supporting Black Lives Matter in the wake of the murders of Breonna Taylor and George Floyd. At best, these actions demonstrate the disconnect between many white academics' self-serving, performative "wokeness" and the day-to-day realities of their treatment of their Black colleagues and complicity in anti-Blackness in the academy more generally. It also reflects the difference (often a chasm) between the ways in which many educated, "liberal" white folks prefer to see themselves and the ways in which people of color more accurately see them. These incidents don't make me feel embarrassment, humiliation, or sadness but rather anger and, at times, disgust. My research focuses on the intersection of race and history, and I am well aware that this is how whiteness operates. Therefore, I expect these kinds of behavior to characterize academia in much the same ways that they characterize any other profession and life in general. As my favorite Black bloggers proclaim, whites are gonna white. It is also why I believe it is important to tell and archive our stories.

A CALL TO LEVERAGE BLACK VOICE

EVELYN B. WINFIELD-THOMAS

My background and identities are Black female, cisgender, licensed psychologist, and tenured full professor with over twenty-five years of higher education professional experience, including seventeen years as an administrator in a large, predominantly white midwestern university. During the midstage of my career, I experienced some unsettling trans-actional encounters in pursuing an internal employment opportunity. A younger white female and junior colleague, with whom I had collab-orated extensively on university-wide initiatives and whose educational endeavors and career pursuits I had supported, intentionally leveraged her privileged identities, social capital, and access to authority in oppo-sition to my effort for advancement.

During the confidential stage of the search process, my colleague ap-proached me and unethically discussed and disingenuously expressed support of my candidacy for an administrative position while politically working against me in support of her own self-interest. She was not sup-posed to know I had applied for this internal position, so I speculated that a fellow colleague and member of the search committee had shared my name with her. Shortly after another Black woman was hired for the position, my junior colleague asked to meet with me. During the meeting she disclosed that she had actively recruited the Black woman to pursue the position as her next supervisor but was now experiencing discontent-ment with her leadership style and decisions. She insensitively expressed to me that my qualifications were stronger, yet she was anxious and fearful about potential and undesirable department restructuring that she as-sumed I would implement. I inferred that she was worried that changes would thwart her plans and opportunities. Now she was hopeful that her concerns would resonate with me and I would join her to help "control" the new Black woman supervisor. This exchange felt like a selfish dump to ease her dissonance so she could move forward. Even though she had approached me earlier, what she revealed was unexpected and disturbing. I was a bit astonished. How dare she come to me with this disclosure! Who does this? At this point, I was offended, irritated, hurt, and pissed off, but I didn't let her know. In the moment, I was not poised to share my true emotional reaction and feelings with her. I chose silence.

After reflecting on our interaction, I requested a follow-up conversation to clarify my understanding of her assumptions, admissions, and actions. The additional information I got from that conversation confirmed my view that her behavior was self-serving and she was likely feeling vulnerable and trying to safeguard her status and position. I perceived her deliberate campaign for another person as undermining and a devaluation and personal affront against me. While it was her privilege to support another candidate, it was quite unprofessional for me to hear about it in this manner, especially after she expressed her dissatisfaction with the person whom she had solicited for the role. I still remained silent.

I came to the realization that I had experienced the impact of racial privileges afforded to white women and a series of racial microaggressions. In a sense, a white woman had exercised her untethered "white voice" as an entitlement to flaunt whenever, wherever, and to whomever. On some level, I was traumatized into a numbness and believed I consciously censored and muted myself as a defense and for protection from the potential risks or negative consequences of communicating and expressing my true thoughts and feelings directly with a member of the "dominant" group. Admittedly, I have suppressed and carried some baggage associated with other situations from being quiet and reserved and wonder whether my narrative would have been different had I used my authentic voice. In retrospect, I regret electing silence over speaking candidly about my reactions to these experiences. While it may be important and helpful to weigh the value and impact of using strategic silence versus Black voice when subjected to racial privilege, racial microaggressions, and other forms of hostile or traumatic encounters, I am embracing and issuing a call to leverage Black voice.

INCIDENTS IN THE LIFE OF A BLACK PROF

A Speculative Curriculum Vitae

VALORIE DIANE THOMAS

Valorie Diane Thomas (she/her/they)
University of Caliban, St. Baartman
Department of Wynter-Laveau Studies
vthomas@liminal.edu
1-800-DIV-RSTY

SCHOLARLY PROFILE

Committed to interdisciplinary scholarship, teaching, activism. Theoretically nomadic with Afrofuturist tendencies. First African American/BIPOC hired as core tenure track faculty in all-white English Department and Africana Studies at current institution. Teaches decolonial approaches to literature and art informed by Black and Indigenous intersectional analyses of race, inclusion, structural relations, misogynoir, anti-Blackness, anti-Indigeneity, and colonizer innocence. Treasures trustworthy, compassionate community and allies. Occasionally optimistic but refuses to sprinkle performative diversity glitter. Neurodivergent. Episodes of snow blindness due to encounters with lateral violence, chronic virtue-signaling, holier-than-thou-ing, civility hallucinations, gatekeeping, and acts of racism and ableism being blamed on the recipient's affect and personality.

EDUCATION

PhD in English, "But . . . No, We're Not Addressing You as 'Doctor.'"
MA in "Next, Get a PhD, So You Can Become One of the Two Percent of
    Tenured Black Women Professors in the United States?"
BA in "Predatory Student Loans, or, We're Charging You $30K on a
    $5K Loan, Coming After Your House, Your Credit, and Your Health,
    and Getting Away with It."

DISTINCTIONS

1998   Believes higher ed is where we pursue excellence
            (*defined by me as eradicating racism, structural violence,

environmental destruction, poverty), circulate knowledge, support next generations, and imagine the possibilities of diversity—multiple ways of being and knowing (i.e., ontoepistemological wherewithal).

Additional information: Positioned to live the metastructural abolition work of inventing inclusion in the space and desegregating at the department and curricular level without acknowledgment of the intellectual labor, health impact, or need for infrastructure and resources. All you really need to know is that on day one of the job the chair walked into the first English Department meeting of my career and asked my white colleagues and my Black self about budgeting with the words, "Are we being too niggardly?" (*how to stealth say the whole N-word and dog whistle racists on day one, or, "Fun with Homophones!")

2000–22 Genius white writer shrieks up and down the department hallway, hollering my name, banging both fists on office doors, and runs screaming out of the building.

Additional information: Someone indicated I had a folder he wanted.

2000–22 I code-switch out loud in a meeting (*I code-switch in all meetings).

Additional information: Apparently, certain people experience hearing AAVE (African American Vernacular English) as violent. Also, my Black body in the room is violent. There could be "disciplinary action" if this "pattern" continues.

2000–22 Requests the college support me in developing a (potentially) national Black organization to foreground the academic accomplishments and interests of Black and BIPOC students and allies, envisioned as a platform for welcoming families, friends, support systems, faculty, staff, community, and professional networks by providing college resources for building one campus conversation centering Black well-being and welcoming anyone who supports and celebrates it. Driven by priorities and programming suggested by student and family or support system participants. Black Study Abroad panels, alumni talks, writing workshops, spoken word programs, and welcome receptions for students, families or support systems, and community are well attended but die out. Budget award: $200 a semester. Other inclusion initiatives like this one: zero.

2000–22   The English Department—in which I've been the senior faculty member for two years and "core" faculty since I was hired, and in which I've participated in hiring, directly or indirectly, literally everyone in the room—holds a vote on whether or not I'm allowed to be in "their" department. Am I allowed to "join" "their" department? I am jointly-appointed in Africana Studies, therefore apparently not actually "in" "their" department. Who really knows the difference between inclusion and exclusion, anyhow? And who cares?

2000–22   Black tax: I have a holistic doctor, a clinician, a nutritionist, a cranio-sacral-fascia MD, a chiropractor, a therapist, a meditation instructor, a breathwork trainer, an acupuncturist, a therapeutic massage specialist, and a yoga instructor. One is covered by health insurance.

2000–22   It is suggested I offer a public apology after I was racially attacked outside a faculty residence. I refuse and press charges. The school installs a dainty wall between the faculty residence and the dorm walkway where the (racial) incident occurred. All (racial memory) will be erased/sanitized/stuccoed and painted beige.

Feb. (all)   Increased peripheral vision by 85 percent due to the amount of side-eye I engage in daily.

Me:

Certain people: "Would you fetch my keys?"

"She, the one Black person in the department, refused to sign our faux Black solidarity statement, but we found a way around her." They are rooting out anti-Blackness wherever it lurks and one insignificant Black woman is not about to get in the cotton-pickin' way.

"Black women can't grow their own hair." Tries to touch my locks.

"Can you wash your hair?" Makes a face.

"I haven't seen you in a coon's age."

"At your request, I am responding to your email. I did change the subject line of the email, as it is offensive to me . . . please be specific, and professional, about . . ."

"I'll thank you to keep a civil tongue in your head or . . ."
"I thought it would be fabulous to meet in the Overseer's Room. She thinks everything is about race. She bullied me."
"She's . . . touchy."

WRITING SAMPLE

Abstract: A close reading for Ms. Saartje Baartman.

This used to be the biology building
Where we penned your ancestor

well-funded experts mumble
you're (not) one of us

skin a mirror
sharded

breath a text
inking the room

triggers silence
dull-knife teeth

makes people
feel a jagged saw

skin a mirroring
margin peeling

my mirror of broken crystal memory
skinned knowledge

my mirror of broken skin
voice chorusing

Black inclusions
under glass

we will continue our dissection
tomorrow

WHAT'S IN A NAME?

TAMEKA PORTER

I was recruited to serve on an advisory committee for an organization that provided engaging professional development experiences for the thousands of academic staff (that is, administrative office staff, undergraduate advisors, grant and scholarship officers) at my former large, tony, and elite research university in the Midwest. Committee members were up-front that I was sought after because I was a Black researcher, a woman, and a recognizable young scholar on campus—of which there were many, but of course, in some circles, there can only be one.

The campus organization was looking to bring Black early- and mid-career academic staff new to the university into the fold, but it had a looming and ongoing public relations problem: it was trying to overcome its historical name and acronym, Engaging New Staff Leverages All Viable Endeavors, or ENSLAVE (please note that I have changed these names to protect both the innocent and the guilty).

Though ENSLAVE was established in the aftermath of campus protests about the destruction and inequities surrounding the Vietnam War, it took a public reckoning, hearing, and vote to change the obviously offensive (to some but clearly not all) moniker—over forty years later.

Think about it: Who wants to be ENSLAVE(d) as a professional learning opportunity? Isn't that how modern anti-Black textbooks are marketing the "Atlantic Triangular Trade" to the next generation of scholars?

Despite having enrolled and retained few Black members, those on the committee—possessing no knowledge of other Black organizations or people on campus and recruiting no other diverse voices—felt my addition to the board and their new brand, Engaging New Staff Locally and All Year (ENSLAY), would be the key to recruitment success. Black enrollment declined. They still wonder why.

ACADEMIC LYNCHING
Chronicles of a Black Scholar's Deleterious
Racialized Experiences at a University in Texas
THELMA "PEPPER" G. MCCOY

A two-year social work master's degree was the fullest extent of my academic ambition as a middle-aged adult after launching multiple children on their own collegiate and professional paths. However, academics in the master's program with close ties to a specific doctoral program convinced me that a scholar of my caliber was highly sought after. In the fall of 2006, I became a PhD student in a cohort of seven multiracial, multiethnic, and multigendered scholars in a social work program at a Texas university. My first impressions of and sense of belonging in what I thought to be an equitable and inclusive doctoral educational experience were quickly dispelled by a number of troubling racialized and disparate social work departmental experiences beyond the full scope of this brief vignette. Instead, the following succinctly chronicled psychological and professional deleterious racialized experiences are by far the most disturbing.

In the fall of 2007, I was on track to complete all prerequisite courses before declaring formal dissertation work. But then my son and I were struck head-on by a drunk and drugged driver. Trapped in the wreckage for nearly an hour, we miraculously survived despite severe, life-threatening injuries. After being hospitalized for weeks, I returned to school in the spring of 2008, aided by a wheelchair. Somehow I managed to complete the coursework and started the dissertation process while undergoing physical, psychological and emotional recovery, and rehab. However, the event that nearly sealed my undoing was when my amicable academic advisor, mentor, and dissertation chair, L. Lein, left the university for a deanship in the Northeast. Beyond overwhelmed, I felt as if the ground had literally opened beneath me, in that I was unceremoniously thrusted into academic purgatory without an advisor for over a year.

Eventually, a new advisor and dissertation chair, D. DiNitto, was acquired, whose friend, the department's then African American dean, B. White, compellingly suggested we work together. Shockingly, D. DiNitto required in the spring of 2010 that I start over my research and writing process after a year and half of solo research, writing, and dataset location work guided by the outline, context, and content of my previous advisor. The stringent, baseless, and tremendously laborious requirement also occurred, irrespective of my physical rehabilitation and lingering PTSD symptoms (headaches, anxiety, depression, and panic attacks) from the accident. An informal appeal to Dean White, additional direct efforts with the chair, and requests for assistance from others in the department to change the senseless requirement were all unsuccessful. Resultantly, an extremely difficult working relationship with the new advisor ensued due to her frequent microaggressions, covert manifestations of chronic ambiguous slights, and race-coded messages, including demonstrative preconceived lack of trust and expectations of substandard work. Similarly, on several occasions I witnessed her exclusionary behaviors, demonstrated by an elated, egregious, and engaging persona with non-Black students and faculty members. She readily provided more generous financial support, advice, writing and publishing opportunities to non-Black graduate students. Whereas her demeanor with me was, more often than not, overtly professional, paternalistic, and minimizing. For example, in the fall of 2011, without any prior discussion, D. DiNitto arranged a meeting with one of her faculty mentees, M. Lopez, whose secondary data, I was informed, would be used in my dissertation, in effect denudating me of the typically honored, expected, and academically recognized freedom and autonomy over one's independent research project. I felt unspeakably blindsided, disrespected, and disempowered in equal measures. Notably, the conundrum weighted even heavier with the sad and sobering realization that given D. DiNitto's lengthy tenure and my previous invalidated and failed attempts at addressing her behaviors and actions, I had absolutely no one in the department to turn to for support.

Eventually, through a convoluted departmental approval process, in May 2012, I participated in the official doctoral cohort graduation ceremony as an ABD (All-but-Dissertation) with the understanding that by December 2012, my graduation would concomitantly become official after a final data analysis chapter and defense—that is, if the faculty mentee, M. Lopez, actually provided the data. I eventually acquired the data in the spring of 2013 in the midst of a cumulative series of calamitous miscommunications and academic discord on the dissertation committee (for example, vague verbal and nonverbal communications conveying rudeness and insensitivity were common). Even when conciliatory attempts were made to address or try to resolve problems, my reality was invalidated or the perpetrator responded in a very conniving, punitive, and derogatory way. These occurrences precipitated the unprecedented need to receive data analysis assistance from outside the department, although the committee included a data analysis member (J. Schwab).

Ominous, yet successful completion of the data analysis chapter ensued in fall 2013, but was quickly overshadowed by the defense delayed scheduling because the dissertation chair (D. DiNitto) quit the doctoral committee in response to my expressed concerns about the onerous and grueling process of her required massive re-editing (that is, copyediting by hand on paper rather than electronically and re-editing her own and other committee members' edits to the final draft of my dissertation). Incredulously and indefensibly, even after quitting the committee she attempted to orchestrate the new dean (L. Zayas) as her chair replacement on my dissertation committee even though an African American associate professor (D. Gilbert) had already accepted my invitation. Furthermore, in response to my adamant refusal to switch the chairperson, Dean Zayas gutted my funding by terminating a graduate teaching assistant position two months prior to the dissertation initial defense. During a requested meeting with additional faculty and the new chair in attendance, when asked directly why my funding was cut, Dean Zayas eventually angrily and emphatically stated, "You don't deserve it!"

This and other undeniably egregious deanship actions, witnessed by multiple departmental faculty and staff, catapulted the aggrieved and anti-Black, racialized social work department into an even more troubling and psychologically crippling environment; an academic sphere I could no longer pretend as tenable, let alone legal, given the obvious disheartening concerted and convoluted efforts for me to discontinue my doctoral education.

As a result, in spring 2014, I acquired faculty ombudsmen advocacy assistance and filed formal grievances and an EEO complaint that advanced to the office of the then university president. Neither laborious attempts for equitable redress were successful. Similarly, the funding and employment gap included a tortuous and suspicious departmental failed dissertation defense (spring 2014) and a subsequent delayed dissertation completion and passed defense (fall 2014). At that time, having been on the job market for nearly two years, I received post–job interview feedback that suggested that on more than one occasion the search committees had received less than favorable responses about me from the Social Work Department supervisory faculty. Now, a decade post-ABD 2012 graduation and with the lack of a tenure-track position, it is exceptionally clear that I was and potentially continue to be academically lynched—namely, the "less visible forms of lynching . . . where academic labor takes place, . . . anti-black rituals that produce belonging within the University" (McCann 2021, 2)—for speaking up and attempting to address obvious retaliatory issues associated with a toxic anti-Black graduate-level academic environment.

Reference

McCann, Bryan J. 2021. "Lynching and the University." *Quarterly Journal of Speech* 107, no. 2 (April): 245–49.

ENCODING ANTI-BLACK RACISM INTO ACADEMIC COMPENSATION STRUCTURES

IJEOMA NNODIM OPARA

I never thought I would tolerate a toxic relationship. I never thought I would be that woman who stayed with the man who hits her, abuses her, and devalues her every day, the woman who shows up in public with the huge sunglasses to hide her black eye, talmbout "I be walking into open cabinets, chyyyyle. Gurl, you know I'm so clumsy!" rationalizing and justifying my own dehumanization when concerned parties queried if everything was all right. I never thought I would tolerate a toxic relationship until I realized I had been doing exactly that for almost four years while working as an assistant professor and attending physician of internal medicine at an academic institution, earning the lowest percentile among my peers despite my clinical, academic, teaching, and service productivity being among the top percentiles.

When I was initially hired, my division chief explicitly informed me that my salary was nonnegotiable and that it was the standard amount offered to all new hires at the time. I had no choice but to accept what was offered and be grateful. I was told the contract included boilerplate clauses that are standard across the board. The only thing I was able to add to the contract was an agreement on the institution's part to sponsor a master's degree in public health to support my global health program, which I was supposed to develop for the university.

Spoiler alert: that promise was never honored. I accepted the offer because, as a newly graduated physician from my residency program, I was naive. At the time, I did not have the mentorship to help me be discerning in my career decision-making. I also had no idea of my value. I had spent the last ten years learning medicine but not the *business* of medicine. I believed what I was told, accepted what I was offered, and was grateful for what I received. In the interim, I developed multiple educational programs; led important initiatives in global health, health equity, justice, and anti-racism; produced scholarship; received grant support; represented the university nationally and internationally; taught and mentored countless medical students and resident physicians; and served on multiple committees—all while seeing patients and producing clinical revenue for the university. In the meantime, I placed my young single-income family on a tight budget—I'm the breadwinner and also paying off student loans.

Four years later, one fine day, I ran into a non-Black former colleague of color at a conference who disclosed that there had been a salary increase of more than $35,000 for the past few years and how nice is that? Wayment . . . say what now? A salary increase? For whom? Where? How? That's when I found out not only that I was earning the lowest amount in my department but that new hires, including my own former trainees, were being paid higher salaries and no attempt had been made to adjust my income. I was livid. I felt humiliated. I felt betrayed.

I was hurt.

On my way home from the conference, I thought about how many times I had felt burned out. I was constantly overworked, overwhelmed, unsupported, under-resourced, under-mentored, unsponsored, and underpaid. I thought about all the times my requests for support had been ignored or excuses had been made for the absence of funds to provide the support needed. I thought about the dysfunction, trauma, and stress I had normalized. I wept hot tears at how I had tolerated a toxic relationship and rationalized the disrespect, dishonor, and dehumanization because I didn't know any better. I didn't know my worth, and I was naive to expect that others would automatically look out for me and do right by me. I felt helpless. I didn't know what to do, but I knew I had to do something. I didn't know whom to trust, but I knew I had to tell someone. I had gotten used to people with titles and apparent authority being completely unhelpful. I decided to take matters into my hands and wrote a letter to my division chief requesting a review of salary that listed all my contributions and demanded pay parity. I found out that I was one of the two lowest-earning faculty persons in my department, and the other one was also a Black woman. I found out that this was a pattern throughout the department and possibly throughout the university. This was clear institutional racial and gender inequity—institutionalized misogynoir.

I went up and down the leadership ladder making my case, involving other senior leadership to advocate on my behalf, to no avail. There were some mutterings that my patient charts were not timely, which may be a fair assessment but one that does not take into account the numerous additional duties I was performing and also is not a factor in determining our salary. It was as if reasons were being constructed from thin air to magically justify my low pay. I was depressed and my feeling of self-worth plummeted. I just wanted to live under my bed forever. I think this issue hurt me so deeply because it was a very personal decision to stay at my institution and serve our predominantly Black community. I received an offer at another institution with a higher salary but decided to stay because the department chair at the time was a Black man who had practically promised me protection, mentorship, and professional development—another promise undelivered, because he ended up leaving the institution a few months after I joined.

There was a rich history of Black leadership at my department relative to other departments, and I felt that I could develop my scholarly niche in a supportive, nurturing environment, the environment where I "grew up," the environment I called home. My significant other. So, when one's significant other, whom one loves and trusts, delivers a punch to the gut, the hurt is more than physical. The hurt is emotional, psychological, and even spiritual.

After almost two years of futile self-advocacy, I was contemplating my next move, which was to leave—a tough option because, frankly, I was afraid. What if I wasn't any good elsewhere? What if this was the only place that could accommodate my needs? What if I deserved this treatment? What if other places were just as bad, if not worse? What about my benefits and health-care coverage? What about my family? The questions twirled and swirled.

Then one day the email popped into my inbox: "Dr. Opara, can you come to my office please?" We had a new chief administrator, a woman of color, and she was cleaning house. I reluctantly visited her office because nothing good ever happens when you are called in to see the principal, you know.

"Dr. Opara, I have been going through the books, and I see here that you are double board-certified, have worked here for six years now, and do A LOT! Your salary is incredibly low; we have to adjust it for pay parity." My eyes widened. Where was this coming from? I had already given up. I was planning to leave, not knowing where I would go, but I knew that if I stayed I would be complicit in my own devaluation. Yet, this woman was about to answer a two-year-long prayer? She didn't know about my fight to achieve pay parity; she had noticed the yawning gap and was trying to correct it. A gap that others were comfortable with. She offered me a number. This time, I countered. She accepted. I felt like I was being pranked, but my subsequent paycheck was proof that it wasn't all a dream. My pay parity was achieved because a woman of color in a position of power just picked up her pen and wrote in equity with dollar signs.

My relationship with my university is not fully healed and may never be healed. The trust is broken. The betrayal is still fresh. The hurt is still present even while writing these words. At the same time, I grew up very quickly as the veil of naïveté was removed from my eyes to see clearly how academia is a function of the mutually reinforcing systems of injustice, inequity, and oppression that pervade society as a whole. I learned to get everything in writing and not move until then. I learned that capitalism is an unfeeling bitch and that "mission" is only mission to the degree it doesn't get in the way of the institution's bottom line. I learned that I was worth so much more than I had been made to believe. Now I know that I won't let anyone ever define my value and that I will not hide my light under a bushel but shine brightly, authentically, and unapologetically.

WHITE PRIVILEGE
AMARDO RODRIGUEZ

1. You are always believed. You are never lying, fabricating, or falsifying anything.
2. You are always doing what is right. Your intentions are always good.
3. You are competent. There are always good and valid reasons for why you fucked up.
4. You are civil and decent. You would never ever do anything insulting or embarrassing.
5. You know what is best. You thus have the right to impose your mediocre bullshit on others and call it excellence.
6. You never have to worry about being heard. Your dumb ass always has something important to say.
7. You never have to worry about being treated cruelly or unjustly. That shit is for others to deal with.
8. You never have to struggle with holding on to your sanity and worrying about what all the rage you are harboring is doing to you.
9. You never have to anguish about whether evil is real and the devil no less so. That burden is for others to bear.
10. You never have to stop hoping and praying for some people to leave, retire, or die so you can have some kind of peace.

This poem came from a place of rage, a deep rage. Black folks know this rage well. bell hooks calls it a killing rage, and rightfully so. You cannot live in this rage. You certainly cannot thrive in it. On the other hand, if you fail to acknowledge this rage, it will come at you sideways and eat you alive. We are now to believe that the struggle is about diversity, equity, inclusion, and access (DEIA). After all, DEIA is now everywhere. But this is a farce. How, for instance, can we have any serious discussion of DEIA without discussing reparations?

Reparations are about reminding us all that the effects of over 350 years of slavery, Black Codes, and Jim Crow are real and enduring. Only revolution will bring about the full redemption of Black folks. To this end, the everyday struggle is about preserving our dignity and humanity in the face of all the cruelties and indignities that we constantly face. It is about refusing to allow ourselves to be disfigured and dehumanized by these cruelties and indignities. It is therefore about refusing to become like those people who subject us to these cruelties and indignities. Thus, the struggle is about being and remaining beautiful, always acting with grace and generosity, dignity and integrity. If we can hold on to our beauty, only then we are different, truly different, beautifully different. Diversity is the struggle for beauty. It is about saving ourselves and each other from all things that are ugly. Thus, when next contemplating a course of action, I would gently advise that you pose this question: "What action will allow me to remain beautiful?"

THE SMALL THINGS ADD UP

THOMAS F. DeFRANTZ

Spotlight Narrative

Microaggressions cohere through time for senior Black faculty. I have been a full professor for over a dozen years now; I worked for ten years before that as an assistant and associate professor. During this time I have been party to several hires that have produced mediocre white colleagues, even as each search counted outrageously accomplished Black candidates, as well as Brown and Asian candidates who were short-listed and even interviewed. But white supremacy and the continuous practices of whiteness that support its operations tend to lead to awkward outcomes.

I've reported to four deans across these many years as an academic: two white women, one Brown man (Middle Eastern), and most recently a Black woman from the US South. Sometimes Black people forget that we are also embedded in systems of oppression, that we learn from these systems, and that we can be racist, misogynistic, homophobic, and colorist. The Black woman dean from the South expressed very little grace toward me during the time we worked at the same institution; I started looking for another position nearly as soon as we met at the president's house for her welcome event. In the blink of an eye, I could see the lack of empathy toward my skin, my scale, my obvious queerness. Like many "church ladies" I have encountered over the years, her expression hoped for me to be somehow different: possibly less visible or more restrained. I wasn't wrong, and within sixteen months she removed me from all leadership positions I had been assigned before she arrived. This crushed my spirit and my self-confidence. It's very hard to work well when one feels disavowed or out of place.

I teach graduate courses in several different units; my work focuses on Black cultural production. I work with the major queer and Black feminist theoretical models available and provide overviews to intersections among these and the more prevalent white masculinist European formations. In these circumstances, there are always, *always*, white students who relate that they are better prepared than I to lead conversations and provide an "accurate" rendering of theoretical materials at hand. These students inevitably reveal that they are only passing through this temporary relationship with me, a Black faculty member, along the way to working with some more famous white faculty.

I have chaired two units and served as director of graduate studies twice. The ceremonial aspects of this sort of leadership invite scrutiny from a larger public. As program director in women's studies, I was tasked to introduce an invited feminist Israeli academic. Confusion reigned when a tall queer midwestern Black American academic performed as the representative of the university and its presumably pro-Israeli, anti-Palestinian leanings. Activist protesters and security guards alike registered uncertainty as I introduced the speaker and moderated the discussion after her talk. Are Black American academics not to be involved in concerns of Palestine, Israel, and the Middle East?

Years later, hosting a visiting former colleague and his friends did not go so well. I arrived late to the intimate dinner reception, coming from some other responsibility. We were three Black senior academics, all men, somehow surrounded by three young white women postdocs who worked on Caribbean topics. One of the young white women, whom I did not know, felt compelled to "interview" us at her pleasure, asking the visitors "what they did." When she turned this weird colonial attention toward me, I was not at all polite. I refused to answer her query about "what I worked on" and "what my position might be" at the university. Note that I was chairing the department that cosponsored the visit of my friend, and I was allocating the departmental funds to pay for the dinner that she enjoyed. The temperature at the table dropped in response to my refusal, and it took the white girl some time to understand that I would not respond to this sort of social maneuver. Clearly, she did not consider the relationships of the people she encountered at the dinner, and on meeting us, felt entitled to perform a colonial maneuver of discovery among us. She behaved with ignorance as a girl might, even though by her age she might have known at least how to respond to a refusal. My friend seemed distraught that I would not lubricate the social event toward happiness. But I refused. I briskly explained that I had not consented to be part of her "anthropological fieldwork." The dinner ended awkwardly. The next day, I wrote to the two white faculty mentors who work with the young woman about their mentee's actions and effect and her lack of understanding that in our cultural traditions, young people do not ask elders personal or inconsequential questions. I expected, and experienced, no particular outcome from that communication.

These sorts of microaggressions cohere to an overall dispiriting experience for me as a Black academic. All too often, I have been expected to perform the labor of explaining these points—the dangers of obviously biased hiring practices, that Black people are able to hurt and intimidate each other, that we know what we're doing as academics and intellectuals, that our interests extend beyond our areas of expertise, and that we have long-established modes of social relationship that nurture and enliven us. Luckily, I have also enjoyed simultaneously a full career as a working artist and crafted creative experiences that explore the potentials of an afroFUTUREqu##r at most every turn. These performances inspire me, alongside the audiences and witnesses who attend them, allowing us to commune briefly outside of the governing racial logics of the universities where I have held positions.

NAVIGATING NATURAL HAIR IN ACADEMIA
CAROLYN DESALU

After I began my career in academia, I fretted about my natural hair, which looked like a short, tight coily 'fro in its wash-and-go state. Depending on how I styled it or how it was cut, my hair sometimes looked larger than Angela Davis's signature Afro or big and billowy like Diana Ross's or Chaka Khan's coif. These were my preferred looks, but in academia, I wondered whether my hair choice would be accepted. Prior to interviewing for a full-time position as a visiting instructor at a university, which later led to a full-time assistant professor position, I scrolled through the photographic list of faculty and staff members. In that specific school, there were almost a hundred people and five were Black women, all of whom wore their hair straight for their faculty photo.

As I prepared a lesson and portfolio for my interview, I also made plans for my hair: flat-iron and then curl it in a loose, bouncy style. I deduced that this style would be more acceptable to my all-white interview committee and that my assimilation—at least in the area of hair like the other Black women faculty members—would somehow better my chances of landing the job. Experience taught me that something as seemingly benign as hairstyle choice was fraught with challenges. With the exception of one employer, I had always worked in predominantly white environments. Previously, at a corporate job, a white woman had walked up to my desk and strongly encouraged me to wear my hair straight because it "looked better." To emphasize her point, she demonstrated "straight" with hand gestures and then strolled off, chuckling. Although I am a gloriously proud Black woman, that white lady wanted me to adhere to a Eurocentric look.

To be fair, Black women in the South offered strange comments about my hair too. At other corporate jobs, they said my natural hair suggested I was "woke," like the Black Panthers of the late 1960s, or simply "not the one to mess with." One had even called me brave, stating that she was too ashamed and scared to wear her hair natural so she had opted for weaves; she never wore braids because those were "too Black" in an office filled with white coworkers.

I presumed the same sentiments would be true of academia and braced myself for similar experiences.

I accepted the university job, and on day one, when I arrived with my hair in the coily 'fro style, previous experiences and conversations flitted through my mind. I felt a mix of excitement about my career and dread for demeaning remarks that could come my way. Several people had commented about my hairstyle change, which made me self-conscious, but none of the comments seemed laced with insult or malice. Internally, I breathed a sigh of relief and looked forward to not justifying my hairdo.

As the months went on, I grew accustomed to inquiries about my 'do from white colleagues (and sometimes Latino, Asian, and other Black colleagues) and hoped that those conversations surrounding hair, Black beauty, and, at the very least, professionalism would prevent me and future Black women faculty members from feeling othered because of hairstyle choice.

Some colleagues often marveled at my Afro and others stood so close I had to take a step back to avoid feeling their breath on my face and the slight stirring of my hair since I didn't use hairspray. The close talkers stared at my hair and perhaps wanted to touch it but didn't dare. At least they maintained a sense of professional decorum.

Except for one who did not.

An older white man, who previously was a congenial and respectful colleague, blatantly disrespected me by attempting to touch my hair without my permission.

We were chatting in his office, and as I started to exit, he said, "I just want to touch your hair. I've never felt hair like yours before." He didn't ask; he stated what he wanted to do regardless of my consent. It was the epitome of white privilege: he tried to control and take ownership of my Black hair and invade my personal space.

I said no.

Instead of letting the topic drop, he asked, "Why not?" At the time, I didn't want to engage him in a conversation about my hair being my crown and the history of personal violation and abuse between white and Black people. Had he not heard of slavery? Had he not heard Solange's aptly titled song "Don't Touch My Hair" or seen the Oscar-winning short animated film *Hair Love*? Did he not know personal space was real? I couldn't vouch for where his hands had been; they may or may not have been clean. At the very least, his attempt to touch my hair was unprofessional.

He reiterated his desire to touch "hair like mine," this time chuckling like it was the most normal thing to do and say.

I laughingly chastised him, but wish I'd been firmer. In retrospect, my laugh minimized the severity of the situation. Though I was greatly offended at his gall and white presumption that it was OK to touch my hair, I didn't want to upset him and had concerns about workplace retaliation. Who I befriended professionally and who was considered an ally mattered, especially since I did not have tenure yet.

As I walked to the door, he walked behind me and said, "There's a piece of lint in your hair. Let me take it out for you."

I believed he was lying and said, "Just leave it," briskly exiting his office.

We were still affable after this incident, but I often made it a point to avoid being within his arm's reach to prevent a similar encounter.

Besides the constant curiosity and the incident with my colleague, I had my own internal hair struggle to address. I waited eight months to take my faculty photo because I didn't want to be the only Black woman with non-Eurocentric-looking hair in my school. I glanced at photos in other schools and departments, and many of the Black women there also had straight-styled hair. Nonetheless, I arrived at my faculty photo session rocking a large Afro and a colorful printed blazer to boot. The university photographer had taken countless pictures, I assumed, and, as a creative, visual person, would know to zoom out the lens so my hair would fit in the frame. When my photo appeared with my name under the faculty list a few days later, I was frustrated because my hair was cropped. I went back and looked at faculty photos again and noticed not everyone had passport-looking pictures. She could have given me the same courtesy.

I don't believe this was racially motivated, however. The photographer's lack of cultural awareness caused her not to consider that my photo with a cropped Afro would look peculiar and smushed. A handful of people at the university and several friends had asked about the cropping of my hair, and a few even chuckled. But there was no levity in the situation for me. It had taken me eight months to find the courage to take the photo, and while I could have requested a redo, in the end, I decided not to bother with it again.

Similar gaffes have been committed by major consumer brands. One apparel company styled a Black child in a monkey sweatshirt, a luxury brand used blackface to sell sweaters, and a fast-food chain advertising burgers to an Asian market used chopsticks.

The personal care brand Dove created racially insensitive ads in 2011 and 2017 but in early 2019 began advocating for Black beauty by co-founding the CROWN Coalition to prevent hair discrimination by supporting the passage of legislation called the Creating a Respectful and Open World for Natural Hair Act of 2022. One of the poignant findings of Dove's research was that 80 percent of Black women were more likely to change their natural hair in workplace settings. While I was not one of the survey respondents, this was true for me as well.

In March 2022, the US House of Representatives passed the Crown Act, which, according to Congress.gov, the official website for federal legislation information, "prohibits discrimination based on a person's hair texture or hairstyle . . . commonly associated with a particular race or national origin" at places including work and for those participating in federal assistance programs, housing programs, and public accommodations. The vote was 235–189 along party lines, and while the bill has the support of President Joe Biden, it still needs to pass in the Senate. In the last three years, however, more than a dozen states, including California, Massachusetts, New Jersey, and New York, passed local bills banning discrimination based on natural hairstyles. I am elated that individual states have recognized and found a way to protect the choice of people like me to wear natural hairstyles and textures.

State-by-state progress is a step in the right direction, but it doesn't necessarily translate into academia, where cultural and ethnic transgressions continue.

There are surveys, research, and cultural criticisms about Black women's hair and discrimination but limited information as it pertains to academia. To help remedy that, I'm working on my own research about it.

Workplace settings, including academia, have changed since the COVID-19 pandemic. Work-from-home saved me from quizzical looks, questions about how often I washed my hair, attempts to touch it, and invasion of my personal space. At home, I opted for vibrant headwraps or big twists like Miss Celie and comfortably sat with my camera on for Zoom calls.

As I continue to navigate a new normal in predominantly white environments like academia, I hope natural hair will be accepted instead of being an anomaly. I hope my white colleagues, in particular, maintain personal space and boundaries. Going forward, I also hope Black women—and more broadly, women and men of color—feel comfortable wearing their hair in natural and ethnic styles without worrying about the white gaze or being scrutinized at work.

CONVENIENT NARRATIVES
HOLDING BACK #BlackintheIvory
ASMERET ASEFAW BERHE

Minutes after he first met me—a Black woman and a recent immigrant from Africa who was already admitted to a top-ranked US institution with a fully funded PhD fellowship—a prominent professor in the graduate program I attended told me he couldn't understand how I got admitted into the program: because I came from Africa. He said that I didn't have the right pedigree to attend the prestigious university, and if I wanted to do the work I was proposing, I should first take the most basic, introductory course in my field that the department offered. He said all this before even checking any of my academic records that demonstrated that I had graduated in the top 5 percent of my undergraduate class in the same field, that I even had conducted undergraduate research in the same area I was proposing for my graduate research, and I had already received a master of science degree from a US institution.

My story is one about how sometimes #BlackintheIvory means enduring the convenient stereotypical and biased narratives that some choose to believe (Berhe 2020). As soon as we step foot in some institutions, we are told we don't belong there. We're told that we don't have the right pedigree to join the ranks of the elite or even learn from them. Further, some choose to believe that we must be incapable of succeeding in our professions. Some even proclaim that the things we accomplish must have been the result of affirmative action or even fraud (Berhe 2020). These statements demonstrate a failure to imagine that scholars from minoritized communities can be intelligent and hardworking. This convenient narrative is common in the academy and is very damaging. It makes our education and professional journey difficult, causes some of us to drop out of educational programs, and is used to rob us of our accomplishments and deny us a seat at the table (Pirtle 2021). Once people buy into a convenient narrative that agrees with their previously held belief, or if the narrative is told by individuals they hold in high regard, it's nearly impossible for us to counter it. The believers of that narrative work very hard to prove it right. Even if there is a mountain of evidence to the contrary. They spend a lot of time and energy to nullify the facts and show that we don't belong. They argue that we should not be given opportunities to prove we have what it takes. They claim that we snuck in through some shady, improper ways. And when proof of our hard-earned work shines through, they argue that there is no way we could have done the work we produced. Therefore, they say there is no possible way we could deserve the accolades, awards, and other recognition we receive for our work. Part of this is, of course, human nature; human beings are sometimes loath to be proven wrong, especially when it comes to sensitive topics like equity and inclusion of people from minoritized groups. But these convenient narratives continue to be important mechanisms for robbing minoritized scholars of the successes we achieve with a lot of hard work and after enduring a lot of heartache due to isolation, bias, discrimination, and more.

Convenient narratives that hold back #BlackintheIvory also show up in our public discourses. Notice that every time a high-profile case of racial harassment or discrimination is reported in the academy, many react to the unacceptable behavior passionately, especially in social media. Many of us are rightfully incensed that these exclusionary behaviors continue to happen under our noses, in the system that we hold very dear, in the environments where we should be training the great minds of tomorrow, the future leaders of the world. We are rightfully offended that some of our students, the best and brightest minds of the coming generation, are having to drop out of graduate school or soon after and will never be the dynamic professors, scholars, and world leaders that we knew they could have been. We know that the despicable behavior of some among our ranks is responsible for the observed trends of very low racial and other forms of diversity in our academic community (Marin-Spiotta et al. 2020). But, especially before the year 2020, very few of us would even dare to publicly acknowledge—even less dedicate time and energy to address—racial harassment and discrimination in institutions of higher learning. Some of the hesitance in countering the convenient narratives, at least publicly, is because of the real (for example, lack of evidence) and imagined (for example, fear of retaliation) issues or consequences of being vocal or of taking action on very serious matters such as race and discrimination. But our reluctance to deal with these real, albeit difficult, issues in the academy has delayed much-needed efforts to address impacts of toxic workplace cultures and climates that have continued to cause under-representation of people from minoritized communities in higher education.

Furthermore, the trauma of having to deal with the toxic behaviors in isolation continues to cause untold damage to those affected by exclusionary behaviors. Working to correct the record on these convenient narratives turns into a continuous, draining exercise for scholars from minoritized communities. It becomes a career-long heartache that contributes to making the academy a vicious, hostile obstacle course that Black and Brown people have to endure. As Toni Morrison puts it, "The function, the very serious function of racism is distraction. It keeps you from doing your work. It keeps you explaining, over and over again, your reason for being. Somebody says you . . . [don't belong or you are not worthy and you spend ages trying to correct the record and prove yourself]. None of this is necessary. There will always be one more thing" (Morrison 1975).

References

Berhe, Asmeret Asefaw. 2020. "Amplifying Black Voices: The Convenient Narratives That Perpetuate Racism (Parts 1 and 2)." *Springer Nature Blogposts: Life in Research*. SpringerNature.com, October 1, 2020. www.springernature .com/gp/researchers/the-source/blog/blogposts-life-in-research/amplifying -black-voices-the-convenient-narratives-of-racism-pt1/18415774.

Marin-Spiotta, Erika, Rebecca T. Barnes, Asmeret Asefaw Berhe, Meredith G. Hastings, Allison Mattheis, Blair Schneider, and Billy M. Williams. 2020. "Hostile Climates Are Barriers to Diversifying the Geosciences." *Advances in Geosciences* 53 (July): 117–27.

Morrison, Toni. 1975. "Black Studies Center Public Dialogue, Pt. 2." Panel by Portland State. Portland State Library Special Collections. Series: Public Dialogue on the American Dream Theme, May 30, 1975. https://soundcloud .com/portland-state-library/portland-state-black-studies-1, 36 min. mark.

Pirtle, Whitney Laster. 2021. "We, Too, Are Academia: Demanding a Seat at the Table." *Feminist Anthropology* 2, no. 1 (January): 179–85.

EMBRACING TEACHING MOMENTS FROM MICROAGGRESSIVE CLASSROOM DISCUSSIONS

ELETRA GILCHRIST-PETTY

In the spring of 2021, my graduate-level Intercultural Communication class discussed how many companies were rebranding themselves and finally becoming more racially sensitive with their packaging. For example, in February 2021 PepsiCo announced that the Aunt Jemima brand would be renamed Pearl Milling Company and the logo would no longer feature a Black woman but rather the company's name. Similarly, after seventy years, Mars Inc. changed Uncle Ben's Rice to Ben's Original in September 2020 and removed the smiling, gray-haired Black man from its packaging. We discussed not only these companies but also many others that have removed insensitive and racist imagery from their logos, names, and designs, such as Land O'Lakes, which, after more than ninety years, removed the image of a Native American woman from its packaging; the football team that for decades was known as the Washington Redskins, which would be announcing its new name in 2022; and the evolution of Eskimo Pie into the more generic brand of Edy's Pie. These actions were taken after years of criticism that the products and companies were stereotypical and racially insensitive. The changes were designed to promote respect and inclusivity.

Our class discussion addressed not only the historical significance of branding but how packaging, names, and logos are communication artifacts that convey meaning, whether intentional or not. The overwhelming majority of students in my class at the predominantly white southern institution applauded the companies' actions, with audible praises consisting of "It's about damn time," "Finally," and "It's a shame this is just now happening." However, the positive affirmations were quickly quelled when a white female student said, "I don't get it. People, especially Blacks, have constantly complained about a lack of representation and being featured in media, but in cases like these when they are featured they still complain and want to be taken off the products and renamed to something more generic. It's like damned if you do, damned if you don't." At first, I and many others in the class were taken aback. From a brief look around the room, I could see looks of shock, disgust, and even rage on my students' faces. Some simply dropped their eyes, lightly shaking their heads. After briefly pausing to digest the statement, I thought of the many ways to handle this situation. Among the options, I could simply ignore the comments and move on with the lesson; I could query the student, all while naturally exposing her ignorance; or I could use this as a teachable moment. The answer was clear; I knew that I had to embrace this teachable moment—after all, this is what it means to be Black in the ivory. I am here to educate my students both on and off the scripted lesson plan.

I knew from anecdotal comments that this student had rarely been around those who are Black, Indigenous, and People of Color (BIPOC). She had even commented that I was the first Black professor to teach her in the five years she had attended the university. So the first thing I did was to facilitate a candid, yet respectful, impromptu lesson on micro-aggressions (a topic we were not scheduled to discuss until the next week). I addressed much of the work by Derald Wing Sue, who not only defined microaggressions but explored them as microassaults, microinsults, and microinvalidations. Interwoven in this discussion was critical information pertaining to implicit bias and representation, whereby I clearly articulated to the class that not all representation is good or desired representation. Perhaps the most impactful teachable moments came when I invited students in the class to contribute to the discussion. There were only two BIPOC students in the class of twenty, but they eagerly embraced the opportunity to share their opinions, with the Black male conveying chilling experiences of how he is always profiled while shopping in stores and driving based simply on how he looks, yet he has never been arrested and is earning his master's degree, all while working full-time. The Black female in the class added that she always feels misrepresented because her hair is in locs. She said that growing up she did not have very many positive role models who were people of color, and it hurt to see the car-icatures of Aunt Jemima and Uncle Ben because they were stereotypical and fed into the negative images she had been exposed to since infancy.

As our conversation progressed, many of the white students chimed in, with some saying that before our class they had never thought about the implicit meanings of names, packaging, and logos, and they appreci-ated now having that knowledge. What pleased me the most is that the white female student who made the comments that diverted our class discussion had an awakening and even said, "I didn't know what I didn't know." Though I was mentally and physically exhausted after our three-hour-long seminar, I felt renewed. Instead of worrying about deviating from our course schedule, I felt grateful that God planted me, a BIPOC person at a predominantly white institution (PWI) where my experiences, background, and expertise equipped me to identify and facilitate teachable moments. While I may not be able to counter all microaggressions that pierce our class discussions, I count each small victory a step in the right direction.

THE ONLY REASON YOU'RE HERE IS BECAUSE YOU'RE BLACK . . .

TIMOTHY E. LEWIS

I was a thirty-two-year-old new hire at a predominantly white institution in rural southern Illinois, joining the Political Science Department as the sole Blackademic. Yet, I was also accepting the task of breaking racial tenure barriers, as the department had never granted tenure to a Black American in its sixty-plus-year history. However, I was optimistic! Perhaps, as I reflect back, I was like Dr. King as he penned his "Letter from the Birmingham Jail"—"I was too optimistic." On the day of new faculty introductions, the other tenure-track and tenured faculty seemed legitimately excited that I had accepted the offer and proudly rallied around me after introductions. I distinctly remember one faculty member joking that the department "needed" me as it struggled to offer courses in identity politics and wanted another strong political theorist.

In all of the welcoming, I could see a gentleman standing off to the side, out of my peripheral vision. From his proximity, I could tell he was affiliated with the department, but I had no idea who he was; I thought the entire department was present at my job talk. As the enthusiasm died down, he made his way toward me and stated that we talk. With my face and body language, I nonverbally communicated, "OK, start talking." However, he insisted that we go to his office and have a private conversation. I took his insistence as importance, and as our offices were in the same building, I saw no reason to deny having this conversation immediately. Once we arrived at his office, he introduced himself and informed me that he was an instructor, not tenured faculty, which is why he was absent from my job talk. He then took a hard shift, seemingly gloating as to how his straightforward conversation style often offended people, bragging about how his directness had led to him being reprimanded in the past. I immediately thought, *That's nothing to brag about, but let's see where this is going.* It was what he said next that ended the conversation for me:

"I'm just going to say it! You know the only reason you're here is because you're Black, right?"

He must have talked for another twenty minutes or so, but for me, the conversation was over. I remember nothing said after his initial statement. I do not even remember whether the conversation cordially ended before I walked out of the small, cluttered office or whether I just walked out. At that moment, I was bombarded with emotions, but the feeling most salient was confusion. How did this person—a supposed highly educated individual serving as faculty at an accredited university—reduce my employment to the genetic differences in tyrosinase that result in my, and most Black people's, rich, darker skin, enlarged and round nasal cavity, and distinctive eye orbit? This white cisgender male sat across from me, insulting me by dismissing my eleven years of postsecondary education, resulting in two bachelor's degrees, a master's degree, a PhD, and thirty-plus provisional and permanent certifications. To him, I was nothing more than a Black man, and perhaps that meant I had no real qualifications.

This insulting display of racism shaped my entire pursuit of tenure. Initially, it inundated me with a feeling that I needed to prove my merit beyond the standards met by my white colleagues, even if I was meeting all the metrics outlined in operating papers. However, I came to understand that no matter what level of success I achieve, to some, like this instructor, I would always be "just" another Black man. So, I stopped trying to prove my worthiness and simply started celebrating my proof; and in a moment of personal celebration, I stood before the Board of Trustees and recalled this very incident moments before they voted to confirm my tenure—making me the first Black American to earn tenure in the department since its creation sixty-plus years ago.

The colleague in this recollection, and many in higher education, are what scholars John Dovidio and Samuel Gaertner (2000) call the aversive racist. Aversive racists cannot see their own racism because they prioritize egalitarianism but simultaneously operate from stereotypes and biases that devalue the qualifications of people of color. I can only speculate, but in this colleague's mind, the only possible way a Black man, particularly one several years his junior, could receive a tenure-track position while he remained an instructor was because of some adaptive affirmative action initiative that gave an advantage to Black people. Perhaps he could not conceptualize that one can be Black and qualified! However, this incident reveals more about the ignorance of the white racist mindset. White aversive racists reduce and diminish Black achievement, opting to embrace Black stereotypes while ignoring the obvious comfort of their privilege. To this colleague, all I needed for employment was Black skin, but he simultaneously disregarded his own white privilege where all he will ever need is white skin!

Reference

Dovidio, John F., and Samuel L. Gaertner. 2000. "Aversive Racism and Selection Decisions: 1989 and 1999." *Psychological Science* 11, no. 4 (July): 315–19.

I AM NOT YOUR MAGICAL NEGRO

AMIR ASIM GILMORE

As I reminisce about my thirteen years (BA to tenure-track professor) within the ivory tower, James Baldwin's sentiments come to mind: "I remain as much a stranger today as I was the first day I arrived" (2012, 190). To be Black in America is to be a stranger and to feel universally strange as you occupy spaces that were *never* designed for you. Your body, presence, and cultural knowledge do not fit the spaces that you enter—and that rings true within academia. Inside the ivory tower, I must rectify that I am a stranger in a white space—just a Black speck within a vast sea of institutional whiteness, disrupting the alleged "natural order of things." As one of the only Black teacher educators who teaches about diversity, pluralism, and social justice at a predominantly white, rural R1 land-grant university, a certain racial calculus impacts my identity as a Black academic. The arrival of my Black body in white spaces is surrounded by an air of mysticism—scripted as marvelously strange, different, unknown, terrifying, and exotic. Through the university's white gaze, I am seen as the *magical token Black man*: the defender of everything Black, the alleged savior of systemic racial injustice, the race specialist offering minority discourse, the facilitator of white racial consciousness-raising. Simultaneously, I am also seen as a pessimistic, race-obsessed rabble-rouser who challenges white authority and seeks to indoctrinate white college students with alleged "Marxist ideologies" such as critical race theory. Who knew that a Black man could wield so much power? Ain't it magical?

So, as a *point of view* and a *point that is viewed*, I am always negotiating my identity. Not only is my existence political, but I must engage in a certain labor—a racial etiquette with white students to ensure that my speech is not considered as mildly unconventional or extremist but is also breathtaking and inspiring. For many of my white teacher candidates, I am usually their first (and only) Black professor, and I teach the required diversity class. The course is dedicated to helping teacher candidates understand how they are implicated in historical and ongoing struggles about educational equity and think critically about the shifting purpose of school and schooling through the social markers of race, class, gender, sexuality, dis/ability, linguistic ability, citizenship status, and adolescence. I am compelled to teach in an uplifting way that must validate white introspection of fragile white feelings, because if I do not, I will be deemed *the problem* (read: the racist). *You don't want to be THAT GUY, Amir.* Therefore, I must be the "right kind" of Black—the mild-mannered Black person who enthusiastically talks about race and racism to white people but will not disrupt their social comfort—you know, not "rock the boat." *You don't want to be THAT GUY, Amir.* As such, every semester I must prepare myself for psychically draining encounters, microaggressions, and conversations mired in bad faith, all for the sake of white racial consciousness-raising. Isn't magic fun?

Being this "Magical Negro" for white people is *exhausting*, considering the ongoing anti-Black violence levied against Black people's minds, bodies, and spirits by the state and white vigilantes. Living through the summer of 2020 *exhausted* me. Bearing witness to the extrajudicial quarantine killings of Ahmaud Arbery, Breonna Taylor, George Floyd, Sean Reed, Tony McDade, and so many others *exhausted* me. Watching white colleagues proceed with their day, productive and totally oblivious to what had occurred, *exhausted* me. The racial injury inflicted upon me was immense because Black suffering and Black death weren't worthy of a damn conversation. That fall 2020 semester—perhaps I was out of *magic*, or maybe I was out of *fucks to give*—I was not seeking pleas to humanize Black people through racial consciousness-raising or the white introspection of white feelings. I centered Black social realities and the myriad of violence that befalls Black people in the so-called post-racial United States.

Well, that did not go over so well with my students, as I challenged them not to find solutions but to *sit* with societal problems that cannot be easily reconciled. Some were dismayed that racial inequities cannot be quickly solved as they are in *Remember the Titans*. I became THAT GUY, and it showed in my teaching evaluations. One student—dripping with privilege—wrote that my class was "too depressing" and was not "inspiring enough" for them. Imagine needing to be inspired by a Black professor to center social justice in your educational praxis. Imagine needing to be inspired to do what is *right* for and by Black children. Imagine always needing to inspire white people to have any semblance of rights in this country (oh wait!). The utter caucacity! I was hurt but mostly angry because this student weaponized their teacher evaluations like white customers utilize customer service satisfaction surveys. Because I was THAT GUY, I became the problem, and they were not satisfied with my performance. But I am so sick of being a plot device for white people. I am so sick of prioritizing and sacrificing white feelings over the pervasive threat of anti-Black violence. My life is not a movie. This ain't *The Legend of Bagger Vance* or *The Green Mile*! I am not white people's Magical Negro! And besides, I kind of like being THAT GUY (wink).

Reference

Baldwin, James. 2012. *Notes of a Native Son*. New York: Penguin Random House.

RACE WORK AT PWIs

VALERIE C. JOHNSON

Like my white colleagues, I fully expected a career engaged in teaching, research, and service, and that's all. However, as a vocal and racially conscious African American woman who teaches on race and socioeconomic inequality, I have been continually pulled into the inescapable web of academic racism. Many have romanticized the academy as the ivory tower, a place of intellectual community that is immune to racism. However, racial inequality is as present in academia as it is in other institutions of American life. And in many ways, it is more impactful, particularly when one considers the academy's greatest commission—training minds.

Before receiving an invitation to interview for my first academic job, the department had been warned that it would lose its faculty line if it did not go back to the drawing board and find someone to interview other than three white males. I was ultimately hired, but that initial focus on race led to a lot of resentment among my white colleagues and followed me through the tenure and promotion process. It probably didn't help that I invited Reverend Jesse L. Jackson Sr. to campus for a meeting with African American state legislators to hold the university accountable for continuing racial disparities. Although some may argue that this should have been an obvious "no-no," I submit that the question to ponder is why I—an assistant professor at the time—would have the added burden of race work as a part of my academic experience. Who poses a greater threat—those who fight for change or those who resist it? I contend that a shift in consciousness is a necessary precursor for change. The mindset that has brought us to this present moment must decidedly be eradicated if we are to create new racial and societal norms.

My application for tenure was denied, but the following year, a white male with a nearly identical record was successful, prompting a courageous tenured senior white female faculty member to pointedly ask how members of the department could justify support for my white male colleague's case after having previously denied mine.

Wedged between my arrival and departure at my first predominantly white institution (PWI) is a long list of racial slights, such as the day when my chair and I were discussing my upcoming conference presentation, and he very innocently asked whether it was for one of my "Black conferences." When I complained to this same chair about an "Ebonics Christmas" email circulated by a junior white male colleague, he asked whether it was possible that a student could have sent this under the faculty member's name. After I engaged the absurdity of such a proposition, he asked me what I thought he should do about it. I responded that I should not be expected to be a victim, judge, and jury and that, as chair, he should work to ensure that all faculty have a workplace free of demeaning racial taunts and harassment.

I recount this story not to call attention to the racial ineptitude of my former chair but to illustrate the racial hegemony that is on daily display at PWIs. I was an impressionable assistant professor, sorely in need of mentorship. Instead, far too many of my encounters with white colleagues left me feeling marginalized and devalued at an institution wholly foreign to me as an African American woman.

When I obtained another job, the one I have occupied for the past twenty years, race labor inevitably followed. Whenever there has been a racial crisis, students of color have faced discrimination, and instances of discriminatory policies and practices have been identified, I have both wittingly and unwittingly become an academic race worker. My experiences in the academy and my analyses of those experiences have evolved through a lens foreign to my white colleagues. They only experience race sporadically when it enters like an unwelcome intruder into their limited experiences. For me, however, race is an everyday reality. Yet, it is their white (institutional) perspective that most shapes university policies and practices. Those in the majority set the tone for everyone else at the university. However, the little-known physical, psychological, and emotional costs associated with the centrality of whiteness at PWIs are never discussed. Faculty of color are expected to bear these costs in the academy and preferably to bear them silently.

I am fully conscious that my every response to institutional inequity has carried risk and has often been considered an affront to the administration and university. Those who identify the problem are often cast as the problem. I have found that to dare broach the R-word (race) at a PWI, oddly enough, signals that I am not a team player and seems as verboten as the N-word. It is a catch-22, to be sure. If I don't speak out and draw attention to inequities, they may persist, but even if I do, they may persist.

This fact alone serves as evidence of systemic bias. Although many officials at PWIs post–George Floyd have declared their commitment to eradicating systemic racism, any person of color who has consistently committed to promoting such change is risking career advancement. This circular pathology, nevertheless, raises the question: Who is the real team player, and who is, conversely, a cog in the wheel of real and meaningful change?

WHAT I WISH SOMEONE HAD TOLD ME

The contributors to this book wrote advice to Blackademic readers under the prompt "What I wish someone had told me" when they were pursuing their undergraduate studies and graduate degrees, moving up the professional ranks, and thinking about alternatives to academia entirely. They range in length, scope, and tenor. The advice from contributors to the "Moving Up the Academic Ranks" section is shared below, but you are encouraged to read advice from contributors in the other sections too because their words may resonate with you.

Being a tenure-track professor is more emotionally and psychologically stressful than being a graduate student. That is, if faculty didn't like me in graduate school, I could remove them from my committee and continue working toward graduation. I wish someone had told me this agency was a privilege that I would not enjoy as an assistant professor and that I would second-guess everything I said for the better part of a decade because I was living precariously close to the wrong side of a disparity.

More importantly, I wish someone had told me that knowing all the race and gender disparities in academia would not—could not—prepare me for living through them. I watched colleagues in faculty meetings disrespect the first Black woman in the United States to earn the prestigious title of dean at a communications school, and I realized that my future depended on these same people. The majority votes on the value of the minority every day in every department on every campus in the United States, and you have to work twice as hard to be thought of as half as good.

—Charisse

It is vital for your own health and well-being that you understand how much your voice matters. You matter, and you do not have to sit in silence or tolerate the intolerable. Intervene when you feel it is appropriate. Do not compromise your values and who you are as a strong and confident Black person. Everything you do has worth to the institution, but it is most important to document how it has worth to you. Your work, your voice, and your passion are going to take you places, so be sure to promote yourself even as others are using your work to promote themselves and their careers.

—Anonymous

As you read the stories in this book, get into the space of the writers. Attempt to feel the presence of their experience and the destiny of the journey. The journey may not always be a good experience, but it is a journey worth the time we walk with, talk to, and encounter each other.

—Herman

You are young, gifted, and Black.

—Anonymous

Working in the academy is a game structured against Blackademics. Our success requires a strategic plan of action. As a Ford Fellow, I have benefited from a community of scholars whose mentoring, advice, and institutional knowledge represent those performing at the highest levels in their respective fields. If Serena Williams, playing at her highest and best level, requires a coach, so do we as scholars.

In my path to tenure and promotion, I hired a professional coach and put my strategic plan into practice. Doing so allowed me to navigate the day-to-day hostile work environment and envision my future. Tailored to my context, my coach supplied real-time engagement. This support helped guide my path and became a critical ingredient in crossing over to the other side. This is the best piece of advice I can offer. Hire a coach and request institutional support. Finally, find your people. Find external support from your department and institution. Find those who are willing to advocate on your behalf. Find those who express a dedicated commitment to your reaching your individual goals. This requires work and self-care. Build and cultivate a community of people who believe in you and the power of your work.

—Mark

"Trust your truth." This means believe your gut instinct and spend time connecting with and trusting your deepest instincts about yourself and the world around you.

—Tamorah

Ask more senior faculty what they wish they knew—or wish someone had told them—during their first, second, and third years in their tenure-track position. Ask within your department and school or college, as well as outside your department and school or college. Ask, even if it is an institution that you otherwise know well through interactions with it as a graduate student or a postdoc, because chances are you were shielded from such politics.

When facing a trade-off, consult with more senior faculty—again, within and outside your department—so that you know all alternative options before giving in to the one that your department or your school or college is presenting you. This is critical to do as a Black woman, because chances are your department and school or college has not done so, nor do they care to.

—Anonymous

I wish someone would have told me when I was twenty-five, "It's OK to take a break from academia"—a year or two away from the classroom to explore other career options, or a year or two to get a professional degree in creative nonfiction writing, journalism, education, something connected to writing for audiences outside of academia. For me, at least, my two stints in higher education have been about bashing my brains up against the Hoover Dam. Academia isn't worth it. To quote Robert Ludlum via Jason Bourne, "Look at us. Look what they make you give." My advice is simple: if you do anything else, anything that brings you joy and provides an income you can prosper on, you should.

The only reason I remain in academia is because of my students (and because I prefer to eat and live in a home over starvation and homelessness). The students frequently are among my inspirations. They are the reason I came back to higher education after a decade in nonprofit work. I do not know how much longer students will sustain me, though. I wish I had known a way to combine this with being a full-time writer, back when I was still young and not sitting at the fountain of middle age.

—Donald

"If you are silent about your pain, they'll kill you and say you enjoyed it." The words of the incomparable Zora Neale Hurston in *Their Eyes Were Watching God* ring true. Our silence, in the name of being strong and resilient, is killing us and protecting those who have caused us harm. We as Black women must speak up about both the intentional and unintentional harm that is being done to us. Find someone with whom to share your story so that your silence doesn't become your narrative or contribute to your demise.

—Tuesday

I wish someone had told me, "You have a voice, and you have the agency to decide when and how to use it." I attended college without the benefit of a support network of more experienced Blackademics. My 12,000-student undergraduate institution had only five Black faculty members. I often lacked the requisite confidence to share my experiences and the implications of those experiences on my academic worldview. Instead of speaking up, I employed a strategy of meticulous observation, gathering as much information as possible in hopes that I could use that information to my advantage in the future. That approach served me well on many occasions. However, waiting for a future opportunity is not always the best option. In some instances, I would have been better served by asking questions and voicing concerns about the roots of biases I perceived in others' messages. Your voice is important. Don't censor yourself. Speak up about the things that matter to you and to future generations of Blackademics. Peace.

—Michael

"Never say you love your job, because your job will never love you back." Someone actually did say this to me—an Asian American professor, and the first person to hire me to teach my own college class, told me this as I started my first academic job search, and it was some of the best advice I've ever received.

He knew what he was talking about. Despite having an epic, field-defining book, he was denied tenure, and his scholarship was dismissed by colleagues as not good enough. It turned out OK—students protested on his behalf, resulting both in him being granted tenure and in the formalization of a new ethnic studies program on that campus. But he learned a hard lesson that he then passed on to me.

I didn't mind years of existing mostly in obscurity at my own institution; I have plenty of friends and a lot of family who aren't on campus. Although my accomplishments went mostly unnoticed and racist slights piled up, I always figured that at least I knew where I stood.

In the last few years, that situation has changed. I've been featured on the college website and been given leadership positions. I appreciate the acknowledgment and the opportunities, but I don't mistake it for love. If I let it, my institution will work me to death (and yours probably will too), put me on an HNIC pedestal as long as that benefits it, and then pull it out from under me when that benefits it more.

I like being a professor: I have a great affinity for my students. I like some of my colleagues. I really like the life that being a faculty member makes possible. But it's not where I get my sense of self-worth, nor is it the community I am most accountable to. I'll never say I love my job, and I'll never expect it to love me.

—Rosamond

The academy was never created with us in mind. Research centering faculty of color shows that from the early years when faculty of color were hired in the academy, the concerns, needs, wants, and struggles have remained the same. Changing, morphing, internalizing, and degrading yourself won't change the system. You have a gift to contribute. The academy needs that gift, even if it doesn't deserve it. Jump in, fully ready to embrace all the power that is within you, and get ready to push your way through. It will probably be difficult and sometimes it will hurt, but together, we can. Find your tribe and fulfill the requirements to secure your position. Those of us who are already here are kicking the walls down to usher you in. Join us!

—Kerri-Ann

Find a Black mentor—preferably in your discipline, preferably tenured or retired—whom you can call twenty-four seven to do these five C's: curse, cry, chuckle, cheer, and celebrate.

—Anonymous

Your authentic Black voice is powerful and transformative, and there is a healing energy in your narratives. Silence allows you to hide, carry, and avoid unpacking an accumulation of extra, sometimes heavy baggage and inhibits your learning, growth, and restoration. Silence challenges your ability to respond to matters in the moment, move forward from your past hurt and pain, and embrace the joys and possibilities of today and tomorrow to live fully and freely.

Practice leveraging Black voice with intention. You may feel vulnerable, uncomfortable, and afraid to share some of your reactions and experiences. Yet, tell your truth bravely and find supportive spaces to share your stories openly in a meaningful way. People are waiting to hear and learn from you to help guide and change their lives in order to thrive. Speak your authentic Black voice so that it can be heard, and leverage that Black voice for the transformation of your life and the lives of others.

—Evelyn

1. Always get it in writing. Keep a journal.
2. Your dues *been* paid. You don't owe anybody anything: time, attention, energy, overtime, stress, uncompensated labor.
3. Cut off all narcissists and gaslighters.
4. Move toward your intuition.
5. People know exactly what they're doing. You don't have to know why they're doing it or how they rationalize it. Act according to what is optimal for your well-being.
6. Say "no" to what you don't want to waste your time on, and don't feel awkward about it. Ever.
7. Make sure you have community outside of academia.
—Valorie

The only things you *have* to do in this world as a Black person are stay Black and die. Everything else is everything else.
—Tameka

Prior to successfully exiting the academic graduate program, it's professionally judicious to minimize demonstratively exhibiting one's academic proclivity or intellectual prowess to avoid the exponential risks of being misappropriated from to advance faculty members' careers or due to covert frugality, insecurities, or repercussions—that is, treated as a threat to inconspicuous advisors' own scholarly aspirations. More importantly, chart a self-actualizing "flourishing" path beyond the university with the necessary life skills and educational aptitude to live a life of financial, psychological, emotional, and spiritual wellness.
—Dr. Thelma "Pepper" G. McCoy, PhD, MSW, LMSW

You are enough. You are more than enough, just as you are. Your hair is enough. Your voice is enough. Your brilliance is enough. Your ideas are enough. Your sashay is enough. Your passion is enough. You are more than enough. Please internalize this fact and know that you are deserving of the best. Do not settle for less and do not accept the limiting beliefs that others may attempt to put on you. Trust your instinct. If it don't feel right, it probably ain't. It is OK to ask for more, demand more, and expect more. If your value is not recognized where you are, it is OK to pick up and move to where you will be appreciated, celebrated, and elevated. I also encourage you to do the daily work of decolonizing and liberating yourself, because our limited beliefs often keep us in toxic, harmful, and dehumanizing places and spaces. Our ill-conceived ideas of value, prestige, self-worth, and insecurities rooted in internalized white supremacist patriarchy tell us we are not valuable unless we are located in certain institutions or have a certain affiliation or title. We are already validated and worthy by virtue of our lineage. We are already validated and worthy by virtue of our inheritance. We are already validated and worthy by virtue of our identity as Black, Brilliant, and Powerful.

—Ijeoma

Establish work boundaries from the start. If you get in the habit of responding to colleague and student emails at all hours and weekends, it sets the precedent for being available any time. Do yourself a favor and turn off your work email after business hours (this may vary for faculty and staff who teach evenings and weekends). An older Black colleague told me this, and while I was initially concerned about backlash for giving the perception of being inaccessible and unavailable, I quickly realized I was giving away my time and energy unnecessarily—both of which I reclaimed. Second, say no when requests are made that force you to go above and beyond your capacity. Things like committee memberships are time-consuming, so accept only the ones you have a genuine interest in *and* for which you have an agenda for executing change instead of talking points about change. In addition to "regular" committees, I was asked to be on a search committee almost every semester because of need and at other times for the sake of diversity. My advice to you is if you're inclined to be a member or chair of a search committee, accept the invitation no more than once per academic year. And when possible, I'd recommend participating only once every three or four semesters, especially early in your teaching career. Boundaries and saying no are acts of self-care, and you'll need them as a Blackademic.

—Carolyn

My entire collegiate experience has been at predominantly white institutions. I was educated at predominantly white institutions (PWIs) and have worked my holistic career, which is nearing two decades, at PWIs. So it's only fitting that I offer some words of advice to my fellow Black academics, especially the novice ones at PWIs. First, know your worth. You deserve to be wherever you want to be—never be reduced to a diversity hire quota. Granted, a targeted hire may have opened the door for you, but let your intellect and ambition be what promotes you through the ranks. Second, never shy away from a teachable moment. Sometimes we have to go off script and deviate from the lesson plan to awaken our students to life's realities and foster a holistic educational experience. Third, and finally, don't be afraid to let your white students see a glimpse of the world through your BIPOC experiences. Many of our students live very encapsulated lives, and you may be the only BIPOC professor they have ever had. So as energy and mental capacity permit, use class discussions, assigned readings, and personal narratives as vessels to foster authentic education, because sometimes our students don't know what they don't know until we enlighten them.

—Eletra

Dr. King closes his "Letter from the Birmingham Jail" by noting a mistake. No, not a mistake in intentionally breaking an unjust Birmingham law, but the mistake of expecting too much from those he termed "White moderates." Dr. King was optimistic and expected those of reasonable intellectual attainment and spiritual awareness to understand the racial tensions of the day and the reality of Black citizens. To Black graduate students and new faculty, remember to temper your expectations and optimism with the reality that racism's pervasive nature has infiltrated every institution of American society, including higher education. Remember that intellectual attainment and academic prowess do not mitigate interpersonal racism. If a racist person obtains a terminal degree and faculty appointment, their intellectual capabilities and professional designation do not remove their racism. They are simply an educated racist! Prepare yourself; protect yourself; provide for yourself!

—Timothy

Always be unapologetically you, when even the institution demands otherwise. Learn to say *no*. Learn to say *hell-to-the-no* to service obligations that do not align with your morals, values, or joys. The ivory tower will utilize you when it deems necessary and cast you aside when you are no longer needed. So, never carve up your identities to receive a crumb of recognition from a social institution that does not love you or your Blackness. Remember, to survive a system, we must *survive*! Rest and rejuvenation are revolutionary! Take care of yourself, love yourself, and hell, make sure to #treatyoself! No matter if you attend a PWI or an HBCU, just know that there are Black people out there who are fighting to center you—me—us. Be brilliant, be bold, and above all else, stay Black, aight?

—Amir

Although it is known that strong teaching, service, and research are the criteria for tenure, it may not be as evident that collegiality is also very important. Faculty of color at a PWI can be a target for those who view their presence as an intrusion on "their" space. As soon as you walk in the door, begin to build alliances. They may come in handy.

—Valerie

Part 4 Seeking Alternatives to Academia

"Alternatives" is a word used broadly here. For some, it can mean identifying resistance strategies and other tactics to remain at their university. But it could also mean quite literally looking for an alternative professional route and leaving academia altogether. One Blackademic who is a champion of being open to the range of possibilities within and outside of academia is Kerry Ann Rockquemore, a successful entrepreneur, founder of the National Center for Faculty Development and Diversity, and former tenured professor. In a series of widely circulated articles such as her *Inside Higher Ed* piece "Do You Need an Exit Strategy?," Rockquemore implores faculty, particularly midcareer faculty, to think openly and honestly about how and why they chose to become a professor and to examine whether their position in academia is serving them. In this particular article, she outlines six steps that faculty should consider as they decide whether to remain in academia or to find the exit door. Similarly, Rockquemore created a twelve-week program for the National Center for Faculty Development and Diversity "designed to provide a space for a group of tenured faculty to pause, engage in a discovery process about what's possible in their next chapter, and build the support network necessary to move powerfully in that new direction" (NCFDD, n.d.). Her work resonates with a goal of this book, which is to remind Blackademics that we have options and also the agency to explore every opportunity related to our professional future. We are not beholden to stay in places where our presence, ideas, and contributions are not celebrated, let alone valued.

It may or may not come as a surprise that this fourth and final professional moment offers far fewer stories than the other three sections. It is important that we pause and make note of this. This book's open call for submissions invited Blackademics from across the nation to submit stories to all four sections, but there were considerably more submissions about graduate school and faculty life. As a trained empirical researcher and social scientist with an extensive background in inductive, qualitative research, I have a responsibility to make sense of the stories as they are told and not to adjust or backfill them so that they reflect how I may want them told. The unevenness is a direct reflection of the data submitted, and so I wanted to analyze them as such. Moreover, and in all honesty, I believe that this final section, while brief, can and should serve as an opportunity for you, the reader, to fill in the gap. Why were there fewer stories submitted by people who sought out an alternative? Are there missing ideas, information, or themes? What more did you hope to read (or want to learn) from the stories in this section? Are you seeking alternatives, and if so, what resources do you need? I will leave you to find your own answers because your critical thinking at this point in the journey is a way to add to the necessary conversations about anti-Blackness and anti-racism, as well as a way to work against forces that seek to keep us bound to a form of labor that undergirds our degeneration physically, mentally, and spiritually. We hold these stories in high regard because they offer a glimpse into what it means to take up one's agency and challenge the norm.

For one scholar, seeking alternatives meant forging her own path. Karida L. Brown, a sociologist and public intellectual, has lent her expertise to outside organizations. That includes serving as a board member for the Obama Presidency Oral History project and as the director of Racial Equity and Action for the Los Angeles Lakers. In her essay, Brown addresses reimagining one's relationships with academia and unapologetically pursuing that vision.

Reference

NCFDD (National Center for Faculty Development and Diversity). n.d. "Post-tenure Pathfinder Programs." NCFDD. Accessed September 12, 2023. www.facultydiversity.org/pathfinders.

SEEKING ALTERNATIVES TO ACADEMIA

KARIDA L. BROWN

Lead Narrative

> *This essay is dedicated to Karen E. Fields,*
> *the one who showed us what it could look like.*

I shifted my relationship to academia because it became clear to me that if left unchecked, I was going to unravel. Before that, though, I always wondered why there were so many stories about Blackademics who just die. They are brilliant and lauded and award-winning—and all too often riddled with vicious cancers, adult-onset autoimmune diseases, and debilitating mental health issues. I mourn the losses of the many Blackademics who have recently been taken from us much too soon. To say the names of a few: my own colleague, neighbor, and friend Mark Q. Sawyer, who passed away at forty-five years old during my first year at UCLA; the fearless journalist, biographer, and guardian of our Black literary genius Valerie Boyd, who was snatched from us after just fifty-eight years of life; and Steven Gregory, the visionary urban anthropologist and faithful steward of Black studies, who transitioned at sixty-eight. There have been so many more, and I mourn for them too.

Publications, awards, keynotes, promotions, fellowships, and other markers of prestige have never inoculated any of us from the slow death of institutional malfeasance. I personally have never been a believer in human exceptionalism. What that means to me is that I am not an exceptional Black person, and neither are you. I am not an exceptional Black woman, and neither are you. I understand that if those premature mental and physical outcomes are a possibility for the many Blackademics in my present and past, they certainly are always already lying in wait for me. They are for you too. In so saying, my decision to recalibrate my relationship to the academy was a conscious attempt to save my own life. Academia was making me sick.

It doesn't take long to figure out the cause of dis-ease. While some predominantly white institutions tolerate a smattering of Black faculty, not one of them welcomes us. According to the Merriam-Webster dictionary, the word *tolerate* means "to allow to be or to be done without prohibition, hindrance, or contradiction" or, more simply, "to put up with," whereas the word *welcome* means "to greet hospitably and with courtesy or cordiality" or "to accept with pleasure the occurrence or presence of." Whether you are presently conscious of it or not, over time the feeling of being tolerated wears on you, mind and body alike. This sensation is experienced in a way that makes it seem like it is our own unexplained Black presence, not the institution's tolerant disposition, that has so many Blackademics unhinged. As much as you try not to internalize the feeling, the vibrational energy of contempt, benign disbelief, disdain, misrecognition, and pity seeps into your cells.

As was the case for many others, the summer of 2020 forced me to decide how I was gonna *be*. It was no longer a question for metaphysical abstraction, comparative historical analysis, or moral philosophy but instead an in-real-life (IRL) question about whether I was going to live or not. I chose me. With that choice, I did a bunch of things that were out of pocket. In many areas of my academic life, I just shut down. Between 2020 and 2022, I stopped responding to all academia-related emails and phone calls. I abruptly discontinued relationships with colleagues and students. And most unlike myself, I did not write for two years.

The contemporary definition of the word *intoxicate* means "(of alcoholic drink or drug) to cause someone to lose control of their faculties or behavior." However, the word originates from the medieval Latin word *intoxicare*, from *in-* + *toxicum* "poison." When a person becomes intoxicated, the body either forces itself to involuntarily expel the toxin, or it blacks out. That is the body's emergency flight response to save your life, as it has entered an untenable state of toxicity from an external poison. For a time, I was intoxicated with academia, and my spirit could no longer tolerate it. In response, I reconfigured the terms of order to bring the relationship into balance.

In June 2020, I joined the Los Angeles Lakers organization as its first director of Racial Equity and Action. I maintained my academic appointment at UCLA until June 30, 2022, and joined the faculty at Emory University on July 1, 2022. I was able to take on the role as a public intellectual with the Lakers largely because I was on academic leave for the 2021–22 academic year.

Derek Chauvin's homicidal act in May 2020 was displayed for public consumption and was the violent tipping point that pierced the conscience of the world, subsequently ushering in a period of moral reckoning around the deep-seated realities of systemic anti-Black racism. One distinct feature about this iteration of moral reckoning was that corporations were confronted with their complicity in the system and whether they would commit to do their part to repair it. Some corporations responded as a result of public shame and others through an attempt to rise to the occasion and make a difference. The Lakers organization was part of the latter group. Because of their commitment, I proudly served as a Laker for two-and-a-half years.

IRL

As academics we are trained to critique. The purpose of critique is to eval-uate and identify positive and negative points and to establish frameworks through which individuals or groups can translate those points into plans for reparative action. Plainly said, the aim is to make the world a better place. As Blackademics, most of us righteously spend our time critiquing the systems, structures, interactions, and belief systems that continue to oppress us. However, the clear and present danger for us is falling into the trap of becoming solely a critic, referring to a person who judges or evaluates and sometimes a person who finds only negative points. The thing about critics is that they are not required to be able to *do* the thing that they are evaluating. For example, food critics do not necessarily need to be good chefs, nor do sports critics need to have ever been great at playing the game that they so harshly judge.

Academic critics are people who find themselves ostensibly *doing* something about their area of expertise but only from a platform of asym-metrical power and voice: in other words, from behind a podium in the classroom, in office hours, on social media, or during an invited lecture. It is so very important for us to envision a world in which we can all be free. What does it look like? How is it structured? Who is there? Who is not? What knowledge systems govern what and how we "know"? How is power distributed? These are the questions. However, I have come to understand that in the unreal bubble of academia, endless criticism unmoored from the lived lives and language of everyday people is a slippery slope to the dead end of moral righteousness. It is safe to be a critic as Twitter Fin-gers, on the pages of a book, or even on a panel discussion among other academics. It is an entirely different story when you are out IRL.

My experience outside of academia has been both affirming and hum-bling. I could not just come into the Lakers organization with grand theo-ries, big words, good intentions, and an outsize bibliography. Ain't nobody got time for that. My time with the organization was a much-needed reminder that everyday people do not live, navigate, and understand their lives or the lives of others through the logics of academia. Instead, it was important for me to be self-aware about how I related to people. How could I show up in a manner that would earn people's trust in a process of institutional change? Unfortunately, those questions are optional for us academics, especially for those of us with tenure. My return to an IRL work environment was so very helpful because it brought me awareness about how I had been seduced by the luxury of the ivory tower. I was spoiled by the faux protection of being able to talk a lot of shit and not really have to do much of anything to change things IRL. I could just sit around being dissatisfied, with no shortage of like company.

I offer this observation not because I believe that we Blackademics are apathetic or effete but instead to point out a key ingredient in the academic Kool-Aid that stands to intoxicate us all. Most Blackademics enter the academy well aware of that sensation of being tolerated, disbelieved, discredited, disrespected, underpaid, and unwelcomed. It is our very own site of oppression, albeit chosen. Therefore, too many of us falsely believe that the university can and ought to be our site of liberation. This belief keeps us tethered to the institution in the unhealthiest and most life-consuming ways. We become intoxicated with an institutional field that seeks to eviscerate our lives, our laughter, our relationships, our activism, our health and wellness, and our physical proximity to our family and support systems when, in fact, academia is just our job.

THREE LESSONS LEARNED

I offer three things I have learned during my time with one foot out of the academy. First, there is a distinct difference between being an academic and being an intellectual. Being the latter is not predicated on the institution. While your institution very well may afford you a platform to express your ideas, it does not license them. Put differently, you do not have to wait for your university or any of the gatekeepers in the institutional field for your ideas to begin to have impact.

Second, alternatives to the academy can show up in many different ways. Yes, you can consider how to leverage your own expertise to create independent revenue streams outside the academy. Many Blackademics do this through the commercial speaker circuit or through contracting their services out to the private sector. However, seeking alternatives to the academy need not stem from a financial impetus. Adopt a local K–12 school and go spend time with the kids or offer your syllabi and lesson plans to the teachers. For example, my husband and I were supposed to take sabbatical for the 2021–22 academic year; however, we decided to go serve at Fisk University for the year. There are countless ways you can meaningfully exercise your intellectualism that do not require permission. That is a much more freeing position to act from because you can just be Blackety-Black and show up as your beautiful, smart, skillful self and contribute. You don't have to always show up as the leader, the know-it-all, or the person who's coming to save the thing. Instead, you can roll up your sleeves and help by being a part of something. Just get in there and do it.

My last point: money. By virtue of attending graduate school, we lose anywhere between five and eight years of earning potential in our formative work years. That equates to nearly a decade of little to no retirement contributions, savings, debt clearance, or wealth accumulation. As we know, when it comes to the time value of money, growth is not linear but exponential. As a people for whom the majority does not come from intergenerational wealth, choosing a career in academia is a high-risk financial decision. For many of us, seeking alternatives to the academy is a matter of necessity. Left to our university compensation alone, too many of us quietly do not have a clear pathway to retirement, are cash poor, and live check to check. The neoliberal university survives on overwork and underpay. Without either intergenerational wealth or a high-income partner, limiting your work solely to the university for most Blackademics is a recipe to being prestige rich and asset poor. Therefore, I urge you, do not restrict yourself from going out and getting it in other ways.

Therefore, my words of wisdom to you are this: If you have ceded too much of your power to the institution, wrench it back for dear life. You are a self-possessed Black intellectual. Period.

GETTING OFF TRACK

KAI MARSHALL GREEN

Spotlight Narrative

When I was thirteen years old, I received a scholarship to attend a private school in my hometown, Oakland, California. I was leaving my under-resourced public school, which didn't have any sports teams or physical education curriculum. My dream then was to become a famous basketball player. At twelve years old I had been a towering five feet ten, and my coach saw potential in my Black body. I went to that school to become a basketball player, but one day my coach sat me down and said, "You are here for this education!" This was his way of saying I was gifted intellectually. He didn't burst my hoop dreams, but he let me know there was something else out there—or rather in me—that might get me out of some tough situations at home.

My first few months of private school were mixed with anxiety, depression, confusion, and anger. I had just entered a world of options that I wasn't used to. I could play in the jazz band or the rock band, and there was a pool where we could take swimming lessons. These were all things I had only imagined when I was in public school. I was one of the only two Black kids to receive a scholarship that year. I blew people away. My teachers saw that I was a writer and encouraged me to be great. But this private school world was just a precursor to what I'd start to experience as I moved along and through some of the most exclusive academic spaces. I made it, but it also broke me. When I started at that private school, I knew these other kids had more tools than my mom, my Oakland public school, or I could ever provide. I was afraid that they'd find out how behind I was. I went from a school where we didn't have books to take home to a school where we were being asked to read, annotate, and analyze. I feared they might kick me out, so I masked what I didn't know. And that mask, though shape-shifting over time, was how I kept myself together. But things would continue to fall apart again and again.

I open with this early experience of education because it is the point at which I started to recognize my impostor syndrome. From that moment, it was as if I was being trained to be a professional scholar in ways that young Black kids like myself are often trained and tracked to be professional athletes.

But what happens if you don't make it to the pros? What grief? And what happens when you do make it? In academia, for me, the result was still great grief.

I write this piece while I am on medical leave for the second time during my five years of employment in my tenure-track position at my small liberal arts college. My body, mind, spirit, and soul collapsed. I have had to take leave twice to take care of my mental and physical health. I have seen all of my Black comrades that I started with five years ago leave under duress. My body said, No! Our bodies continually say, NO! My institution can't hold our grief—this Black body that is not just my own body.

Once, a senior Black faculty member told me it was the "golden handcuffs" that kept them at our institution. I took that to mean the stability of things like health care, housing, and a steady paycheck. I wonder to myself whether there is a way to be here and not wear those handcuffs, whatever the material may be: handcuffs are handcuffs and a type of unfreedom. What do we do when our livelihoods are bound up in unfreedom? The ivory tower can be a kind of prison, and it is the track that is supposed to keep us in line—disciplined.

Black people and specifically Black queer people, whether we want to or not, are made to be bridge-people and do bridge-Werq in the academy and in other institutions. A recurring theme in my professional evaluations has been a concern regarding my boundaries and tendency to overextend myself. As a response to this fair critique, I decided to do some deep reflection. I went on research leave after my first medical leave, and it was the first time I had ever gotten to sit with myself as myself, not as a student or teacher. I hadn't had that space since preschool. I was on the track. I used my research leave to gain more clarity regarding my own boundaries and goals. I finally had the time to sit with my multiple ideas and my actual human capacity. I came to the conclusion that my Werq is and will always be informed by my Black queer feminist lens and politic, and this may not always be in alignment with what my committee and my college desires of me.

I further concluded that the Werq I am made to do as a Black trans professor often stifles the Werq I'd like to do. For example, I organized a Black trans writing retreat where a dean came to welcome the attendees and in his welcome misnamed me and mispronounced my name multiple times. It was an embarrassing moment for me and the college. It proved why my work was important but also how I and my work were devalued and disrespected. I cannot accurately talk about my teaching, scholarship, and service without naming how my Black queer and transgender body is negatively impacted by the anti-Blackness and transphobia that exists in my academic institution.

My auto-ethnographic accounts in both of my forthcoming monographs, *Gender Trappin'* and *A Body Made Home: My Black Trans Love*, share Black queer bridge-Werq stories by centering people who have acted as bridges from one community to another. The relationships between bridge-people and our communities can be difficult to maintain and even detrimental because bridge-people are expected to not simply do the Werq; no, we are often forced to also be(come) the Werq. To be(come) the Werq often means to be(come) the physical manifestation and representation of radical change, and this often occurs without one's explicit consent. This is a positionality of suffocation and social and sometimes even physical death as it leaves no room for the possibility of individual transformation. Here, the individual who becomes a bridge and Werq versus the individual who does bridge-Werq is the individual forced into acting as solid infrastructure. If or when individuals become Werq, we, our bodies, then become the infrastructure that gets walked on or crossed over. As bridges stretched out in the name of Black queer loving, I am concerned about what happens when we get sick, tired, and transition.

We cannot be(come) the infrastructure for transformation in the academy, though that is how we often are used. It will harm us mentally and physically. Our bodies are not durable infrastructures, and we need infrastructure that has the capacity to exist and hold even when individuals cannot.

The greatest lesson I learned this past year is that capitalist and ivory tower time kills, and before it does that, it makes you sick. I write this from a place of being in an institution that views me as the Werq (to be), an infrastructure that I have experienced as lacking the capacity to be able to understand, respect, and value the creative and scholarly bridge-Werq that I do (to do) both inside and outside of the academy. I share this with you while my body is in great pain. I struggle to take in a complete breath. I am sick and I am tired. I can no longer be the Werq, for it is killing me. I want to be here to continue the dynamic creative and scholarly research and teaching that I have been called to do. But I refuse to get in line and follow this track that thrives off keeping me unwell.

In the academy, we are pressured to stay in line and on track, and that is how success is measured. But many of us come from something or somewhere bigger and seek something deeper like radical change. The academy loves the diversity we bring to the institution as Black bodies but not always what we bring in terms of our Black thought. We often exceed this track life and pose a threat to the very foundation of the academic industrial complex. From the vantage point of the ivory tower this may look like failure, but for many Black academics, getting off track might be the very thing that saves our lives. And this is what I wish someone would have told me and showed me how to do.

WHEN A MORAL IMPERATIVE ISN'T ENOUGH

PAUL C. HARRIS

Spotlight Narrative

When I finished my doctoral degree in 2009, I did not submit any applications for faculty jobs, because I wanted to continue working in the field
as a school counselor as I had done full time while writing my dissertation.
I did that, then briefly served in an administrative role at a large urban
high school, and eventually I applied for an adjunct faculty position in
counselor education at a local university. For a year, I worked as a school
counselor by day and adjunct faculty member by night. While I enjoyed
how the two informed each other and my overall thinking around education policy, practice, and research, I decided it was time to transition
from the K-12 environment. So, I submitted applications for full-time
faculty positions so that I could more actively pursue a research agenda
in addition to my teaching. I was offered two positions in my first round
of applications for full-time jobs: one was a tenure-track assistant professor role in a nationally acclaimed counselor education program and the
other a non-tenure-track assistant professor role in a program that was
rebuilding. I accepted the non-tenure-track assistant professor position
in counselor education and began in August 2011 at a predominantly
white institution on the East Coast after negotiating the opportunity to
transition to a tenure-track role pending a successful third-year review.
I was particularly excited about working for this institution, as it was
my alma mater and had been the space within which I had cultivated
meaningful relationships with peers and mentors alike, particularly those
who identified as African-American. My hope was to give back to students
and the community at least a percentage of what I'd gained during my
undergraduate and graduate experiences.

In 2014, after three years of executing my non-tenure-track responsibilities (which did not include research) and conducting research, I received
a successful review and switched to a tenure-track role. I continued to
receive positive annual reviews in scholarship, teaching, and service every
year on the tenure track, including a positive pre-tenure review in 2017.
Thus, I expected a successful tenure review in 2019, which would have
been the first for a Black man in the over fifty-year history of the program.

However, on Friday, January 31, 2020, at 11:30 a.m., my dean informed me that I was *not* recommended for tenure. This meant that I would not be given lifetime job security and that my financial compensation would increase at a slower rate should I decide to stay at the university in a non-tenured position. Specifically, I would not have the academic freedom that protects tenured faculty members from being fired no matter how controversial their research or ideas are. Though quite disillusioned, I soon realized that many of the data points cited in my denial letter as the basis for the negative recommendation were inaccurate. For example, the citation count presented was grossly incongruent with the actual source that was cited, publications that had impact factors were not considered as such, an article I'd written was deemed self-published, and other things were simply untrue. Upon realizing this, it was clear that I needed to appeal to the provost.

The next few months involved consultation with mentors, legal counsel, family, and mental health counselors about how best to pursue justice while also caring well for my well-being and that of my family. The advice, based on the evidence, was singular: fight it. Specifically, I was encouraged to challenge the decision by focusing solely on the facts presented in all written communication. That *should* be enough to at least have your case reopened, everyone said. The stress, shame, guilt, sense of betrayal, trauma, and feelings of powerlessness were real in their impact on me, my wife, and three children. This was an institution my entire family had given ourselves to, including my consistently going above and beyond my job responsibilities. I'd had formal and informal discussions with mentors and senior colleagues and supervisors who reviewed my career productivity every year and affirmed my positive trajectory toward tenure. To hear the antithesis of such ongoing and consistent feedback in the final decision was overwhelming, to say the least.

I drafted a lengthy appeal detailing my case and submitted it for the provost's review in March 2020. It was denied in May 2020, with the provost's review citing a lack of procedural errors. This meant there had been no step in the process that was skipped over. However, in my appeal I argued just that—that many steps in the documented process had been overlooked, including but not limited to policies that were not adhered to early on that tainted the rest of the review process. I later received a favorable appeal review from the university's faculty senate appeals committee (a separate university appeals process less advertised to faculty) after the provost denied my appeal. My story was also picked up by several media outlets and amplified via social media. Naturally, I was nervous about the increased exposure, but as time went by, I quickly realized my advocacy was not just about my case but about the many that had never been heard, though greatly impactful to those involved. The increased exposure led to more national discussion about promotion and tenure processes in general and eventually to a reversal of the negative recommendation in my particular case in July 2020.

While I am grateful that the right decision was eventually made in my case, I am more inspired by those who recognized that a moral imperative to do the right thing is not always enough and thus raised their voice in support of justice—for my case and beyond. In other words, the facts detailed early on in my appeal process *should* have been enough. However, it took significantly more effort and emotional labor on my family's part, as well as on the part of the many who supported my case and those in the media who raised a national conversation about it. I remain indebted to those whose work exposed the flaws and bias in promotion and tenure processes many years prior to the situation I found myself in (for example, see Matthew 2016). I am in awe of my wife who interrogated racism in America through her writing (Harris 2020). I am honored by the actions of a student who heard about my case and designed a website detailing the errors made in my review ("Tenure for Doctor Paul C. Harris," n.d.). I am moved by the actions of former students and colleagues who penned an open letter to the provost and dean highlighting bias in my case along with broader equity issues at the institution and securing over 4,000 signatures in support. I am encouraged by the dozens of letters sent to the university administration by nationally recognized faculty across the country. I am proud of #BlackintheIvory, a hashtag that created space for Black academics to share their experiences. I am hopeful about the impact of news coverage sharing Black academics' experiences with anti-Black racism (see ABC News interview with Paul Harris, "Uphill Battle for Black Professors"; *Inside Higher Ed* articles by Colleen Flaherty; *Chronicle of Higher Education* articles by Megan Zahneis; and *Diverse: Issues in Higher Education* articles by David Pluvoise and Walter Hudson). And I am consoled by the thought that my family's unnecessary and psychologically violent experience does not have to be wasted. May what we absorbed in the form of unnecessary resistance by those in power, hate mail, and institutional inefficiencies lead to more scrutiny of current practices and less professional malpractice that other faculty have to endure.

The wanton tenure ordeal cost my family time, money, emotional labor, psychological strain, and concern about our well-being throughout and even beyond the overturned decision. This reality cannot be overstated. Being awarded tenure did not undo that damage. However, I am encouraged by the story told about the biblical character Joseph in the fiftieth chapter of the book of Genesis. To be clear, my case is far from Joseph's, but my perspective remains similar. In verse 20, Joseph faces his family who had previously betrayed him and hurt him deeply, "You intended to harm me, but God intended it for good to accomplish what is now being done, the saving of many lives." While I do *not* subscribe to the notion that God ordained my tenure drama, I am convinced that what *could have* crushed me and my family could be redeemed for the good of those around us and those who come after us. Or perhaps for the good of those whose tenure denials never got publicized but wreaked just as much psychological, emotional, and professional havoc in their lives as it did in mine. Or for the good of those pondering academia and needing to hear that you do not have to navigate the terrain of academia alone. Or for the good of those who need to hear that tenure is not everything but that it should be *your thing* when you have earned it. Or for the good of those who need encouragement to recognize when a moral imperative is not enough for the right thing to be done and to not wait for it to begin righting the myriad injustices in the world.

References

Harris, Taylor. 2020. "Whiteness Can't Save Us." Catapult, June 10, 2020. https://catapult.co/stories/taylor-harris-on-police-violence-racism-church-parenting-black-kids.

Matthew, Patricia A, ed. 2016. *Written/Unwritten: Diversity and the Hidden Truths of Tenure*. Chapel Hill: University of North Carolina Press.

"Tenure for Dr. Paul C. Harris." n.d. Google Sites. Accessed September 12, 2023. https://sites.google.com/view/tenureforpaulharris/home.

CLAIMING A FREE BLACK SCHOLARLY SELF

MARIA S. JOHNSON

How did I free myself from oppression related to being Black in the ivory? In 2018, after four years on the tenure track, I walked away from an assistant professor position to chart a new scholarly course. Leaving was a difficult but right decision for me. The culturally taxing work and environment drained the energy, focus, and curiosity that had brought me to the academy. For me to reengage my interests and passions, I had to undertake two critical steps: leave my faculty position and more fully embrace the issues and activities that drew me to the academy. I embraced the truth in Toni Morrison's *Beloved* that "freeing yourself was one thing; claiming ownership of that freed self was another." Since leaving academia, I have continued to center Blackness and intersectionality in my research and writing and have published scholarly pieces in traditional academic outlets like peer-reviewed journals and edited volumes. As an independent scholar, I even serve on the editorial board of a top-ranked academic journal. My greatest joy, however, has involved applying my research and theoretical knowledge to the field of philanthropy. I created and run a donor-advised fund dedicated to distributing grants to organizations led by or serving Black women and girls. I use my research and expertise on the status of Black women and girls broadly to identify and select grantees, distribute funds, and design and facilitate educational workshops. My day-to-day work and collaborations are energizing and affirm my focus on Black communities. Centering my passions and skills became my radical act of self-love and liberation. No one approach to freedom is better than another path. I share my story only to illuminate one journey. May we all boldly and bravely claim for ourselves what it means to be free and Black in the ivory.

WHAT I WISH SOMEONE HAD TOLD ME

The contributors to this book wrote advice to Blackademic readers under the prompt "What I wish someone had told me" when they were pursuing their undergraduate studies and graduate degrees, moving up the professional ranks, and thinking about alternatives to academia entirely. They range in length, scope, and tenor. My advice is shared below, but you are encouraged to read advice from contributors in the other sections too because their words may resonate with you.

Be honest about the aspects of the academy that are (not) serving you and identify aspects of the job that you can change to make it more life-giving. After doing this work (leaning on help from trained counselors, certified therapists, and trusted confidants), take the intentional steps to make changes in your career that prioritize yourself, your skill sets, your needs, your well-being, your passion, and (if you know it) your divine purpose. You have the *authority* to make the ivory tower work for you if you deem it a place where you want to remain. And you also have the *right* to leave if you find that the situation is not viable. Remember, your professional life does not have to be ridden with pain, sorrow, and angst. In the words of the great Maya Angelou, "My mission in life is not merely to survive, but to thrive; and to do so with passion, some compassion, some humor, and some style." Academia is not the only profession that values your master's or doctorate. You have a degree and skill set that are undeniably valuable, and *no one* can take them away from you. Find a way to leverage the resources that are within your grasp so that your professional life is breathing life into you rather than sucking you dry day in and day out. As bell hooks poignantly wrote, "When you wake up and find yourself living someplace where there is nobody you love and trust, no community, it is time to leave town—to pack up and go (you can even go tonight). And where you need to go is any place where there are arms that can hold you, that will not let you go."
—Shardé

EPILOGUE

*I feel most colored when I am thrown against a sharp white background.
. . . Among the thousand white persons, I am a dark rock surged upon,
and overswept, but through it all, I remain myself. When covered by the
waters, I am; and the ebb but reveals me again.*
—Zora Neale Hurston

The stories in this book, written by Blackademics across the nation, convey struggles of anti-Black racism and anti-Blackness that are often not validated by the dominant culture. That is, the stories told by dominant groups are generally legitimized and provide members of these groups with a shared sense of identity within society and its institutions. Their identities and life experiences are also reflected in dominant discourses and practices, are viewed as mainstream and natural, and are widely accepted as the "truth." Such reflections of "truth" can determine and limit who gets to speak, be heard, and be trusted. What individuals value as knowledge (ontology) and how they know what they know (epistemology) are defined within the confines of white supremacy, which is why telling stories that inherently counter the dominant social order of white supremacy puts us at great risk. This is especially true when Blackademics (are asked to) share stories in white academic spaces such as colloquiums, public events, faculty meetings, and even published scholarship. Not only is our truth delegitimized, but our mere existence is undermined through a distortion of time.

Like reality, time is also socially constructed: it has no meaning until individuals collectively ascribe meaning to it. One's culture provides the lens through which individuals understand time, and Americans have agreed that time is a tangible and fixed resource. Edward T. Hall referred to this orientation as monochronism and argued that individuals from monochronic societies, such as the United States, complete tasks sequentially, fiercely uphold schedules and deadlines, emphasize punctuality, and believe that a disrespect of time engenders serious repercussions. Nearly every decision, activity, and commitment are ruled by the clock. Indeed, many idioms reflect the high value Americans place on time, such as "beat the clock," "be early," "save time," "free time," and "spare time." Whether we are conscious of it or not, the United States is governed by the mono-chronic perception of time. And according to Brittney C. Cooper, if time in the United States had a race, it would be white. In her 2016 TED Talk, Cooper advanced that white people own time; they are the "world makers" who master how time is used. But Black people are pitted against time as "space takers." Cooper suggested that time is used to displace us; we either live a life of "perpetual urgency" or are urged to complacency with ubiquitous messages to "extend grace" and "just be patient." Cooper also maintained that, historically, time has been stolen from Black people, which has resulted in a delay of progress (in various domains) for people across generations. In the current world order, white people own time and dictate how it is used in the social sphere, who can use it, and when. Ultimately, the displacement, distortion, and delegitimization of time, truth, and reality have created the environment for anti-Black racism to persist.

One critical point of intervention is counterstorytelling. This book offers a competing narrative that challenges the dominant version with the hope of opening new windows into reality. These stories are the con-tributors' truth—a truth that rarely gets told or held in high regard and should be handled as such.

THE EXPERIENCE OF READING #BLACKINTHEIVORY®

One of the important aspects of anti-Black racism and anti-Blackness in academia is that it does not discriminate according to one's discipline, pro-fessional rank, (inter)national recognition, social identities, or other points of difference. While it is imperative to consider differences across experi-ences and hone in on particular subpopulations of Blackademics, this book necessarily widens the scope to consider anti-Black racism as a systemic issue that has been institutionalized by American colleges and universi-ties. By using storytelling as a subversive tool, this book seeks to unearth how racism is the culprit for the traumatizing experiences of many Black-ademics and to galvanize action among readers. No matter one's fame or distinction, anti-Black racism is a cruel, equalizing force that levels us all. Across space, place, and time, a few key ideas have emerged from and are repeated across the stories in this book. These ideas have been studied and formally conceptualized by scholars, particularly Black scholars, across academic fields. Here, I necessarily contextualize the emergent ideas with these race-based theoretical and conceptual frameworks to allow you, the readers, to understand and process them more fully.

While anti-Black racism occurs at four levels (internalized, inter-personal, institutional, and structural), the Twitter hashtag #BlackintheIvory speaks directly to anti-Black racism at the institutional and structural levels. Denotatively speaking, *institutional racism* occurs when unfair policies and discriminatory practices of particular institutions (such as colleges and universities) routinely produce racially inequitable outcomes for people of color and advantages for white people. *Structural racism* occurs among institutions and across American society. It involves the cumulative and compounding effects of an array of societal factors, including American history, culture, ideology, and interactions of institutions and policies that systematically disadvantage people of color and privilege white people. The current dominant discourse in the United States has focused on how racism significantly affects Black people in various social domains: housing discrimination (for example, redlining), government surveillance, social segregation (for example, legalizing racial segregation in PreK-12 schools), racial profiling (such as stop and frisk police policy), predatory lending, mistreatment in health care (for example, doctors ignoring and pathologizing Black pain), and mandatory minimum sentences for convictions. Up until recently, higher education was rarely publicly scrutinized for (re)producing race-based inequities through policies, procedures, and practices. Yet these inequities enforce structural anti-Black racism by normalizing historical, cultural, and institutional practices that benefit white people and disadvantage Black people. The stories in this book illuminate examples from each type of practice, but the most notable are at the institutional and structural levels. For example, scholars of color—and specifically Blackademics—with excellent dossiers are often denied tenure. This topic consistently garners national attention as more and more cases enter into the news cycle, like that of Paul Harris, who, in his vignette, details his tenure denial case and the emotional, psychological, and relational strain he experienced because of it. Earning tenure is lauded as the pinnacle of one's academic career, and sadly, many Blackademics confront formidable barriers to reach that end. Charisse L'Pree, a faculty person in a tenure-track position, also exposes the flaws in the tenure system in her vignette. Her faculty colleagues convinced her that she could get tenure, even though no Black woman had earned tenure in the department in the previous fifty-five years, nor had many other women or people of color. She had no viable pathway to tenure and experienced a litany of other issues in the workplace, and it seemed as though the system was structured for her to fail rather than succeed.

When thinking about race, one has to also consider how it intersects with other critical identities such as gender, class, ability, and sexuality. Gabriella Gutiérrez y Muhs, Yolanda Flores Niemann, Carmen G. González, and Angela P. Harris examine the intersections of race and class for women in academia in their critically acclaimed edited volumes, *Presumed Incompetent*. The books extend an opportunity to name the issues that women of color faculty encounter across their careers. A long line of other scholars have focused on the experiences of Black women as well—for example, Stephanie Y. Evans, with her seminal 2008 book, *Black Women in the Ivory Tower, 1850–1954: An Intellectual History*, and Deborah G. White, with her 2009 book, *Telling Histories: Black Women Historians in the Ivory Tower*. Black women have a unique experience because gender barriers, such as misogyny and sexual harassment, interact with racial components, such as colorism and texturism, and not to forget the other formidable societal issues that may also be present, such as xenophobia and anti-African sentiments. The stories in this book illuminate that even with the passing of time and significant strides in civil rights for women and Black people, the issues documented by Evans and White remain in present day. For instance, according to the US Department of Education, Black women represent no more than 4 percent of full-time tenure-track faculty and less than 3 percent of tenured faculty in the United States. And with many colleges and universities having a total number of Black women faculty that can be counted on one or two hands, it comes as no surprise that Black women have been treated as the "unicorns" of the academic system. Black women possess the ingenuity and intellectual prowess of their counterparts. However, in the eyes of many within academic institutions—in particular, white men and women—Black women are seen as anomalies, tokens, or work mules ripe for exploitation.

This book also illuminates LGBTQIA+ issues as queer and transgender Blackademics engage with every facet of their holistic identities and find space for themselves while being oppressed in multiple ways. Andraya Yearwood shares how she reckons with being both a Blackademic and a trans woman within the academic space, an intersection of identities that gets less attention and even less empirical study—so much so that there is a dearth of available national data about the percentages and experiences of Black trans* students and faculty. The formidable barriers Blackademics face only compound when other isms and phobias are folded in, a point E. Patrick Johnson makes in his essay about his experience as a Black southern queer man in a faculty position at a predominantly white institution. Across the stories, some Blackademics contended with xenophobia and anti-Blackness, including Diane Ezeh Aruah, who writes about her peers' and faculty advisors' prejudicial attitudes and sheer ignorance about her Nigerian heritage and, relatedly, what it means for people from the continent of Africa to study in America.

While most Blackademics narrate instances of anti-Black racism (and its intersection with other identities) at the institutional and structural levels, the stories also highlight incidents at the internalized and interpersonal levels. It may come as no surprise to read in these narratives examples of internalized racism and anti-Blackness among white people, whereby they have a learned form of prejudice toward Black Americans. More specifically, the stories illuminate how internalized racism can manifest as *internalized privilege*, occurring when white people (sub)-consciously believe in their racial superiority over Black people. But *internalized anti-Blackness* is also present among people of color. Over centuries, many non-Black people of color have bought into colonial lies and anti-Black stereotypes in an attempt to gain access to structures of power and be accepted within whiteness. The price of assimilating into structures of power has often meant stepping on the heads of people who are closer to the lower rungs on the ladder of power. These acts, particularly when committed by well-intentioned individuals who champion issues of social justice and solidarity, clearly show that many people of color can have an implicit bias and undertake actions that are indicative of a dominant worldview that reifies white supremacy and anti-Blackness. A number of stories discuss how non-Black people of color have a stake in the systemic injustice of Black people and the Black experience and can reproduce it. For example, in his lead narrative, Eduardo Bonilla-Silva refers to these individuals as "Brown and Black snakes" that "talk radical stuff in public but keep their younger colleagues or senior 'competitors' in check." He maintains that because departments usually have so few faculty of color, some of these individuals position themselves as the "HNIC" (or "Head N—— in Charge"), sometimes stymieing the advancement of other scholars of color. Acknowledging the ways Black people can be disproportionately affected by specific kinds of racial prejudice by people from other minoritized racial groups is vital in order to dismantle these entrenched hierarchies that pit historically oppressed groups against each other rather than unite us all and optimize collective solidarity to confront the true enemy—white supremacy.

A bit more complex are the stories that narrate acts of anti-Blackness by Blackademics. As Black people are victimized by racism, it makes sense that we might internalize it. Best known as *internalized racism*, this behavior can manifest as a form of internalized oppression, according to sociologist Karen D. Pyke. Internalized racism involves both conscious and subconscious acceptance of a racial hierarchy in which the white racial group is consistently ranked above people of color. This definition encompasses a wide range of instances, including (but not limited to) belief in negative stereotypes, discrimination against individuals with a dark skin tone, adaptations to white cultural standards, and thoughts that support the status quo (for example, denying that racism exists). We can see a few instances of internalized racism in the stories. For instance, in one anonymous vignette, a Black woman graduate student explains how an issue with her TA assignment was escalated to the office of the associate dean (a position focused on spearheading issues on diversity, equity, and inclusion and occupied by a Black woman). The dean not only was dismissive but also tone-policed and gaslit the student. In the vignette, the anonymous writer makes sense of this issue as internalized misogynoir, a form of oppression where Black women (sub)consciously uphold a distrust, dislike, or prejudice against Black women and project these beliefs onto each other. The writer expresses dismay that sometimes these issues can come from "one of our own." Rather than shy away, this book leans into this concept because talking about anti-Blackness among Blackademics is a vital step toward subverting the system altogether. In fact, Donna Bivens maintains in her 2005 monograph chapter "What Is Internalized Racism?" that discussing internalized racism among and within Black people is not intended to "blame the victim." Rather,

> it is meant to point out the unique work that people of color must
> do within ourselves and our communities to really address racism
> and white privilege. . . . As experiences of race and structural racism
> become more confusing, complex and obscured, it is imperative
> that people of color explore and deepen our understanding of
> internalized racism. As more anti-racist white people become
> clearer about whiteness, white privilege and "doing the work"
> with white people, people of color are freed up to look beyond our
> physical and psychological trauma from racism. We can then focus
> on other challenges to our ability and need to create what we want

for ourselves, our communities, our larger U.S. society, our world. (Bivens 2005, 45)

In the same vein, this book intends to spark vital conversations about the ways in which Blackademics, especially those in positions of power (such as university administrators, department heads, and dissertation chairs), might interrogate the specific source of this destructive behavior and engage in candid yet constructive conversations about this concept so that people can be open to accountability, correction, and recourse.

Overt racism against Blackademics is prevalent in academia, with some high-profile national cases crystalizing its presence: the denial of tenure for Pulitzer Prize–winning journalist Nikole Hannah-Jones at the University of North Carolina at Chapel Hill and for Cornel West at Harvard University; the slew of hate crimes and racial assaults against Black students on college campuses; and effigies and ropes hanging from trees on student campuses and banana peels being left in Black student spaces. These national events are a mere reflection of the countless cases of overt racism that are "on display" on far too many campuses across the United States, including the ones recounted in this book. One anonymous writer shares an incident about a black sock and rope that fashioned a hanging in effigy on campus. Sadly, the white administration had a non-response to the hate crime and also summoned the Blackademic to instruct administrators on what to do after the Blackademic called them out for carelessly disregarding the safety of Black students and the severity of the incident. In another vignette, Jewell Stewart Lay writes about the small crosses erected in the campus courtyard of a predominantly white Catholic school as a protest against abortion. But to increase the impact, protesters tied colored ribbons around the crosses to indicate the race of the women who had abortions—and most of the ribbons in that courtyard were black. Lay expresses the horror of seeing a field of black, how the ribbons made her feel targeted as one of only a few Black students on campus, and the dismay when her impassioned remarks about the protest fell on deaf ears.

Overt racist acts are often the easiest to see and describe as racism, unlike the more insidious, covert forms of racism. Chester Pierce, a prominent psychiatrist, coined the term "microaggressions" in the 1970s to describe the bifurcation of overt and covert discriminatory behavior, and Derald Wing Sue and his colleagues later expanded upon Pierce's work, defining *"racial microaggressions"* as (un)intentional indignities that "communicate hostile, derogatory, or negative racial slights and insults" and that can take different forms such as verbal, nonverbal, behavioral, or even environmental (Sue et al. 2007, 278). The work done by Pierce and by Sue and his colleagues demonstrates that microaggressions are ubiquitous in the United States and provoke various psychological, mental, and communicative responses from Black people who are targeted. The stories in this book provide lived examples, and they vary considerably. For instance, Precious Boone talks about a white professor in a social work program who upheld gross stereotypes about Black and Brown people who live in South Central Los Angeles. Rosamond S. King expresses rage in her vignette over her white faculty colleagues who wanted to write a statement condemning the sexist language that a faculty member on campus used in a personal blog but who ignored prior opportunities to write a statement when racist incidents happened on campus, particularly those involving Black students. King writes how energy-depleting it was when her white (women) colleagues went out of their way to explain why the incident about sexism was different, worse, and more worthy of attention than past issues of racism.

The subtle nature of racism leads Blackademics to doubt our internal mechanism for detecting racism: "Did that really happen? Was that deliberate? Can I call that racist?" For example, a few stories in the book reveal Blackademics who had to assess whether an incident (or a series of incidents) was, in fact, racist. In her vignette, Paris Wicker writes about experiencing rejection and avoidance by peers during group work in a statistics course, leaving Wicker to work alone. The incident left Wicker to expend considerable cognitive energy discerning whether the avoidance was actually happening and, if so, why—was it racially motivated? Was it a personal attack on her methodological prowess? Sue and his colleagues identified in their 2007 qualitative study that racial microaggressions correspond to a great deal of psychological distress for Black Americans in most (if not all) interracial encounters. Microaggressions activate "energy-depleting attempts" where targets have to determine whether incidents are racially motivated or not. If the event is deemed to be a racial microaggression, then the target has emotional, psychological, and behavioral responses, all of which require even more time and effort. Racial discrimination can be a constant source of stress and anxiety and can trigger the long-standing psychological challenges that Black people face, including trauma, isolation, and internalized oppression, according to Black psychologists such as Thelma Bryant-Davis, Jioni Lewis, and Aisha Holder.

Microaggressions can promote feelings of powerlessness among Black people, who often believe direct confrontation with aggressors is a futile endeavor. Many Blackademics, as they recount in their stories, chose not to confront their peers or push back against their superiors because their risk assessment showed that doing so might result in more psychological harm and professional repercussions.

The insidious nature of covert racism also provides convenient opportunities for people, such as aggressors and bystanders, to conjure a number of plausible explanations for discriminatory acts and can leave room for people to diminish the act altogether. For example, Sue and his colleagues noted in their 2007 article on racial microaggressions that most white Americans perceive themselves to be good, moral, and decent human beings who uphold important cultural values such as equality and democracy. Thus, they may cling to a belief that they cannot possess biased racial attitudes or engage in behaviors that are discriminatory. Additionally, acts of racial microaggression can typically be justified or explained away, which can make it difficult for aggressors, targets, and bystanders alike to call the incident for what it is—racist. For example, some readers of this book may have judged the narratives' veracity or perhaps deduced that Blackademics experienced microaggressions for individual reasons such as a character flaw, a personality clash with peers, a poor work ethic, or low productivity. Something to keep in mind is that, after making a mistake, white-identified individuals often receive second chances such as the benefit of the doubt, help from others, and respect for their point of view. For instance, a white male student who is known to be terse and unapproachable can have his demeanor reframed as "serious about his work." But a Black student who conducts herself in a similar manner can be denied opportunities because she has a "bad attitude." Or, faculty in a department may assess that a Black graduate student's writing does not meet the department's standard, and as a result the student is considered ill-equipped and unfit for a PhD program. But the same group of faculty may determine that a white student with a similar writing style and technique just needs more guidance, help, and mentorship. Accomplices in this work on anti-Black racism and anti-Blackness in academia must be aware that some of the formal and informal evaluative measures for hiring, tenure, promotion, admissions, publication, and grading are highly subjective, which lends itself for covert racism to occur. Minimizing the seriousness or severity of a microaggressive act (whether intentional or not) can also make Black people feel as though racism *can* be nullified, thereby compromising their sense of sanity and prompting them to question one's ability to address it.

Not surprisingly, verbal, nonverbal, and environmental assaults on Blackademics can have very real consequences and affect how Blackademics choose to react. As a result, responses to anti-Blackness and anti-Black racism vary considerably across the stories, and much of this has to do with the nature of the racist act (overt or covert), the nature of one's relationship with the aggressor (someone with power or a peer), how long the aggressor has committed these acts (first offense or repeat offender), and the types of consequences that may ensue from responding. Some Blackademics had a nonresponse or an inactive response. This self-protective strategy is understandable given the amount of risk involved in naming an incident as racist or confronting an aggressor. Unfortunately, Black people in the United States do not have the power or privilege to address every racist incident and might determine that they do not have the emotional capacity for confrontation or even know how to engage if the desire was there. Remaining silent or even removing oneself from the situation is a viable strategy used by some Blackademics in this book. At the end of the day, Blackademics have the right to choose the tactic that works for them and befits the specific situation.

Other Blackademics address their situations head-on, though this takes different forms. Some use their voice as power and confront the aggressor immediately or in a follow-up encounter. Some handle the situation by pursuing legal action against the individual or university on account of discrimination. Resistance also takes the form of documenting the encounter by reporting it to the department head, dean, or an upper administrator. Another way Blackademics respond is by creating and retreating to their own community. This community has been formally conceptualized as a *counterspace*. Grounded in critical race theory by education scholars such as Daniel Solórzano, Micere Keels, Carla Hunter, and Andrew Case, counterspaces are where marginalized persons can challenge each other to push beyond stereotypical narratives, develop counterstories, and learn adaptive strategies from others who are navigating similar struggles. In educational settings, counterspaces can work to facilitate collective processing of discrimination and promote well-being. For Blackademics, counterspaces provide timely opportunities to gather in critical numbers, validate the truth of their lived experiences as targets of racism on campus, and critique the dominant narrative that emerges from their experiences with the larger institution.

While many of the aforementioned responses are demonstrative in nature, some of the more common responses are emotive: frustration, fear, sadness, resentment, bewilderment, and anxiety. For example, Clifton Boyd writes about the fear of challenging a senior white faculty person who assaulted him by telling Boyd's classmates that they "should lynch him" in response to Boyd's excellent performance during class. Black feminist scholar Audre Lorde validated our temperament by establishing that anger is a viable emotional response, referencing her own experiences of racism in academia in her famous keynote address at the 1981 National Women's Studies Association Conference in Storrs, Connecticut. In that speech, Lorde stated that anger has the potential to "become a powerful source of energy serving progress and change. And when I speak of change, I do not mean a simple switch of positions or a temporary lessening of tensions, nor the ability to smile or feel good. I am speaking of a basic and radical alteration in those assumptions underlining our lives." In many of the stories, righteous indignation emanated as a notable emotion. Some Blackademics struggle with knowing that they have a right to be angry even though their peers and colleagues communicate otherwise. May the words of Lorde continue to inspire us to embrace and sit with whatever emotion is invoked by incidents of racism.

Finally, some of these narratives don't convey an ending to the story. That is, some people do not engage an aggressor, formally address the issue with people in positions of power, or file a report. There are also some instances where the situation is in progress. For instance, Tuesday L. Cooper ends her essay by stating that she is playing the "wait and see" game after serving as a witness on a racial discrimination case filed by her Black woman faculty colleague. Without the protection of tenure, Cooper contends with the risk of breaking her silence. The sobering reality is that anti-Blackness and anti-Black racism still exist, and there is no subversion to this system in the immediate future. Perhaps readers of this book need to sit with the discomfort of having no closure, mirroring the way that Blackademics rarely experience closure to our circumstances.

LONG-TERM EFFECTS OF ANTI-BLACK RACISM

Some racist accounts discussed in the book are explicit and overt, while many more are implicit—an individual is not recognized for an award, not invited to a department party, or not trusted when answering a question in class. Nevertheless, they all work in tandem and over time can have a significant and long-lasting impact that manifests in one's psychological, mental, and physical well-being.

As previously mentioned, anti-Black racism, especially micro-aggressions, can encourage Blackademics to question their own internal mechanism for detecting racism. Informed by the notion of gaslighting, *racelighting* is a concept advanced by J. Luke Wood and Franklin Harris III to represent a unique type of gaslighting experienced in the daily, normalized realities of Black people, Indigenous people, and other people of color. Racelighting is when racialized messages cause people of color to question their own lived experiences with racism. When racelighted, Blackademics, for example, may question their interpretation of reality and begin to wonder whether they are being overly sensitive. They can also feel invalidated and become overwhelmed by feelings of inferiority and self-doubt. The persistence and fervor with which such messages are delivered can make them seem verifiable and reasonable. According to Wood and Harris, racelighting is a way to explain why many Blackademics struggle with impostor syndrome and even start to believe stereotypes that their community is less than smart, capable, disciplined, or even worthy. These beliefs may lead Blackademics to dismiss any academic or career-related achievement and justify it with external factors such as beginner's luck or filling a perceived quota (for example, "I was offered the internship only because they needed a Black woman intern").

Another long-term effect of anti-Black racism is *spirit murdering*, a concept that was originally conceived by Patricia Williams (one of the original architects of critical race theory) and later expanded by Bettina Love (2016) and other scholars (for example, Garcia and Dávila 2021). According to this body of work, spirit murder is a slow death of the spirit intended to reduce, humiliate, and destroy people of color. Spirit murdering occurs every single day in academic settings, virtually unnoticed, unchecked, and all in the name of some arbitrary norm created by a white person. Bettina Love likened these (implicit) forms of oppression to a blatant murder that ends someone's life. While not named directly, there are a number of Blackademics in this book who suggest that their fervor for research, learning, serving, or teaching has been squelched. The stories convey a sense of exasperation, particularly by those who have experienced incessant racial assaults.

Blackademics experience *daily* battles in attempting to deflect racism, stereotypes, and discrimination in predominantly white spaces; they must always be on guard or wary of the next attack they may face. Both the anticipation and experiences of racial trauma contribute to *racial battle fatigue*, a term coined in 2008 by critical race theorist William Smith. It was originally used in reference to the experiences of Black men in the United States but is now expanded to describe the negative and racially charged experiences of all people of color in the United States. Racial battle fatigue causes people of color to suffer various forms of mental, emotional, and physical strain that can lead to psycho-physiological symptoms, such as tension headaches, trembling and jumpiness, chronic pain in healed injuries, elevated blood pressure, and a pounding heart-beat. When people of color with racial battle fatigue anticipate racially motivated conflicts, they may experience rapid breathing, an upset stomach, or frequent diarrhea and urination. Race-based discrimination can materialize for Blackademics in academia in ways that negatively affect one's mental and physical health.

Across the stories, Blackademics mention the physical toll of racism, such as weight gain and hair loss, as well as mental health issues, such as stunted job performance, disengagement from work and personal life, and depression. While morbid to think about, there are instances where the weight of these issues is too much to bear and can be fatal. In fact, in 2018, Thea K. Hunter died from conditions related to being overworked and having a lack of health care, according to Adam Harris's 2019 article "The Death of an Adjunct," published in *The Atlantic*. Described by colleagues as a "brilliant scholar" and "beautiful writer," she landed a tenure-track job after completing graduate school. Reports assert that as a Black woman professor at a state university in Connecticut, she encountered discrimination and harassment that made her life in academia unbearable. She resigned two years later, leaving her position for part-time adjunct appointments that came with long hours for little pay and a heavy teaching load outside of her area of expertise. She reportedly slid into a downward employment spiral, resulting in her death a little over a decade later. Other Blackademics in the book speak about their physical degeneration and the implications that racism has on their overall health. In one vignette, Mark Broomfield speaks to this exact point when he admits that exhaustion and depression, sleepless nights, and weight gain all followed attacks and microaggressions by his mentor and colleagues, who faced no form of accountability for their actions. Broomfield states that his experiences are best described as post-traumatic stress disorder. In fact, Robert T. Carter's *race-based traumatic stress theory* (2006) suggests that experiences of racial discrimination are akin to a psychological trauma and may elicit a response comparable to post-traumatic stress. Stated differently, racial trauma can cause symptoms that mirror those of PTSD. Externalizing the stress of discrimination, through death or PTSD, are just some ways in which the body responds to racism.

Not surprisingly, considering the gravity of these effects, Blackademics who experience racial discrimination over time can develop racial trauma, which is the emotional, psychological, and physical reaction to ongoing or persistent acts of hate, bias, discrimination, or intolerance. It can come directly from other people (for example, racial discrimination) or can be experienced within a wider system. Expanding on a hypothesis by psychiatrist Alvin Francis Poussaint and journalist Amy L. Alexander, Joy DeGruy (2005) advanced the idea of *post-traumatic slave syndrome* to build upon the work on racial trauma for Black Americans. DeGruy argues that post-traumatic slave syndrome is a result of unresolved post-traumatic stress disorder arising from the experience of slavery and transmitted across generations to people in the present day, along with the stress of contemporary racial prejudice. This manifests as a psychological, spiritual, emotional, and behavioral syndrome that results in a lack of self-esteem, persistent feelings of anger, and internalized racist beliefs. DeGruy stated that post-traumatic slave syndrome is not a disorder that can simply be treated and remedied clinically; rather, it requires profound social change in individuals and institutions that continue to reify inequality and injustice toward the descendants of enslaved Africans.

These psychological frameworks—racial battle fatigue, race-based traumatic stress theory, and post-traumatic slave syndrome—set an important theoretical foundation for Blackademics to necessarily contextualize our experiences in academia and identify the source(s) of our general well-being and its degeneration.

A JOURNEY TOWARD HEALING

Acknowledgment and validation that racial trauma is real play a critical role in moving toward restoration and healing. Blackademics may find themselves having a very difficult time feeling calm, safe, or even empowered when they are reminded of the racial injustices occurring nationally and globally. Blackademics should know that they are not alone and that this reaction is warranted and normal. There is not a "right" way of processing or reacting to racial trauma, but the first step is recognizing it and learning about it.

So, what is the solution? It is not through individual grit or respectability, nor is it dependent on Blackademics being more hardy or resilient. The best and most effective way to address these issues within academia is to eradicate and uproot anti-Black racism. This will take time and the effort of many. bell hooks wrote in *Yearning: Race, Gender, and Cultural Politics* that "true resistance begins with people confronting pain . . . and wanting to do something to change it" (1990, 229). hooks explained how critical it is that we acknowledge and confront the pain that we have experienced in order to transform and move beyond that pain. When looking holistically, one could argue that America has not fully reckoned with the harm that was inflicted on different racialized communities. No recompense, for example, has been offered to descendants of enslaved African people at the federal level despite repeated arguments for it, such as Ta-Nehisi Coates's 2014 article in *The Atlantic* titled "The Case for Reparations." In order for society to evolve, there must be a full acceptance and recognition of the generational trauma, hardship, and suffering inflicted on various communities while working collectively to create solutions that promote repair and healing. Failure to reconcile with the country's past transgressions will inhibit growth and continue the cycle of trauma and pain. Finding viable entry points to subvert anti-Black racism is important work that accomplices can shoulder.

BLACKADEMICS

Taking steps to be open and honest about traumatic experiences can be challenging and even downright scary. Several ways to begin one's journey to healing might include having *therapeutic conversations* with those whom you trust such as a therapist, counselor, or other Blackademic colleagues who have the capacity, maturity, and skill set to hold space for you. If *spirituality* plays an important role in your life, utilize your belief system as a way to cope—connect with others who share your spiritual beliefs, confide in your spiritual leaders, or participate in your spiritual rituals (such as prayer, meditation, listening to spiritual music, or chants). Cultivate a positive *cultural identity*. A strong sense of self is particularly helpful in combating race-related stress, stereotype threat, and the impostor phenomenon. Take classes that focus on the historical experiences and contributions of Black people in American society and join campus organizations and follow social media pages that celebrate the layers and textures of Black culture. Also, consider engaging in self-care routines. According to Audre Lorde's famous rallying cry, "Caring for myself is not self-indulgence, it is self-preservation, and that is an act of political warfare" (2017, 53). Contrary to the commercialization of self-care that equates it to buying a candle, getting a massage, purchasing an expensive herbal tea, or any other form of consumerism, *self-care* is the sustenance that supports our ability to enact change and progresses our community. So, engage in activities that bring pleasure and promote a healthy life-style, such as having a weekly video chat with a loved one, taking breaks throughout the day to do deep breathing exercises, or employing ground-ing techniques throughout the week (for example, go outside and place your bare feet in the grass or submerge your body in water).

Another helpful resource is the "Racial Trauma Toolkit," developed by Maryam M. Jernigan, Carlton E. Green, and colleagues at the Institute for the Study and Promotion of Race and Culture at Boston College. This seven-phase process outlines how individuals can devise a strategic plan to begin the healing journey; you can find this chart and other useful information about devising this plan on the Black in the Ivory website (www.blackintheivory.net).

ALLIES AND ACCOMPLICES

As Blackademics embark upon a journey of recognition and healing from the devastating blows of anti-Black racism and anti-Blackness, acts that are both overt and covert yet engender lasting consequences, there re-mains much work to be done to "reimagine the ivory in Black"—that is, work that subverts traditional notions of meritocracy, truth, knowledge production, professionalism, productivity, and labor so that these pillars are no longer rooted in the legacy of slavery and white supremacy. Indi-viduals who wish to confront anti-Black racism in academia play a critical role in restructuring these pillars. In order to move this work from theory to action, it is important to understand your role as an accomplice—and not just as an ally. *Allies* recognize that though they're not a member of the community, they support it. They are aware of their privilege and make a concerted effort to better understand the struggle every single day. But *accomplices* take it a step further, using their privilege to challenge existing conditions at the risk of their own comfort and well-being. Being an accomplice is more than just listening to Blackademics talk about our struggles; sitting on a diversity, equity, and inclusion committee; or attending a Black History Month event. It is about devising and carrying out short-term and long-term courses of action that enable you to subvert and eradicate anti-Blackness and anti-Black racism within your sphere of influence. Such action is likely going to be uncomfortable, challenging, and fraught with confrontation because it is a commitment to disrupting the status quo. And it will likely cost you something, because advocacy and comfort rarely go hand in hand; these losses may include your money, time, personal and professional security, and reputation.

Some of you were inspired during the summer of racial reckoning to "do something," and you rightfully took up the responsibility to take action in your department, university campus, and local community. A few years have passed since then. To what extent has the momentum and fervor from the summer of racial reckoning translated to lasting changes in your day-to-day personal and professional life? What progress has been made because of *your* specific action? Have you (in)formally assessed if Blackademics within your sphere of influence are actually benefiting from your work? I urge you to use this book as an alarm clock to wake you up and put you back into a place of urgency and movement. Are you confused about what action you can take now that time has passed? There has been much conversation about what accomplices can do, and these suggestions have been documented in journal articles, books, keynote speeches, podcasts, TED Talks, YouTube series, Twitter threads, workshops, websites, online classes, blog posts, and even infographics. And many of these educational resources are open source, at no cost to the user. As an accomplice in this fight, it is your responsibility to continually educate yourself about the issues, and you can use this book as a starting place. At the same time, remember that this book is the beginning of the conversation, not the end; one resource is not the only resource.

As you do this work, know that some Blackademics may not accompany you at various points of your journey. Blackademics do not have the capacity to exist, heal, and enact change at the same time. But that should never stop accomplices from doing the work—self-educate, advocate, remain open to feedback and accountability, hold space for us, listen when we deem it safe to share, and take heed when we need you to show up for us in a different way.

There may be readers who understand these concepts broadly but are less familiar with the particulars of academia. For instance, some of you may be Black professionals in other industries and fields who can empathize with the accounts of anti-Blackness and anti-Black racism because you, too, experience these issues in your workplace. As mentioned throughout this book, anti-Black racism in academia is one sprout from a toxic seed that has been planted into the bedrock of America. Sadly, there are many others. But this also means that working to subvert or even uproot a system of oppression against Black people can have lasting effects for us all, not just Blackademics. This book presents an opportunity for you to think more deeply about these issues and devise your own course of action—whether that is championing the work of #BlackintheIvory; spearheading your own movement to elevate issues that are specific to your industry, field, or profession; or embarking on a journey of healing to contend with the way anti-Black racism and anti-Blackness reverberates in your life.

A FINAL WORD

To each and every reader, thank you for making the time to come along on this journey. I am certain there were moments that made you pause, feel angry or even enraged, chuckle, or perhaps even cry. I continue to urge you to sit with whatever emotions this book stirred in you and, in the spirit of Audre Lorde, use that emotion as a productive tool to fight against racial injustice. To the Blackademic reader, this book was written just for you. Many of you have been overlooked, ejected, exploited, assaulted, patronized, dehumanized, and traumatized. Please know that you are not crazy. Your anger is rightful. And despite what people and the academic environment may tell you, you do belong. With that said, just because you have a *right* to be there doesn't mean that you are obligated to enter or stay.

To all the Blackademic contributors: words cannot express how profoundly indebted I feel to each of you for standing in your right and speaking your truth. Thank you for trusting me and rocking with me along the course of editing this book. I know this road was not easy. It required great courage to bring forth such emotional and traumatizing events, as many of you expressed in your emails, phone calls, and text messages to me. Yet here we are with all of these counterstories published for the world to read. Please know that I remain committed to use whatever platform I have to amplify our collective Blackademic voices. This book is certainly not the end of the journey, Blackademics near and far can continue to speak truth and by doing so open readers' minds and hearts to receive, understand, and validate our experiences. With many of us doing the work internally and collectively, I believe we can begin to dismantle the "ivory tower," reimagine it in Black, and construct a more inclusive, hopeful, and brighter future for academia.

References

Bivens, Donna. 2005. "What Is Internalized Racism?" In *Flipping the Script: White Privilege and Community Building*, edited by Maggie Potapchuk, Sally Leiderman, Donna Bivens, and Barbara Major, 43–51. Silver Spring, MD: MP Associates.

Carter, Robert T. 2006. "Race-Based Traumatic Stress." *Psychiatric Times* 23, no. 14 (December): 37–38.

DeGruy, Joy. 2005. *Post Traumatic Slave Syndrome: America's Legacy of Enduring Injury and Healing*. Portland, OR: Joy DeGruy Publication.

Garcia, Nichole Margarita, and Erica R. Dávila. 2021. "Spirit Murdering: Terrains, Trenches, and Terrors in Academia: Introduction to Special Issue." *Journal of Educational Foundations* 34, no. 1 (Spring): 3–13.

Harris, Adam. 2019. "The Death of an Adjunct." *The Atlantic*, April 8, 2019. www.theatlantic.com/education/archive/2019/04/adjunct-professors-higher -education-thea-hunter/586168/.

hooks, bell. 1990. *Yearning: Race, Gender, and Cultural Politics*. Boston: South End Press.

Lorde, Audre. 2017. *A Burst of Light: And Other Essays*. Mineola, NY: Ixia Press.

Love, Bettina L. 2016. "Anti-Black State Violence, Classroom Edition: The Spirit Murdering of Black Children." *Journal of Curriculum and Pedagogy* 13, no. 1 (May): 22–25.

Sue, Derald Wing, Christina M. Capodilupo, Gina C. Torino, Jennifer M. Bucceri, Aisha M. B. Holder, Kevin L. Nadal, and Marta Esquilin. 2007. "Racial Microaggressions in Everyday Life." *American Psychologist* 62, no. 4 (May–June): 271–86.

Wood, J. Luke, and Frank Harris III. 2021. "Racelighting in the Normal Realities of Black, Indigenous, and People of Color: A Scholar Brief." San Diego, CA: Community College Equity Assessment Lab.

ACKNOWLEDGMENTS

Where to begin?! So many individuals supported me on the journey to get this book across the finish line, and (as the saying goes) I would be here all day if I tried to name you all. To all of the sistah friends in my inner circle, to my church family, to my blood-linked family, to my closest confidants in academia, and to my university and departmental colleagues: thank you. Over the years as I spearheaded this book from inception to print, you all provided undying support, a safe space to talk through ideas, and also some welcomed distractions when the topic of the book was all too heavy. I am also so thankful for every Blackademic who submitted a vignette to be considered for this book and all the contributors who were chosen to bravely share their stories with the world. Thank you for trusting me and making this "labor of love" feel less like labor and more like love. In addition to my village, there are four specific women who made the completion of this book possible (quite literally).

First, I must honor my mama, who is the captain of my cheerleading squad, my "Day o," my darling shuga, and the anchor in my life. Your ceaseless prayers, "Baby, I know it's hard, but just know I believe in you" pep talks, and random Zelle transfers with instructions for me to grab a coffee or take myself out to dinner to celebrate a small victory offered a unique type of support that I didn't even know I needed. I felt your love and warm embrace even though you were multiple states and sometimes countries away from me. Thank you for *always* loving me as I am and holding me down in the light and dark moments.

I also honor my Queen Mother God in all of her divine glory. As the scripture-based song by Dorinda Clark-Cole goes,

> If it had not been for the Lord
> Who was on my side,
> I wanna know where I'd be?

I can't imagine going on this journey without God by my side, guiding me every step of the way. While various life events tossed me to and fro, God (and my mama) remained the anchors that kept me still and sane. Relatedly, I honor the womanist theologians whose works radically shifted my perception of God and scripture at the most critical time in my life.

The ideological and theological shifts in my spiritual life were so divinely timed as I worked on editing this book, providing a new set of tools that allowed me to think more critically about the world around me and my position in that world.

I must also thank my *phenomenal* assistant, Lola. This book *would not* have happened without you. You are apt, thorough, devoted, kind, genuine, patient, committed, punctual, and diligent, and for these and so many other reasons I honor you and the support you have offered me and #BlackintheIvory.

Last but never least, I must thank my editor at the University of North Carolina Press, Cate. There is more to say than what space allows, but I will do my best. Since the summer of 2020, you have communicated so much support to me and my ideas. While you do not identify as a Black-ademic, you have always understood the assignment—which is to ensure (as best as you can) that the agency, authority, and authenticity of the contributors' stories are not compromised. Thank you for being so willing to take a meeting, serve as a sounding board when I needed to verbally process an idea, and offer solutions and viable alternatives rather than blank stares and dead ends. You have set the bar so high for any editor I work with in the future.

APPENDIX
BLACKADEMIC AFFIRMATIONS

Working and being successful in academia can take a lot of work, confidence, and commitment. And it typically involves a tough road ahead, especially for Blackademics. Racism is ubiquitous in the United States, and as individual people, we do not have 100 percent control over systemic racism or its effects on our lives. However, affirmations are one way to fight against the toll that racism can exert on us. Affirmations can allow you to reprogram your own subconscious mind to be more optimistic and boost your motivation and outlook so you can better achieve your academic, professional, and personal goals despite working in a space where racism is pervasive.

Many individuals use affirmations to focus positive energy on the things that are vital to success, such as passing exams, getting into a graduate school of choice, and earning tenure.

If you are new to affirmations, just know that the science is simple: We all carry thoughts and habits in our subconscious mind. If we keep telling ourselves negative things, then those negative things are more likely to happen. But if we tell ourselves positive things, the possibilities abound for us to achieve higher goals. Thus, through the repetitive nature of affirmations, we can train our subconscious mind to enact and believe positive thinking. There is no right or wrong way to use affirmations, but it is essential that you repeat them daily and as many times as you're comfortable doing so. Most individuals typically repeat them in the morning and evening or throughout the day whenever they have a spare minute. Through affirmations, you can change for the better the way you think and shape your Blackademic future. I hope you find some affirmations below that align with your personal and professional goals.

The following are seven categories of positive affirmations that pertain to the Blackademic experience: Perspective and Reframing, Admissions, Studying and Taking Exams, Writing and Conducting Research, Jobs and Promotion, Expertise and Skill Set, and Identity and Belonging.

PERSPECTIVE AND REFRAMING

Some Blackademics may have internalized the negative messages targeting our capabilities, scholarly aptitudes, and overall possibilities for success. The statements below allow you to shift those negative internal mindsets and perspectives, therefore transforming doubts, unproductive brooding, and damaging personal thoughts into positive statements of what you will accomplish professionally and personally.

1. I acknowledge all that makes me human. I am a work in progress, always growing, always changing, and always evolving into the best version of myself.
2. Failure is not fatal. It is an opportunity to learn and grow. I choose to celebrate progress over perfection and celebrate all of my wins no matter their size.
3. I am smart and capable, and my passions are worth the pursuit.
4. I trust in the knowledge I have and my ability to achieve anything I desire.
5. I know that my words and thoughts are powerful. I will speak only positive words no matter the situation.
6. Every day is a gift, and I will do my best to be present and enjoy each second of it.
7. I will get out of my comfort zone so that I can see new opportunities coming my way.
8. I will do more than just exist; I will live life to the fullest and thrive!
9. I embrace challenges because they can help me reach a new level of success.
10. I am a magnet for blessings, and I attract happiness and joy into my life.
11. I will be present in all areas of my personal and professional life and make room for all the abundance of good that is to come.

ADMISSIONS

The pressure to succeed academically and be admitted into top-ranked colleges or universities is felt by many Blackademics. Say these affirmations to relieve this pressure, to accept whatever admissions outcome you receive, and to be grateful for your future academic opportunities.

1. Submitting my applications was itself an arduous process, and I will stop to celebrate myself for completing this monumental task.
2. No matter the outcome of my application, success is still in my future.
3. My future is bright at whichever university I attend, and I know that I will make a big impact on any environment that I am in.
4. My worth is never determined by a school's decision—and this is true whether I am admitted or not.
5. I recognize that awaiting the admission decisions can be tough and will do my best to work through whichever emotions and negative thoughts arise so that they do not occupy permanent space in my body.
6. Regardless of which school(s) I am accepted to, I will remain focused on what is in my best interest, what feels good to me, and what can elevate me to the next level.
7. I am confident I have made the right choice in taking a chance on myself and turning my academic dreams into reality.
8. I know that one door closing does not mean I cannot continue to work toward opening the one that will be right for me.
9. I acknowledge the pressures that come with striving for a place at the best institution. As I move through this process, I will be easy on myself, assured that what is meant for me will come to me.
10. There is no doubt that I will perform at my best at my chosen school. My skills and talents will be on full display day in and day out.
11. I am excited about attending my future school because there are a lot of positive experiences ahead of me.

STUDYING AND TAKING EXAMS

Taking exams is a part of the academic journey that is often accompanied by feelings of stress and anxiety. To combat this, repeat the following affirmations to boost your confidence in successfully studying for and taking exams. They will help you believe in your ability to succeed academically, no matter how challenging the information.

1. Studying and learning new things can be a pleasurable process that helps me grow to my full potential.

2. I trust in my brain's ability to absorb all the information that I am studying.

3. I will not allow my brain to become cluttered and chaotic as I prepare for exams. I will be patient with myself, and I will not overload my mind.

4. In the moments when I feel overwhelmed and overloaded while studying, I will take the time to rest, recover, and regroup.

5. My brain has the capacity to recall information when answering questions on the exam.

6. I strive to create the best study habits for myself so that I can easily retain information and remain knowledgeable even after completing exams.

7. I do not feel exam stress or anxiety. My body, mind, and spirit are nourished enough to push me toward success.

8. My hard work and studying practices are the tools for building my academic success.

9. When I'm taking my exams, the questions will feel familiar to me.

10. I have worked and studied hard and trust that I did my best to prepare.

11. I will always celebrate my efforts in studying and finishing exams, regardless of whether I pass or fail.

WRITING AND CONDUCTING RESEARCH

Conducting research and synthesizing literature to write papers can seem daunting. To overcome the mental block associated with starting these intensive projects, practice positive self-talk. By repeating these positive affirmations daily, Blackademics can put the tasks into perspective and recognize that writing and research are gradual, continuous processes that need to be taken one step at a time and yet are always within our capacity as valuable knowledge producers.

1. As I read literature, I can make use of material that is relevant to my work. Even if I do not fully understand it or it is off topic, it is still useful and meaningful information.

2. I am more than capable of keeping the facts organized and accurate and handling data with care.

3. I recognize that some writing, even just a little, is a great step forward.

4. I will take this process one step at a time. I have faith in myself that my consistency will push me toward my desired results.
5. My mind is logical, and my writing is sufficient.
6. I am an excellent writer in the making, and I trust the process to help me reach that end.
7. I can write freely now and edit later. I trust that my words and ideas will transform into something beautiful in the end.
8. I will allow others to read my writing in draft form and maintain confidence in my abilities as they do so.
9. I am allowed to listen to my body and take breaks from writing so that I can clear my mind.
10. I know I have expended considerable time, effort, and knowledge to the process, and my work will speak for itself.
11. I trust myself, and I am proud of the progress I have made throughout the writing process.

JOBS AND PROMOTION

These affirmations will help Blackademics affirm their professional future. The stress of advancing one's career can be significantly reduced by repeating these affirmations and acknowledging that work is manageable, goals are attainable, and progress is not linear.

1. I am grateful to myself for recognizing that my talents deserve to be showcased at the next and highest level.
2. All I can ever do is offer my best self, and that will always be enough.
3. No matter how hard things get in my job search, I am equipped with all that is needed to be successful within and beyond academia.
4. Hearing "no" is part of the process; I will be patient as I wait for the "yes."
5. I am worthy of a job that I am qualified for and interested in.
6. I am at liberty to say "no" to what does not match my spirit, align with my values, help me carry out my desires, or meet my nonnegotiables.
7. Opportunities will always come my way. Despite being good, they may not be good for me.

8. I am worthy of receiving tenure and getting promoted. My contributions to my academic community are enough and sufficient.

9. No matter the outcome of my tenure and promotion case, I remain in control over my professional future.

10. I can be successful and still root for my peers as they progress professionally. It will not undo or diminish all that I have achieved.

11. I have the agency to control my success and happiness, and nothing should stand in the way of me attaining my dream job.

EXPERTISE AND SKILL SET

As a Blackademic, you undoubtedly have faced great adversity. You do not have to doubt yourself when presented with professional or academic challenges. They do not define who you are; your ambition does. Repeat these affirmations to reaffirm and acknowledge the dedication, expertise, and skill set it took to become who you are today.

1. I possess excellent skills that are beneficial to me and my communities.

2. I will show up and show out! No more shrinking, hiding, or playing small.

3. I am not perfect, and my flaws are what make me human.

4. I will receive constructive feedback with an open mind and a willingness to improve.

5. I know my work better than anyone, and therefore I have the last word.

6. External criticisms do not determine the strength of my skills and abilities.

7. When things get difficult, I will still put in the work to turn my ideas into reality.

8. There is a solution to any problem I come across.

9. My talents are valuable, and I have received exactly what I need to make the biggest and best impact that I can.

10. I have worked hard to sharpen my skills and competencies, and I will use them to achieve great success.

11. I trust that my skills have prepared me for the tasks ahead.

IDENTITY AND BELONGING

When constantly faced with discrimination in the academic world and beyond, it may be difficult to separate myths, stereotypes, misinformation, and disinformation from the truth that, yes, you as a Blackademic *belong* in academia. These affirmations allow you to reclaim and fight back against racism and ultimately to remind yourself that you have a rightful place in academia if you choose to be a part of it.

1. I am always deserving of unconditional respect as a person. I do not need to beg for it, nor do I need to earn it.
2. My skin color should never determine my place. I will not sacrifice my sanity or health to justify my belonging in academia, and I will take up as much space as needed.
3. Regardless of the time or place, I have the right to present my hair, clothes, and speech in an authentic form, unapologetically.
4. I was made with divine purpose and intention. I will not apologize for being all that I am and all that I am destined to be.
5. I am honoring my ancestors by believing in myself and my abilities.
6. With gratitude and humility, I will confidently walk down the paths that my ancestors blazed for me to succeed.
7. I am not marginal; I have been marginalized. I have the power to resist external forces that attempt to eject me from my rightful place in any environment that I choose to occupy.
8. I am unique and there is no one in the world like me. Therein lies my power.
9. I am proud of who I am. To outsiders I may be "too this" or "too that," but I affirm that I am "just right." I will always show up for myself, as myself.
10. I will not diminish or dismiss my value by forcing myself to fit into spaces where my presence and worth are not recognized and appreciated.
11. I am proud of my culture and do not have to role-flex or code-switch if I don't want to. My way of being is to be celebrated and showcased, not concealed.

GLOSSARY

As you read this book, you may encounter new terms or terms that you have seen before but may not know the meaning. In an effort to enhance clarity, this glossary lists words that are directly referenced in the book and their definitions. It also includes terms that are not directly referenced but that you might find useful as you deepen your understanding of anti-Black racism and anti-Blackness in higher education.

academia/academe/the academy: The community of all individuals involved in scholarly or academic work at colleges and universities.

adjunct/adjunct professor: A part-time employee of the college or university institution who can teach up to twelve credits during a single term (and is paid by the number of credits taught as opposed to an annual salary).

agency: The capacity of individuals to act on their free will and express their individual power.

all but dissertation (ABD): A stage in the process of obtaining a PhD (or equivalent research doctorate) where the student has completed the preparatory coursework, qualifying examinations, comprehensive examinations, and defended his/her/their dissertation proposal and simply needs to carry out the proposed research and write the dissertation to complete the degree.

anti-Blackness: Racist attitudes and practices that try to destroy the worth of what it means to be Black while reifying institutional structures that keep Black people at a disadvantage.

anti-Black racism: A system of prejudiced and biased thoughts, attitudes, and actions toward Black individuals (as a marginalized group) that is perpetuated through institutional structures of power such as education, health care, and criminal justice, as well as through policies, practices, and norms.

anxiety: In the context of racism, concerns and thoughts of panic experienced by marginalized racial groups due to constant institutional, historical, and individual exposure to and experiences with racism, discrimination, and prejudice.

assistant professor (non-tenure-track): An individual employed by the university to primarily teach, having the necessary academic requirements of either a doctoral or professional degree and a track record of dedicated work in regard to previous teaching and research experiences while being active in departmental college affairs. This person is expected to successfully perform in the missions of teaching and service and upon review is reappointed to their position every year or few years.

assistant professor (tenure-track): An individual employed by the university who has the necessary academic requirements of either a doctoral or professional degree and a track record of dedicated work in regard to research and previous teaching experiences while being active in service to one's department, university, and professional associations. What distinguishes tenure-track assistant professors is that they are in the process of following the outlined steps in exhibiting superior academic performance when teaching, when conducting research, and in college affairs to reach the goal of tenure (i.e., job security).

associate professor: An individual employed by the university reaches this job level after meeting the experience and educational requirements of an assistant professor. Additionally, this person goes above and beyond in his, her, or their dedication and commitment to research and teaching and is active beyond departmental college affairs.

bias: Attitudes and thoughts, either conscious or subconscious, that are prejudiced toward individuals, groups, or ideas, typically resulting in unfair treatment.

BIPOC: An acronym that stands for Black, Indigenous, and People of Color who are severely impacted by systemic racial injustices as a result of white supremacist ideology. The term was created to acknowledge the unique relationship that Black and Indigenous people in the United States have to white supremacy.

Black joy: The happiness associated with proudly identifying as a Black individual, acknowledging the legacy of chattel slavery and present-day racism and prevailing despite these circumstances.

Blackness: The shared feelings of connectivity and closeness in the Black community as a result of similar racial, social, and economic experiences and the recognition of Black individuals' roles in forming societal structures throughout history.

Black tax: Describes the economic and psychological burden placed on individuals who identify as Black due to the cycle of inequality in the United States that routinely disadvantages Black individuals in obtaining education, wealth, and other resources.

brave space: A space in which guidelines for conversations and behavior are established to allow individuals to engage with one another with honesty, sensitivity, and respect, especially in the discussion of topics related to racism and social justice for the purpose of mutual learning, respect, and liberation.

college: An institution smaller than a university where education continues at a level beyond high school and where students learn from faculty members and earn a two-year or four-year degree in a specialty subject.

colorism: A racist ideology present both within and among racial groups, that has led to individuals with a light-skin complexion (in this context, within the Black community) receiving preferable treatment and more opportunities than those who have a darker skin tone.

cope/coping: Traditionally known as the cognitive effort one exerts to manage stress and anxiety about a distressing situation, although coping can also occur with the collaboration of others (also known as communal coping).

cultural tropes: Stereotypical depictions, prejudices, and expectations of the cultures of specific racial groups in face-to-face interactions, mass media, and more.

curriculum vitae (CV): A type of résumé that is used in the academic realm listing one's educational background, qualifications, research activity, and other professional experiences for the purpose of future employment.

depression: Feelings of despair and hopelessness, in this context, specifically in relation to racial groups experiencing institutional racism and the inability to change one's situation because of limited access to resources.

discrimination: Unjust, prejudicial treatment that can harm an individual or group based on certain generalized characteristics such as race.

doctor of philosophy (PhD): An academic degree that is awarded to individuals who have earned both a bachelor's degree and a master's degree. PhD students have to do a great deal of investigative research under the guidance of a faculty advisor on a designated topic with the goal of producing a dissertation at a college or university.

economic hardship: The lack of adequate access to financial resources that, in this context, directly impacts an individual's ability to pursue educational or career goals that involve obtaining a degree at a college or university or working at these institutions.

elitism: The belief that a select group of people perceived as having an intrinsic quality—high intellect, wealth, power, notability, special skills, or experience— are more likely to be constructive to society as a whole and therefore deserve influence or authority greater than that of others.

emotional labor: As marginalized racial groups continuously experience racism in the workforce, many of these individuals feel drained by the need to work harder to prove themselves professionally in order to combat these stereotypes.

endowment: The pool of financial resources that a college or university receives from a variety of donors to uphold the educational and research standards of the institution.

epistemic exclusion: A form of academic gatekeeping and scholarly devaluation rooted in disciplinary and identity-based biases that impedes faculty members who are a part of racial minority groups from securing jobs, promotions, and more by colleges or universities.

epistemic exploitation: The act, typically by white individuals, of asking those in racial minority groups to explain what discrimination and oppression are. This can cause members of these racial minority groups to feel uncomfortable and drained from the constant need to explain these struggles in academic settings.

equal employment opportunity (EEO) complaint: An allegation of discrimination at work on the basis of race, color, religion, sex, national origin, age, disability, or genetic information.

faculty advisor: A faculty member who is assigned or chosen to provide support, resources, guidance, and advice regarding various academic requirements for undergraduate and graduate students because of the faculty person's research experience, expertise, and alignment with the students' research and professional interests.

full professor: An individual who has surpassed the job position of an associate professor, who has met the requirements of both an assistant and associate professor, who has exceptional experiences in his/her/their scholarly field, advising, and teaching, and who goes above and beyond in developing a program of research that is recognized (inter)nationally.

grader: Academically qualified university employee, typically a graduate student, who grades student work as well as additional tasks at the discretion of the supervising professor.

graduate assistant (GA): Academically qualified graduate student who aids a professor in the instruction of students, in research, or in other duties related to students' intellectual growth and the graduate assistant's professional development.

graduate school: A higher education institution which awards post-graduate degrees most commonly master's and doctoral.

healing: A multifaceted phenomenon that can be thought of as the transcendence of suffering or, from another vantage point, a restorative process whereby an individual seeks wholeness in physical, psychological, spiritual, or mental health and wellness.

higher education (higher ed): Education beyond the level of either public or private high school to obtain a degree at a college or university (typically to go into a specialized professional field that requires a certain level of education).

Hispanic serving institution (HSI): A college or university that has a certain percentage of Hispanic undergraduate students enrolled and that actively includes these students by providing additional resources and opportunities to help them succeed academically and professionally.

historically Black colleges and universities (HBCUs): Educational institutions founded prior to 1964 with the principal mission to provide educational resources to Black students and support these individuals in obtaining their degrees and succeeding in the job market.

implicit bias: Prejudiced thoughts, attitudes, and actions toward individuals or groups, typically marginalized groups, that people adopt without their knowledge.

institutional racism: Unfair policies and discriminatory practices of particular institutions that regularly limit the access that people of color have to resources and opportunities in education, health, employment, housing sectors, and the criminal justice system (to name a few).

invisible labor: The unnoticed hard work and successes of people of color (and other historically minoritized groups) due to discrimination, implicit or explicit biases, and prejudices that result in the decreased likelihood of their efforts being rewarded professionally in institutional structures (for example, Black faculty who do work, such as university service, that goes unnoticed, uncompensated, or is not considered for promotion or the opportunity for tenure).

ivory tower: Academic institutions such as colleges and universities that are not racially diverse enough and are typically composed of a majority of white individuals. As a result of this lack of diversity, students and faculty of color enrolled or working at these institutions struggle to be accepted and face institutional racism and discrimination.

McNair Scholars Program: Funds awarded to colleges or universities from the US Department of Education to support students from underrepresented groups to pursue a PhD degree. In these programs, students have the opportunity to engage in scholarly activity that prepares them for a PhD, learn how to successfully complete their degree, and receive guidance while they apply to PhD programs.

mentorship: The guidance, advice, and other resources provided by a mentor, especially an experienced person in an educational institution such as a more senior colleague.

misogynoir: The unique intersection of misogyny and racism leading to the specific hatred, dislike, distrust, or prejudice directed toward Black women.

on-campus living: Housing options for undergraduate and graduate students that are provided by universities and colleges. They include dormitories, apartments, or suites that are located strategically around campus; students who live in these facilities pay a cost in addition to tuition and student fees.

oppression: Cruel harm through which persons are systematically and unfairly constrained, burdened, or reduced by societal forces, thereby limiting and preventing them from attaining resources, opportunities, and freedom.

outsider within: Not being included within a group or area due to systems of oppression based on race even though one has the credentials, knowledge, or right to be involved. This is racially motivated, and people of color feel as if they do not belong because of discrimination and prejudice within institutions (for example, Black women can feel this way in academia as they have the credentials and access to the resources of the community but are excluded and marginalized by those in power just enough so that they cannot gain statuses comparable to those who are in control).

overt vs. covert racism: Overt racism is the act of knowingly discriminating against individuals or groups because of the color of their skin in an open and obvious way, usually through prejudiced words and actions. Covert racism is a more subtle and concealed discrimination through (conscious or subconscious) biased thoughts, attitudes, and actions against people of color by either individuals or institutional structures to limit access to vital resources.

postdoctoral (postdoc): A professional position that individuals take after completing their doctorate degree to continue in-depth scholarly research and training.

post-traumatic slave syndrome: A theory explaining the root of the survival behaviors that many Black Americans enact as a consequence of the multigenerational oppression of Africans and their descendants resulting from centuries of chattel slavery.

predominantly white institutions (PWIs): Colleges and universities where the majority of students attending are white. Typically these institutions lack the diversity or inclusion of racial minority groups.

prejudice: Preconceived notions learned from one's environment (for example, parents, school, peers) about an individual or group that are not inherent, inborn, or based in reason and that prevent the objective examination of an individual, group, or idea.

professional doctorate: A doctoral degree that is different from a PhD in that students must use past data and research in their chosen field of study to solve a current problem in academia or society in general (through the publication of a doctoral capstone or the successful completion of an equivalent milestone). Professional doctorates include doctor of medicine (MD), doctor of theology (ThD), doctor of education (EdD), and juris doctor (JD).

publications: Documents such as articles in peer-reviewed journals, book monographs, or book chapters written by an individual researcher or members of a research team. For such work to be published, other field experts have to review the document and provide suggestions before the findings are accepted.

race: A socially constructed, arbitrary categorization of people into populations or groups (on the basis of various sets of perceived or real physical characteristics) that maintains systems of power inequity.

racial identity: An individual's self-concept, focusing on that person's membership in and perception of socio-politically constructed racial groups.

racial identity development: The ways in which we are socialized to understand where we and others fit into socially constructed racial categories particular to the society in which we live.

racial macroaggressions vs. microaggressions: Racial macroaggressions consist of obvious and aggressive discriminatory thoughts, attitudes, and actions toward racial minority groups that are perpetuated by and built into regulatory laws and structures of institutions based on the construct of race. On the other hand, racial microaggressions are more subtle, repeated instances of racism toward racial minority groups that are done consciously or subconsciously by those in power.

racial socialization: A communicative process between children of color and their primary socializing agents (usually parents). In a racialized social system that is steeped in normative white supremacy and anti-Blackness, it is common for Black children to go through some process, starting at a very early age, wherein they learn about racial injustice, their place in society, and information and skills deemed necessary to survive.

racial trauma: The mental and emotional injury caused by major experiences with racial bias and ethnic discrimination, racism, and hate crimes, as well as the cumulative traumatic effect of everyday discrimination and microaggressions.

racism: The belief in the superiority of one race (white) over another (people of color), resulting in discrimination and prejudice toward individuals and groups based on the construct of race.

research: Academic scholarly work in which university faculty members design a study, develop a set of hypotheses or research questions, collect and analyze the data, and review the findings alongside past literature to draw a new conclusion (standards of research are usually set by the Institutional Review Board).

research assistant (RA): A student who helps a faculty person with his/her/their research by completing various assigned tasks, which are later evaluated.

research team: A team of researchers including a principal investigator, a coinvestigator, and regulatory and data coordinators who work together to investigate a formulated set of hypotheses and research questions, collect data to test an idea, and publish their findings to the related academic community.

resilience: The process of adapting well in the face of adversity, trauma, tragedy, threats, or significant sources of stress, influenced by a plethora of biological, psychological, social, and cultural determinants.

resistance: An oppositional force that undermines a dominant culture, idea, or group that is trying to enforce conformity.

respectability politics: Within marginalized groups, the tailoring of an individual's (notably, a Black woman's) societal image of behavior and sexuality to fit the normative public expectations set by white individuals in order to combat racial stereotypes.

revise and resubmit (R&R): The process by which an editor at an academic journal returns a manuscript to its author for revisions, with the expectation that the manuscript will be resubmitted for additional review. Once it is resubmitted, an editor at the journal ultimately decides whether the manuscript should receive an additional R&R, a rejection, or publication in that journal.

safe space: An environment that enables empowering, meaningful dialogue, usually on sensitive topics related to racism and social justice, to generate action-focused outcomes.

social support: The experience of being valued, respected, cared about, and loved by individuals, groups, and communities present in one's life, especially in the midst of physiological, psychological, cultural, and social stress.

structural racism: The normalization and legitimization of an array of dynamics— historical, cultural, ideological, institutional, and interpersonal—that routinely advantage white people while producing cumulative and compounding adverse outcomes for people of color.

student activism/student-led social justice movements: Campus-wide rallies or protests to fight for both institutional and societal changes at the university and national level.

student-athletes: Students who are signed to a college's or university's athletic team who may or may not have been offered a scholarship to be in these competitive programs, which range from Division I (most competitive level of college sports) to Division III (least competitive level).

student body (president/leader): A group of students who are often elected by the student population to create positive change in their college or university campus environment.

survival strategies: Plans of those who are students or faculty at colleges or universities that detail how to succeed and the ways to do so to reduce the stress of academics or academia (for example, effective organizational and time management skills). As for those who are students or faculty of color, these plans have unfortunately evolved to include ways to combat racism and to overcome discrimination by peers or those in power.

teaching assistant (TA): An individual, typically a graduate student, who assists a professor with instructional responsibilities such as creating and delivering materials in a course, lecturing and tutoring, holding office hours, and any other appropriate duties at the discretion of the supervising professor.

teaching evaluations: The formal process used to review teacher performance and effectiveness in the classroom, ensuring that teachers are highly skilled, well resourced, and motivated to best serve their students.

teaching professor/professor in residence: Academically and professionally qualified individuals who primally teach and are involved in department affairs at colleges and universities.

tenure: A professor's employment status within a higher education institution that guarantees him, her, or them job security and stability to safeguard academic freedom. Assistant professors who are hired into *tenure-track* positions have six years to publish a certain number of publications, serve their academic communities, and teach (under)graduate courses. They are expected not only to meet these standards but also to do so with excellence and (at times) exceptionalism. This time frame is often referred to as the *tenure clock*. At the end of their fifth year, assistant professors go up for tenure. During the *tenure process*, individuals have to present their work in the form of a *tenure file* (also referred to as a tenure portfolio or a tenure dossier) that details their credentials, experience, and reasoning behind the contents of their tenure file. This file or portfolio of accomplishments undergoes an extensive *tenure review* by a panel of respected and notable members of the person's academic community (also known as *external reviewers*), the tenured faculty in the person's home department (sometimes referred to as the *Promotion and Tenure Review Committee*) and department chair, the dean, the provost, and then the university's board of trustees. After review, it is determined whether the individual is *denied tenure* or *granted tenure*, an exceptional privilege and honor.

third-year review: Those in academia who are on the tenure track have an initial review in their third year by the upper administration of universities to determine whether a faculty member is making good progress toward tenure.

thriving: Individuals in academia who are succeeding in work and projects by properly managing stress associated with completing tasks in scholarly institutions.

types of degrees/educational background: Students may begin their plans of study by obtaining a two-year associate's degree, or students who are first enrolled in the university's undergraduate program may obtain a four-year bachelor's degree, followed by the increasingly difficult programs to earn a master's degree and, finally, a doctoral degree.

types of socializing messages: Includes preparation for anti-Black racism, pride in being Black, the need for healing spaces, and coping with racial trauma, among others.

underrepresented minority: Those who identify as part of a racial or ethnic group that is considered inadequately represented in the larger population of their job, institution, or community as a whole. This includes individuals whose racial or ethnic makeup is African American/Black, Asian, Hispanic/Latinx, Native/Indigenous or Alaska Native, Native Hawaiian or Pacific Islander, or two or more races or ethnicities.

university: A larger accredited educational institution similar to a college where students attend to earn either a bachelor's degree or a graduate degree.

upper administration/upper administrators: Individuals who hold notable upper-level positions in a college's or university's administration, such as the president or chancellor, provost, dean, and department chair. The roles of a president or chancellor, provost, dean, and chair all share the common goal of ensuring the institution runs smoothly and that educational as well as social needs are met at both the student and faculty levels. The president or chancellor is often seen as the face of the university or college and ensures that upper administration is working efficiently. A dean specifically looks at the department side of the university, such as faculty members and other staff, whereas a provost's goals include making sure all aspects of educational operations are met. The position of chair provides general oversight within each university department through organizational tactics. Overall, all upper administration positions at universities hold paramount importance in ensuring the welfare of students, faculty and staff, and the institution as a whole.

weathering hypothesis: The decreased health of racial minority groups due to discrimination in social and economic sectors, therefore leading to a higher prevalence of medical issues in these communities.

white women's tears: Due to the stereotypical role of white women as victims, when they shed tears about being the aggressor in a racist instance, the impact of the incident on a person of color is overlooked and societal change is hindered.

SUGGESTED READINGS

Everyone has the responsibility to seek out further education about anti-Black racism and anti-Blackness in higher education and may use the stories in this book as a starting point. But there are a vast number of resources—books, chapters, and academic journal articles—that can supplement what you have learned from the stories shared in this book. The entries below include readings referenced throughout the book, such as the section introductions, stories, and epilogue— as well as a vast number of other readings.

Monographs

Anderson, Myron R., and Kathryn S. Young. 2020. *Fix Your Climate: A Practical Guide to Reducing Microaggressions, Microbullying, and Bullying in the Academic Workplace*. Greenwood Village, CO: Academic Impressions.

Berlak, Ann, and Sekani Moyenda. 2001. *Taking It Personally: Racism in the Classroom from Kindergarten to College*. Philadelphia: Temple University Press.

Bradley, Stefan M. 2018. *Upending the Ivory Tower: Civil Rights, Black Power, and the Ivy League*. New York: New York University Press.

Carmichael, Stokely, and Charles V. Hamilton. 1967. *Black Power: The Politics of Liberation in America*. New York: Vintage.

Cole, Eddie R. 2020. *The Campus Color Line: College Presidents and the Struggle for Black Freedom*. Princeton, NJ: Princeton University Press.

Daniel, Jack L. 2019. *Negotiating a Historically White University while Black*. Chatham, NJ: R. R. Bowker.

DeGruy, Joy. 2005. *Post Traumatic Slave Syndrome. America's Legacy Of Enduring Injury And Healing*. Portland, OR: Joy DeGruy Publication.

Delgado, Richard, and Jean Stefancic. 2017. *Critical Race Theory: An Introduction*. 3rd ed. New York: New York University Press.

Evans, Stephanie Y. 2008. *Black Women in the Ivory Tower, 1850–1954: An Intellectual History*. Gainesville: University Press of Florida.

Finney, Carolyn. 2014. *Black Faces, White Spaces: Reimagining the Relationship of African Americans to the Great Outdoors*. Chapel Hill: University of North Carolina Press.

Glasker, Wayne. 2002. *Black Students in the Ivory Tower: African American Student Activism at the University of Pennsylvania, 1967–1990*. Amherst: University of Massachusetts Press.

Harris, Michelle, Sherrill L. Sellers, Orly Clerge, and Frederick W. Gooding Jr. 2017. *Stories from the Front of the Room: How Higher Education Faculty of Color Overcome Challenges and Thrive in the Academy*. Lanham, MD: Rowman and Littlefield.

Hersey, Tricia. 2002. *Rest Is Resistance: A Manifesto*. Hachette, UK: Little Brown Spark.

hooks, bell. 1989. *Talking Back: Thinking Feminist, Thinking Black*. Boston: South End Press.

——. 1990. *Yearning: Race, Gender, and Cultural Politics*. Boston: South End Press.

——. 1994. *Teaching to Transgress: Education as the Practice of Freedom*. New York: Routledge.

——. 2000. *Feminist Theory: From Margin to Center*. London, UK: Pluto Press.

Keels, Micere. 2019. *Campus Counterspaces: Black and Latinx Students' Search for Community at Historically White Universities*. Ithaca, NY: Cornell University Press.

Lorde, Audre. 2017. *A Burst of Light: And Other Essays*. Mineola, NY: Ixia Press.

Lyiscott, Jamila. 2019. *Black Appetite. White Food: Issues of Race, Voice, and Justice within and beyond the Classroom*. New York: Routledge.

Martínez, Elizabeth Sutherland. 1998. *De Colores Means All Of Us: Latina Views For A Multi-Colored Century*. Boston: South End Press.

McMillan Cottom, Tressie. 2018. *Thick: And Other Essays*. New York: New Press.

McNair, Tia B., Estela M. Bensimon, and Lindsey E. Malcolm-Piqueux. 2020. *From Equity Talk to Equity Walk: Expanding Practitioner Knowledge for Racial Justice in Higher Education*. Hoboken, NJ: Jossey-Bass.

Myers, Lena Wright. 2002. *A Broken Silence: Voices of African American Women in the Academy*. Westport, CT: Bergin and Garvey.

Nzinga, S. 2020. *Lean Semesters: How Higher Education Reproduces Inequity*. Baltimore, MD: Johns Hopkins University Press.

Omi, Michael, and Howard Winant. 2014. *Racial Formation in the United States*. New York: Routledge.

Porter, Lavelle. 2019. *The Blackademic Life: Academic Fiction, Higher Education, and the Black Intellectual*. Evanston, IL: Northwestern University Press.

Rockquemore, Kerry, and Tracey A. Laszloffy. 2008. *The Black Academic's Guide to Winning Tenure—without Losing Your Soul*. Boulder, CO: Lynne Rienner.

Ross, Lawrence C. 2016. *Blackballed: The Black and White Politics of Race on America's Campuses*. New York: St. Martin's Griffin.

Shabazz, Amilcar. 2004. *Advancing Democracy: African Americans and the Struggle for Access and Equity in Higher Education in Texas*. Chapel Hill: University of North Carolina Press.

Smith, Annie. 2013. *It's Not Because You're Black: Addressing Issues of Racism and Underrepresentation of African Americans in Academia*. Lanham, MD: University Press of America.

Tuitt, Frank, and Annie Howell. 2003. *Race and Higher Education*. Cambridge, MA: Harvard Educational Review.

Wilder, Craig Steven. 2013. *Ebony and Ivy: Race, Slavery, and the Troubled History of America's Universities*. New York: Bloomsbury Press.

Williams, Lonnie R., and Charles F. Robinson II. 2010. *Remembrances in Black: Personal Perspectives of the African American Experience at the University of Arkansas, 1940s–2000s*. Fayetteville: University of Arkansas Press.

Edited Volumes

Arday, Jason, and Heidi Safia Mirza, eds. 2018. *Dismantling Race in Higher Education: Racism, Whiteness and Decolonising the Academy*. London: Palgrave Macmillan.

Brooks, Jeffrey S., and Noelle Witherspoon Arnold, eds. 2013. *Confronting Racism in Higher Education: Problems and Possibilities for Fighting Ignorance, Bigotry and Isolation*. Charlotte, NC: Information Age Publishing.

Chambers, Crystal Renée, and Rhonda Vonshay Sharpe, eds. 2012. *Black Female Undergraduates on Campus: Successes and Challenges*. Bingley, UK: Emerald Publishing.

Crenshaw, Kimberlé, Neil Gotanda, Gary Peller, and Kendall Thomas, eds. 1995. *Critical Race Theory: The Key Writings That Formed the Movement*. New York: New Press.

Croom, Natasha N., and Tyson E. J. Marsh, eds. 2016. *Envisioning Critical Race Praxis in Higher Education through Counter-Storytelling*. Charlotte, NC: Information Age Publishing.

Davis, Dannielle J., Patricia G. Boyer, and Malcom Tight, eds. 2013. *Social Justice Issues and Racism in the College Classroom*. Bingley, UK: Emerald Publishing.

Douglas, Ty-Ron M. O., Kmt G. Shockley, and Ivory Toldson, eds. 2020. *Campus Uprisings: How Student Activists and Collegiate Leaders Resist Racism and Create Hope*. New York: Teachers College Press.

Hilton, Adriel A., J. Luke Wood, and Chance W. Lewis, eds. 2012. *Black Males in Postsecondary Education: Examining Their Experiences in Diverse Institutional Contexts*. Charlotte, NC: Information Age Publishing.

Ladson-Billings, Gloria, and James A. Banks, eds. 2021. *Critical Race Theory in Education: A Scholar's Journey*. New York: Teachers College Press.

Lynn, Marvin, and Adrienne D. Dixson, eds. 2021. *Handbook of Critical Race Theory in Education*. New York: Routledge.

Majors, Richard, Karen Carberry, and Theodore S. Ransaw, eds. 2020. *The International Handbook of Black Community Mental Health*. Bingley, UK: Emerald Publishing.

Matthew, Patricia A., ed. 2016. *Written/Unwritten: Diversity and the Hidden Truths of Tenure*. Chapel Hill: University of North Carolina Press.

Museus, Samuel D., María C. Ledesma, and Tara L. Parker, eds. 2015. *Racism and Racial Equity in Higher Education*. San Francisco: Wiley Subscription Services.

Niemann, Yolanda Flores, Gabriella Gutiérrez y Muhs, Carmen G. González, eds. 2020. *Presumed Incompetent II: Race, Class, Power, And Resistance Of Women In Academia*. Louisville: University Press of Colorado.

Patton, Lori D., and Natasha N. Croom, eds. 2017. *Critical Perspectives on Black Women and College Success*. New York: Routledge.

Taylor, Edward, David Gillborn, and Gloria Ladson-Billings, eds. 2009. *Foundations of Critical Race Theory in Education*. New York: Routledge.

Watson, Dyan, Jesse Hagopian, and Wayne Au, eds. 2018. *Teaching for Black Lives*. Milwaukee: Rethinking Schools.

White, Deborah G., ed. 2009. *Telling Histories: Black Women Historians in the Ivory Tower*. Chapel Hill: University of North Carolina Press.

y Muhs, Gabriella Gutiérrez, Yolanda Flores Niemann, Carmen G. González, and Angela P. Harris, eds. 2012. *Presumed Incompetent: The Intersections Of Race And Class For Women In Academia*. Louisville, CO. University Press of Colorado.

Chapters, Journal Articles, and Dissertations

Alfred, Mary V. 2001. "Reconceptualizing Marginality from the Margins: Perspectives of African American Tenured Female Faculty at a White Research University." *Western Journal of Black Studies* 25, no. 1 (Spring): 1–11.

Allen, Quaylan. 2018. "(In)Visible Men on Campus: Campus Racial Climate and Subversive Black Masculinities at a Predominantly White Liberal Arts University." *Gender and Education* 32, no. 7 (October): 843–61.

Allison, Donnetrice C. 2008. "Free to Be Me? Black Professors, White Institutions." *Journal of Black Studies* 38, no. 4 (March): 641–62.

Apugo, Danielle L. 2017. "'We All We Got': Considering Peer Relationships as Multi-purpose Sustainability Outlets among Millennial Black Women Graduate Students Attending Majority White Urban Universities." *Urban Review* 49, no. 2 (June): 347–67.

Beamon, Krystal. 2014. "Racism and Stereotyping on Campus: Experiences of African American Male Student-Athletes." *Journal of Negro Education* 83, no. 2 (Spring): 121–34.

Beatty, Cameron C., Tenisha Tevis, Lorraine Acker, Reginald Blockett, and Eugene Parker. 2020. "Addressing Anti-Black Racism in Higher Education: Love Letters to Blackness and Recommendations to Those Who Say They Love Us." *Journal Committed to Social Change on Race and Ethnicity* 6, no. 1 (2020): 6–27.

Bell, Myrtle P., Daphne Berry, Joy Leopold, and Stella Nkomo. 2021. "Making Black Lives Matter in Academia: A Black Feminist Call for Collective Action against Anti-Blackness in the Academy." *Gender, Work and Organization* 28, no. S1 (January): 39–57.

Benjamin, Shann, Roxanne Donovan, and Joycelyn Mood. 2016. "Sacrifices, Sisterhood, and Success in the Ivory Tower." *CLA Journal* 60, no. 1 (September): 84–92.

Bivens, Donna. 2005. "What Is Internalized Racism?" In *Flipping the Script: White Privilege and Community Building*, by Maggie Potapchuk, Sally Leiderman, Donna Bivens, and Barbara Major, 43–51. Silver Spring, MD: MP Associates.

Buchanan, NiCole T. 2020. "Researching while Black (and Female)." *Women and Therapy* 43 (1–2): 91–111.

Caldera, Altheria L. 2020. "Eradicating Anti-Black Racism in US Schools: A Call-to-Action for School Leaders." *Diversity, Social Justice, and the Educational Leader* 4, no. 1 (February): article 3.

Carter, Robert T. 2006. "Race-based Traumatic Stress." *Psychiatric Times* 23, no. 14 (December): 37–38.

Chambers, Crystal R. 2012. "Candid Reflections on the Departure of Black Women Faculty from Academe in the United States." *Negro Educational Review* 62, no. 1–4 (January): 233–60.

Christy, Kayonne, and Gabriel Etienne. 2021. "The Lotus Flower: Black Students Learning and Loving through the Anti-Black Labyrinth of Higher Ed." *Canadian Review of Sociology* 58, no. 3 (August): 443–46.

Coleman, Major G. 2005. "Racism in Academia: The White Superiority Supposition in the 'Unbiased' Search for Knowledge." *European Journal of Political Economy* 21, no. 3 (September): 762–74.

Coleman, Raphael D., Jason K. Wallace, and Darris R. Means. 2020. "Questioning a Single Narrative: Multiple Identities Shaping Black Queer and Transgender Student Retention." *Journal of College Student Retention: Research, Theory and Practice* 21, no. 4 (February): 455–75.

Constantine, Madonna G., Laura Smith, Rebecca M. Redington, and Delila Owens. 2008. "Racial Microaggressions against Black Counseling and Counseling Psychology Faculty: A Central Challenge in the Multicultural Counseling Movement." *Journal of Counseling and Development* 86, no. 3 (Summer): 348–55.

Croom, Natasha N. 2017. "Promotion beyond Tenure: Unpacking Racism and Sexism in the Experiences of Black Womyn Professors." *Review of Higher Education* 40, no. 4 (Summer): 557–83.

Dade, Karen, Carlie Tartakov, Connie Hargrave, and Patricia Leigh. 2015. "Assessing the Impact of Racism on Black Faculty in White Academe: A Collective Case Study of African American Female Faculty." *Western Journal of Black Studies* 39, no. 2 (Summer): 134–46.

Dancy, T. Elon, Kirsten T. Edwards, and James Earl Davis. 2018. "Historically White Universities and Plantation Politics: Anti-Blackness and Higher Education in the Black Lives Matter Era." *Urban Education* 53, no. 2 (February): 176–95.

Dancy, T. Elon, and Gaetane Jean-Marie. 2014. "Faculty of Color in Higher Education: Exploring the Intersections of Identity, Impostorship, and Internalized Racism." *Mentoring and Tutoring: Partnership in Learning* 22 (4): 354–72.

Daniel, Beverly-Jean. 2018. "Teaching while Black: Racial Dynamics, Evaluations, and the Role of White Females in the Canadian Academy in Carrying the Racism Torch." *Race Ethnicity and Education* 22 (1): 21–37.

Davids, M. Noor. 2018. "'Don't Judge a Book by Its Colour': Black Academic Experiences of Discrimination in an Education Faculty at a South African University." *Journal of Black Studies* 49, no. 5 (July): 427–47.

Davis, Maxine. 2021. "Anti-Black Practices Take Heavy Toll on Mental Health." *Nature Human Behaviour* 5, no. 4 (February): 410.

Delgado, Richard. 1989. "Storytelling for Oppositionists and Others: A Plea for Narrative." *Michigan Law Review* 87, no. 8 (August): 2411–41.

Dickens, Danielle, Maria Jones, and Naomi Hall. 2020. "Being a Token Black Female Faculty Member in Physics: Exploring Research on Gendered Racism,

Identity Shifting as a Coping Strategy, and Inclusivity in Physics." *Physics Teacher* 58 (5): 335–37.

Domingue, Andrea. D. 2015. "'Our Leaders Are Just We Ourself': Black Women College Student Leaders' Experiences with Oppression and Sources of Nourishment on a Predominantly White College Campus." *Equity and Excellence in Education* 48 (3): 454–72.

Dumas, Michael J. 2015. "Against the Dark: Antiblackness in Education Policy and Discourse." *Theory into Practice* 55 (1): 11–19.

Dumas, Michael J., and Kihana Miraya Ross. 2016. "'Be Real Black for Me': Imagining BlackCrit in Education." *Urban Education* 51, no. 4 (April): 415–42.

Essed, Philomena, and Karen Carberry. 2020. "In the Name of Our Humanity: Challenging Academic Racism and Its Effects on the Emotional Wellbeing of Women of Colour Professors." In *The International Handbook of Black Community Mental Health*, edited by Richard Majors, Karen Carberry, and Theodore S. Ransaw, 61–81. Bingley, UK: Emerald Publishing.

Foster, Kevin M. 2005. "Diet of Disparagement: The Racial Experiences of Black Students in a Predominantly White University." *International Journal of Qualitative Studies in Education* 18, no. 4 (June): 489–505.

Frazier, Kimberly N. 2011. "Academic Bullying: A Barrier to Tenure and Promotion for African-American Faculty." *Florida Journal of Educational Administration and Policy* 5, no. 1 (Fall): 1–13.

Garcia, Nichole Margarita, and Erica R. Dávila. 2021. "Spirit Murdering: Terrains, Trenches, and Terrors in Academia: Introduction to Special Issue." *Journal of Educational Foundations* 34, no. 1 (Spring): 3–13.

Garibay, Juan Carlos, Christian West, and Christopher Mathis. 2020. "'It Affects Me in Ways That I Don't Even Realize': A Preliminary Study on Black Student Responses to a University's Enslavement History." *Journal of College Student Development* 61, no. 6 (November–December): 697–716.

Gashaw, Amen. 2021. "In the Oppression Olympics, Don't Go for the Gold." *Harvard Political Review*, 24, 2021. https://harvardpolitics.com/in-the-oppression-olympics-dont-go-for-the-gold/.

Glover, S. Tay. 2017. "'Black Lesbians—Who Will Fight for Our Lives but Us?': Navigating Power, Belonging, Labor, Resistance, and Graduate Student Survival in the Ivory Tower." *Feminist Teacher* 27 (2–3): 157–75.

Gray, Darrell M., Joshua J. Joseph, Autumn R. Glover, and J. Nwando Olayiwola. 2020. "How Academia Should Respond to Racism." *Nature Reviews Gastroenterology and Hepatology* 17, no. 10 (October): 589–90.

Grey, ThedaMarie Gibbs, and Bonnie J. Williams-Farrier. 2017. "#Sippingtea: Two Black Female Literacy Scholars Sharing Counter-Stories to Redefine Our Roles in the Academy." *Journal of Literacy Research* 49, no. 4 (December): 503–25.

Grier-Reed, Tabitha L. 2010. "The African American Student Network: Creating Sanctuaries and Counterspaces for Coping with Racial Microaggressions in Higher Education Settings." *Journal of Humanistic Counseling, Education and Development* 49, no. 2 (Fall): 181–88.

Griffin, Kimberly A., Meghan J. Pifer, Jordan R. Humphrey, and Ashley M. Hazelwood. 2011. "(Re)Defining Departure: Exploring Black Professors' Experiences with and Responses to Racism and Racial Climate." *American Journal of Education* 117, no. 4 (August): 495–526.

Griffin, Rachel A. 2016. "Black Female Faculty, Resilient Grit, and Determined Grace or 'Just Because Everything Is Different Doesn't Mean Anything Has Changed.'" *Journal of Negro Education* 85, no. 3 (Summer): 365–79.

Griffith, Aisha N., Noelle M. Hurd, and Saida B. Hussain. 2017. "'I Didn't Come to School for This': A Qualitative Examination of Experiences with Race-Related Stressors and Coping Responses among Black Students Attending a Predominantly White Institution." *Journal of Adolescent Research* 34, no. 2 (March): 115–39.

Grundy, Saida. 2017. "A History of White Violence Tells Us Attacks on Black Academics Are Not Ending (I Know Because It Happened to Me)." *Ethnic and Racial Studies* 40, no. 11 (September): 1864–71.

Harley, Debra A. 2007. "Maids of Academe: African American Women Faculty at Predominately White Institutions." *Journal of African American Studies* 12, no. 1 (March): 19–36.

Harlow, Roxanna. 2003. "'Race Doesn't Matter, but . . .': The Effect of Race on Professors' Experiences and Emotion Management in the Undergraduate College Classroom." *Social Psychology Quarterly* 66, no. 4 (December): 348–63.

Harper, Shaun R. 2012. "Race without Racism: How Higher Education Researchers Minimize Racist Institutional Norms." *Review of Higher Education* 36, no. 1 (Fall): 9–29.

Harper, Shaun R., Ryan J. Davis, David E. Jones, Brian L. McGowan, Ted N. Ingram, and C. Spencer Platt. 2011. "Race and Racism in the Experiences of Black Male Resident Assistants at Predominantly White Universities." *Journal of College Student Development* 52, no. 2 (March–April): 180–200.

Harris, Angela P., and Carmen G. González. 2012. Introduction to *Presumed Incompetent: The Intersections of Race and Class for Women in Academia*, edited by Gabriella Gutiérrez y Muhs, Yolanda Flores Niemann, Carmen G. González, and Angela P. Harris, 1–14. Logan: Utah State University Press, an imprint of University Press of Colorado.

Harwood, Stacy A., Margaret B. Huntt, Ruby Mendenhall, and Jioni A. Lewis. 2012. "Racial Microaggressions in the Residence Halls: Experiences of Students of Color at a Predominantly White University." *Journal of Diversity in Higher Education* 5, no. 3 (September): 159–73.

Hawkins, Darnell F. 2021. "A Racism Burnout: My Life as a Black Academic." *Race and Justice* 11, no. 3 (July): 301–17.

Haynes, Chayla, and Kevin J. Bazner. 2019. "A Message for Faculty from the Present-Day Movement for Black Lives." *International Journal of Qualitative Studies in Education* 32, no. 9 (September): 1146–61.

Henry, Wilma J., and Nicole M. Glenn. 2009. "Black Women Employed in the Ivory Tower: Connecting for Success." *Advancing Women in Leadership Journal* 29 (2): 1–18.

Holmes, Sharon L. 2008. "Narrated Voices of African American Women in Academe." *Journal of Thought* 43, no. 3–4 (Fall–Winter): 101–24.

Jack, Anthony A. 2019. "Poison in the Ivy: Race Relations and the Reproduction of Inequality on Elite College Campuses." *Contemporary Sociology: A Journal of Reviews* 48, no. 3 (May): 292–93.

Jackson, Jenn M. 2019. "Breaking Out of the Ivory Tower: (Re)Thinking Inclusion of Women and Scholars of Color in the Academy." *Journal of Women, Politics and Policy* 40, no. 1 (January–March): 195–203.

Johnson, Azeezat. 2019. "Throwing Our Bodies against the White Background of Academia." *Area-Wiley Online Library* 52, no. 1 (March): 89–96.

Johnson, Lamar, and Nathaniel Bryan. 2017. "Using Our Voices, Losing Our Bodies: Michael Brown, Trayvon Martin, and the Spirit Murders of Black Male Professors in the Academy." *Race Ethnicity and Education* 20 (2): 163–77.

Joseph, Ameil J., Julia Janes, Harjeet Badwall, and Shana Almeida. 2019. "Preserving White Comfort and Safety: The Politics of Race Erasure in Academe." *Social Identities* 26 (2): 166–85.

Ladson-Billings, Gloria. 2005. "The Evolving Role of Critical Race Theory in Educational Scholarship." *Race Ethnicity and Education* 8 (1): 115–19.

———. 2006. Foreword to *Critical Race Theory In Education: All God's Children Got A Song*, edited by Adrienne D. Dixson, Celia K. Rousseau Anderson, and Jamel K. Donor, v–xiii. New York: Taylor & Francis.

———. 2012. "Through a Glass Darkly: The Persistence of Race in Education Research and Scholarship." *Educational Researcher* 41, no. 4 (May): 115–20.

Laster Pirtle, Whitney N. 2021. "We, Too, Are Academia: Demanding a Seat at the Table." *Feminist Anthropology* 2, no. 1 (May): 179–85.

Lewis, Jioni A., Ruby Mendenhall, Stacy A. Harwood, and Margaret Browne Huntt. 2013. "Coping with Gendered Racial Microaggressions among Black Women College Students." *Journal of African American Studies* 17, no. 1 (March): 51–73.

Louis, Dave A., Glinda J. Rawls, Dimitra Jackson-Smith, Glenn A. Chamber, LaTricia L. Phillips, and Sarah L. Louis. 2016. "Listening to Our Voices: Experiences of Black Faculty at Predominantly White Research Universities with Microaggression." *Journal of Black Studies* 47, no. 5 (July): 454–74.

Love, Bettina L. 2016. "Anti-Black state violence, classroom edition: The spirit murdering of Black children." *Journal of Curriculum and Pedagogy* 13, no. 1 (May): 22–25.

Love, Bridget H., Emerald Templeton, Stacey Ault, and Onda Johnson. 2021. "Bruised, Not Broken: Scholarly Personal Narratives of Black Women in the Academy." *International Journal of Qualitative Studies in Education* 10, no. 1 (October): 1–23.

Luney, L. 2021. "Coping to Survive the 'Wild West': Black College Womxn and Femmes Enduring Anti-Black Gendered Racism in a University of the American West." PhD diss., University of Colorado at Boulder.

Marbley, Aretha F., Aliza Wong, Sheryl L. Santos-Hatchett, Comfort Pratt, and Lahib Jaddo. 2011. "Women Faculty of Color: Voices, Gender, and the

Expression of Our Multiple Identities within Academia." *Advancing Women in Leadership Journal* 31 (1): 166–74.

Maseti, Thandokazi. 2018. "The University Is Not Your Home: Lived Experiences of a Black Woman in Academia." *South African Journal of Psychology* 48, no. 3 (September): 343–50.

Matias, Cheryl, Danielle Walker, and Mariana del Hierro. 2019. "Tales from the Ivory Tower: Women of Color's Resistance to Whiteness in Academia." *Taboo: The Journal of Culture and Education* 18, no. 1 (September): article 4.

Mbebe, Keolebogile. 2018. "Whites Cannot Be Black: A Bikoist Challenge to Professor Xolela Mangcu." *Theoria: A Journal of Social and Political Theory* 65, no. 1 (March): 24–47.

McGee, Ebony O., and Lasana Kazembe. 2015. "Entertainers or Education Researchers? The Challenges Associated with Presenting while Black." *Race Ethnicity and Education* 19 (1): 96–120.

McGowan, Brian L., Connie T. Jones, Ayesha S. Boyce, and Sharie E. Watkins. 2021. "Black Faculty Facilitating Difficult Dialogues in the College Classroom: A Cross-Disciplinary Response to Racism and Racial Violence." *Urban Review* 53, no. 5 (December): 881–903.

McKay, Cassandra L. 2010. "Community Education and Critical Race Praxis: The Power of Voice." *Educational Foundations* 24, no. 1–2 (Winter–Spring): 25–38.

McMillion, Desiree Y. 2017. "'We Must Keep Reaching across the Table and Feed Each Other': Life Stories of Black Women in Academic Leadership Roles in Higher Education at Predominantly White Institutions." PhD diss., University of Illinois at Urbana-Champaign.

Miller-Kleinhenz, Jasmine M., Alexandra B. Kuzmishin Nagy, Ania A. Majewska, Adeola O. Adebayo Michael, Saman M. Najmi, Karena H. Nguyen, Robert E. Van Sciver, and Ida T. Fonkoue. 2021. "Let's Talk about Race: Changing the Conversations around Race in Academia." *Communications Biology* 4 (1): article 902.

Mukandi, Bryan, and Chelsea Bond. 2019. "'Good in the Hood' or 'Burn It Down'? Reconciling Black Presence in the Academy." *Journal of Intercultural Studies* 40 (2): 254–68.

Mustaffa, Jalil B. 2017. "Mapping Violence, Naming Life: A History of Anti-Black Oppression in the Higher Education System." *International Journal of Qualitative Studies in Education* 30 (8): 711–27.

Neal-Jackson, Alaina. 2020. "'Well, What Did You Expect?': Black Women Facing Stereotype Threat in Collaborative Academic Spaces at a Predominantly White Institution." *Journal of College Student Development* 61, no. 3 (May–June): 317–32.

Newman, Christopher B., J. Luke Wood, and Frank Harris III. 2015. "Black Men's Perceptions of Sense of Belonging with Faculty Members in Community Colleges." *Journal of Negro Education* 84, no. 4 (Fall): 564–77.

Osbourne, Lateesha, Julie Barnett, and Leda Blackwood. 2021. "'You Never Feel So Black as When You're Contrasted against a White Background': Black Students' Experiences at a Predominantly White Institution in the UK." *Journal of Community and Applied Social Psychology* 31, no. 4 (July–August): 383–95.

Ossom-Williamson, Peace, Jamia Williams, Xan Goodman, Christian I. J. Minter, and Ayaba Logan. 2020. "Starting with I: Combating Anti-Blackness in Libraries." *Journal Articles: Leon S. McGoogan Health Sciences Library* 9 (December).

Overstreet, Mikkaka. 2019. "My First Year in Academia or the Mythical Black Woman Superhero Takes On the Ivory Tower." *Journal of Women and Gender in Higher Education* 12 (1): 18–34.

Parsons, Eileen R. C., Domonique L. Bulls, Tonjua B. Freeman, Malcom B. Butler, and Mary M. Atwater. 2016. "General Experiences + Race + Racism = Work Lives of Black Faculty in Postsecondary Science Education." *Cultural Studies of Science Education* 13 (2): 371–94.

Patton, Tracey O. 2004. "Reflections of a Black Woman Professor: Racism and Sexism in Academia." *Howard Journal of Communications* 15 (3): 185–200.

Payton, Fay C., Lynette Yarger (Kvasny), and Anthony T. Pinter. 2018. "(Text)Mining Microaggressions Literature: Implications Impacting Black Computing Faculty." *Journal of Negro Education* 87, no. 3 (Summer): 217–29.

Pittman, Chavella T. 2012. "Racial Microaggressions: The Narratives of African American Faculty at a Predominantly White University." *Journal of Negro Education* 81, no. 1 (Winter): 82–92.

Platt, Manu O. 2020. "We Exist. We Are Your Peers." *Nature Reviews Materials* 5, no. 11 (November): 783–84.

Roberson, Mya L. 2020. "On Supporting Early-Career Black Scholars." *Nature Human Behaviour* 4, no. 8 (August): 773.

Robinson, Michael A. 2017. "Black Bodies on the Ground: Policing Disparities in the African American Community—An Analysis of Newsprint from January 1, 2015, through December 31, 2015." *Journal of Black Studies* 48, no. 6 (April): 551–71.

Roby, ReAnna S., and Elizabeth B. Cook. 2019. "Black Women's Sharing in Resistance within the Academy." *Taboo: The Journal of Culture and Education* 18, no. 1 (September): article 2.

Rollock, N. 2021. "'I Would Have Become Wallpaper Had Racism Had Its Way': Black Female Professors, Racial Battle Fatigue, and Strategies for Surviving Higher Education." *Peabody Journal of Education* 96 (2): 206–17.

Ross, Henry H., and Willie J. Edwards. 2014. "African American Faculty Expressing Concerns: Breaking the Silence at Predominantly White Research Oriented Universities." *Race Ethnicity and Education* 19 (3): 461–79.

Seraphin, Wideline. 2017. "Blackademic Negotiations When the Ivory Tower Isn't Enough: Finding Pathways to Activism as an Emerging Black Scholar." *Journal of Critical Thought and Praxis* 6 (2): 95–102.

Shelby-Caffey, Crystal, Lavern Byfield, and Edwin Ubéda. 2015. "'Black Sheep' in the Ivory Tower: Academics of Color Explore Racial Battle Fatigue and Microaggressions in 'Post-Racial America.'" In *Racial Battle Fatigue: Insights from the Front Lines of Social Justice Advocacy*, edited by Jennifer L. Martin, 141–52. Santa Barbara: Praeger.

Singer, John N. 2005. "Understanding Racism through the Eyes of African American Male Student-Athletes." *Race Ethnicity and Education* 8 (4): 365–86.

———. 2016. "African American Male College Athletes' Narratives on Education and Racism." *Urban Education* 51, no. 9 (November): 1065–95.

Smith, D. 2020. "Black while Leading: Unmasking the Anti-Black Lived Experiences of Senior-Level Black Men Administrators at Historically White Institutions." PhD diss., Illinois State University.

Smith, William A., Walter R. Allen, and Lynette L. Danley. 2007. "'Assume the Position . . . You Fit the Description': Psychosocial Experiences and Racial Battle Fatigue among African American Male College Students." *American Behavioral Scientist* 51, no. 4 (December): 551–78.

Smith, William A., Jalil B. Mustaffa, Chantal M. Jones, Tommy J. Curry, and Walter R. Allen. 2016. "'You Make Me Wanna Holler and Throw Up Both My Hands!': Campus Culture, Black Misandric Microaggressions, and Racial Battle Fatigue." *International Journal of Qualitative Studies in Education* 29 (9): 1189–209.

Smith, William A., Tara J. Yosso, and Daniel G. Solórzano. 2007. "Racial Primes and Black Misandry on Historically White Campuses: Toward Critical Race Accountability in Educational Administration." *Educational Administration Quarterly* 43, no. 5 (December): 559–85.

Solórzano, Daniel G., and Tara J. Yosso. 2002. "Critical Race Methodology: Counter-Storytelling as an Analytical Framework for Education Research." *Qualitative Inquiry* 8, no. 1 (February): 23–44.

Souto-Manning, Mariana, and Nichole Ray. 2007. "Beyond Survival in the Ivory Tower: Black and Brown Women's Living Narratives." *Equity and Excellence in Education* 40 (4): 280–90.

Stewart, Terah J., Joan Collier, and Marvette Lacy. 2019. "Naming and Claiming the Reality of Anti-Blackness in Student Affairs." In *By and By: Mid-Level Professionals*, edited by Monica Galloway Burke and U. Monique Robinson, 165–75. Vol. 2 of *No Ways Tired: The Journey for Professionals of Color in Student Affairs*. Charlotte, NC: Information Age Publishing.

Sue, Derald Wing, Christina M. Capodilupo, Gina C. Torino, Jennifer M. Bucceri, Aisha M. B. Holder, Kevin L. Nadal, and Marta Esquilin. 2007. "Racial Microaggressions in Everyday Life." *American Psychologist* 62, no. 4 (May–June): 271–86.

Tevis, Tenisha, Marcia Hernandez, and Rhonda Bryant. 2020. "Reclaiming Our Time: An Autoethnographic Exploration of Black Women Higher Education Administrators." *Journal of Negro Education* 89, no. 3 (Summer): 282–97.

Thomas, Kecia, and Leslie Ashburn-Nardo. 2020. "Black Lives Matter . . . Still: Moving beyond Acknowledging the Problem toward Effective Solutions in Graduate Training and Education." *Equality, Diversity and Inclusion: An International Journal* 39, no. 7 (August): 741–47.

Walker, Sharon. 2020. "Racism in Academia: (How to) Stay Black, Sane and Proud as the Doctoral Supervisory Relationship Implodes." In *The International Handbook of Black Community Mental Health*, edited by Richard Majors, Karen Carberry, and Theodore S. Ransaw, 93–111. Bingley, UK: Emerald Publishing.

White, Khadijah. 2016. "Black Lives on Campuses Matter: Reflecting on the Rise of the New Black Student Movement." *Soundings*, no. 63 (July): 86–97.

Whitehead, Melvin A. 2021. "Whiteness, Anti-Blackness, and Trauma: A Grounded Theory of White Racial Meaning Making." *Journal of College Student Development* 62, no. 3 (May–June): 310–26.

White-Lewis, Damani K. 2020. "The Facade of Fit in Faculty Search Processes." *Journal of Higher Education* 91 (6): 833–57.

Williams, Charmaine C. 2001. "The Angry Black Woman Scholar." *NWSA Journal: An Official Publication of the National Women's Studies Association* 13, no. 2 (Summer): 87–97.

Yearwood, Gabby. 2018. "Playing without Power: Black Male NCAA Student-Athletes Living with Structural Racism." *Transforming Anthropology* 26, no. 1 (April): 18–35.

Yeboah, Amy O. 2018. "Reflections on the Second Wave of 'Make America Great Again': A Glimpse from a Historically Black College and University." *Women, Gender, and Families of Color* 6, no. 1 (Spring): 136–43.

Young, Jemimah L., and Dorothy E. Hines. 2018. "Killing My Spirit, Renewing My Soul: Black Female Professors' Critical Reflections on Spirit Killings while Teaching." *Women, Gender, and Families of Color* 6, no. 1 (Spring): 18–25.

CONTRIBUTORS

AJ is a PhD student in electrical engineering at the University of California Los Angeles.

Anonymous. The anonymous essays were written by eight different authors.

Michael Irvin Arrington (PhD, University of South Florida) is an associate professor of communication studies at Sam Houston State University. His scholarship bridges the medical humanities and social sciences, investigating intersections of interpersonal communication, health, narrative, and diversity. He received the Distinguished Journal Article Award from the National Communication Association's Family Communication Division in 2012 and the Southern States Communication Association's Excellence in Teaching Award in 2013.

Diane Ezeh Aruah is an assistant professor of mass communication at Tennessee State University. Her research focuses on the intersections of media and communication and women's health and gender studies.

Molefi Kete Asante is a professor and the chair of the Department of Africology at Temple University. He is the founder of the theory of Afrocentricity, a cofounder of Afrocentricity International, and the president of the Molefi Kete Asante Institute for Afrocentric Studies. Asante was an honorary professor at Zhejiang University, Hangzhou, China, and is Professor Extraordinarius at the University of South Africa. He is the founding and current editor of the *Journal of Black Studies* and was the first director of UCLA's Center for Afro-American Studies in 1969. Asante, often called the most prolific African American scholar, has published ninety-four books, among the most recent of which are *The Perilous Center, or When Will the African Center Hold, Radical Insurgencies*, and the memoir *As I Run toward Africa*. Asante has also published more than 500 articles and is considered one of the most quoted living African authors as well as one of the most distinguished thinkers in the African world. He has been recognized as one of the ten most widely cited African scholars and one of the most influential leaders in education. He has been named a "HistoryMaker" with an interview in the Library of Congress. In 2019, the National Communication Association named him an NCA Distinguished Scholar, its highest honor, saying that his writings were "spectacular and profound." He has directed more than 100 PhD dissertations, making him one of the top producers of doctorates among African American scholars.

Barnabas (PhD) is an associate specialist in botany at a large research institution on the West Coast. They serve the community as a peer reviewer and contribute to making academia a welcoming place for the next generation.

Asmeret Asefaw Berhe is a professor of soil biogeochemistry, Falasco Chair in earth sciences and geology, and interim associate dean for the graduate division, University of California, Merced.

Eduardo Bonilla-Silva is James B. Duke Distinguished Professor of Sociology in the Department of Sociology at Duke University.

Precious Boone received her master of social work degree in 2013. She works with those experiencing homelessness. She is also a student at Saybrook University, where she is pursuing a PhD in integrative social work. She is interested in preslavery history, as she has learned from scholars such as Runoko Rashidi and Ivan Van Sertima that it is an injustice to teach Black youth that their history begins with slavery.

Clifton Boyd (PhD, music, Yale University) is a music theorist and scholar-activist whose research explores themes of (racial) identity, politics, and social justice in American popular music. He is currently visiting assistant professor of music at New York University, where he will transition into his role as assistant professor of music in 2024. He is also the founder of Project Spectrum, a graduate student–led coalition committed to increasing diversity, equity, and inclusion in music academia.

Dominique Branson (PhD, Point Park University) studies African American language, anti-Black racism, gender, intersectionality, and criminal justice with the aim to discover and dismantle the ways in which evaluations of Black language perpetuate anti-Black racism.

Mark Broomfield (PhD, MFA) is an associate professor of English, the founder and director of Performance as Social Change™, and a scholar/artist with numerous publications in the areas of race, gender, sexuality, and dance performance. His book *Black Queer Dance: Gay Men and the Politics of Passing for Almost Straight* is forthcoming by Routledge. His independent film *Danced Out* will be released soon. Broomfield is the recipient of the Career Enhancement Fellowship and the Ford Foundation Fellowship.

Karida L. Brown is a professor of sociology at Emory University and the author of several books, including *The New Brownies Book: A Love Letter to Black Families* (2023) with Chronicle Books and *The Battle for the Black Mind*, forthcoming with Legacy Lit by Hachette Book Group.

Donald Earl Collins (PhD, history, Carnegie Mellon University) is a contributing writer with Al Jazeera English and a visiting professor in African American history at Loyola University Maryland. His articles have also appeared in the *Washington Post*, *The Atlantic*, *Salon*, *NBC News THINK*, the *Guardian*, *HuffPost*, *Teachers College Record*, and *Academe Magazine*, among others. He is also the author of *Fear of a "Black" America: Multiculturalism and the African American Experience* (2004) and *Boy @ The Window: A Memoir* (2013).

Tuesday L. Cooper earned an EdD in higher education administration from the University of Massachusetts Amherst and a JD from the Western New England College School of Law. She is a professor of criminal justice at Manchester Community College. Her research interests include race and justice and critical race theory. She serves as a reviewer for the *Journal of Negro Education* and has authored *The Sista' Network: African American Women Faculty*

Successfully Negotiating the Road to Tenure and *Diversity on Campus* (2nd ed., coauthored with D. Schuman and C. Pillow).

Thomas F. DeFrantz (PhD) is a professor at Northwestern University. DeFrantz specializes in African diaspora aesthetics, dance historiography, and the intersections of dance and technology. DeFrantz received the 2017 Outstanding Research in Dance award from the Dance Studies Association and has been a faculty member at Hampshire College, Stanford, Yale, MIT, NYU, Duke, and the University of Nice. DeFrantz believes in our shared capacity to do better and to engage our creative spirit for a collective good that is anti-racist, anti-homophobic, protofeminist, and queer-affirming.

Carolyn Desalu (MFA in creative writing nonfiction, University of North Carolina at Wilmington) was a full-time assistant professor in the Journalism Department at Elon University, where she taught feature writing, media writing, strategic writing, and freelancing and consulting. She is the recipient of a fellowship from the Scripps Howard Journalism Entrepreneurship Institute at the Walter Cronkite School of Journalism and Mass Communication at Arizona State University. Desalu is also a freelance lifestyle writer for the *Atlanta Journal-Constitution* and *Architectural Digest*'s *Clever* magazine. Her editorial work also appeared in *Food52, Thrillist, Paste, Essence, JET, EBONY, Zora, Philadelphia Inquirer, America's Test Kitchen,* and the *Globe and Mail* (Toronto).

Nicole Eugene (PhD, Ohio University) is an assistant professor of communication at the University of Houston-Victoria, uses autoethnography, narrative inquiry, cultural studies, and qualitative research methods to examine hidden disability as a lived experience. She is an interdisciplinary scholar who is also a disability advocate. She has published research on a range of conditions, including bipolar disorder, obsessive-compulsive disorder, Parkinson's disease, and narcolepsy.

Bernadette M. Gailliard (PhD, University of California Santa Barbara) is assistant dean for Diversity, Equity, and Inclusion at Rutgers University School of Communication and Information and a scholar and research consultant whose work examines the experiences of underrepresented groups within organizations, focusing on identity issues and career socialization. She also supports organizational leaders with the development and implementation of diversity, equity, and inclusion initiatives. Her published research can be found in *Management Communication Quarterly, Annals of the International Communication Association,* and *Human Relations.*

Danielle Geathers is a senior mechanical engineering major at the Massachusetts Institute of Technology and a two-term Undergraduate Association president, the first Black woman to serve in this capacity in MIT's 159-year history and the first president to serve two terms with the same vice president. Geathers was recognized as a Coca-Cola, Foot Locker, Burger King, and National AP Scholar. She has completed collegiate internships with McKinsey Consulting and GH Smart.

Eletra Gilchrist-Petty (PhD, University of Memphis) is a professor and the chair of the Communication Arts Department at the University of Alabama, Huntsville. Gilchrist-Petty researches instructional, intercultural, and interpersonal communication and has authored three books and two dozen other publications. She has held several offices with the National Communication Association and Southern States Communication Association and is a past NCA Division winner of the Top Journal Article and recipient of the UAH Distinguished Teaching Award.

Amir Asim Gilmore received his PhD in cultural studies and social thought in education at Washington State University. He is currently an assistant professor in cultural studies and social thought in education and the associate dean of Equity and Inclusion for Student Success and Retention at WSU. Amir's current research examines how anti-Black confrontations impede the lives of Black boys inside and outside of schooling. Follow him on various social platforms @amir_asim.

Alexis Grant (ScM, Brown University; PhD, University of Illinois Chicago) is a teacher, evaluator, and researcher. Her research involves the processes of cross-sector collaboration for community health interventions. As a graduate student, she cofounded the Black Graduate Student Association at her university to provide a space for support and encouragement.

Kai Marshall Green (PhD, American studies and ethnicity, University of Southern California; 2014 certificate in women's, gender, and sexuality studies) is an assistant professor of women's, gender, and sexuality studies at Williams College.

Candis Harris attended Georgia Southern University, where she completed her undergraduate work in psychology. She went on to complete her MA in rehabilitation counseling from South Carolina State. Harris entered the doctoral program at the University of Iowa and graduated in 2014 with a doctorate in rehabilitation counseling. Currently, Harris is the director for Office of Accessibility Services at Brenau University in Gainesville, GA.

Johnesha Harris (MA in communication studies, Louisiana State University) is the public speaking dual enrollment coordinator and instructor in the Department of Communication and Media Studies at Southeastern Louisiana Universtiy. She is also a creative director for small businesses. She has research interests in ethnography, autoethnography, classroom instructional design, food journalism, and community.

Paul C. Harris (PhD, University of Maryland) is the founder of Integrity Matters, LLC, which exists to build a just world. He is a former tenured associate professor at Penn State University and the University of Virginia. Harris's work focuses on: investigating the college- and career-readiness process of underserved students, analyzing the identity development process of Black male student-athletes, and examining pre- and in-service school counselor training related to promoting equity in schools.

Lucy Anne Hurston earned an MA in sociology from the Ohio State University and spent her entire academic career at Manchester Community College (professor emeritus).

Carol Ann Jackson is a PhD candidate in sociology at the University of Connecticut. Her professional and personal interests include interrupting inequality; education; healing; empowerment of youth, women, and marginalized peoples; poetry in praxis; mental health awareness; creative purists; nature therapy; body movement and liberation; and mysticism and spirituality.

E. Patrick Johnson (PhD, Louisiana State University) is dean of the School of Communication and the Annenberg University Professor at Northwestern University. Johnson is a member of the American Academy of Arts and Sciences. His work has greatly impacted African American studies, performance studies, and gender and sexuality studies. He is the author of several books, including *Appropriating Blackness: Performance and the Politics of Authenticity* (2003), *Sweet Tea: Black Gay Men of the South—An Oral History* (2008), *Black. Queer. Southern. Women. An Oral History* (2018), and *Honeypot: Black Southern Women Who Love Women* (2019), as well as essays and plays, and he has contributed to a number of edited and coedited collections.

Maria S. Johnson (PhD, University of Michigan) is the founder and chairperson of the Black Women and Girls Fund, which awards grants to organizations led by or serving Black women and girls. She writes about the intersections of race, gender, and class discourse within Black families; social policy; culture; and philanthropy. Johnson has published in top research journals, including *Gender & Society* and the *Du Bois Review: Social Science Research on Race.*

Valerie C. Johnson (PhD, University of Maryland, College Park) is the associate provost of diversity, equity, and inclusion (DEI) and an associate professor of political science at DePaul University in Chicago. She teaches and researches on issues of race and socioeconomic inequality.

Herman O. Kelly Jr. has a bachelor of arts degree in education from Morehouse College, a master's degree in education from Springfield College (Massachusetts), a master of divinity degree from Boston University School of Theology, and a doctor of ministry degree from Memphis Theological Seminary. Kelly is presently a pastor at Bethel African Methodist Episcopal Church and an adjunct instructor in African and African American studies at Louisiana State University; he also teaches at River Parishes Community College in Gonzales, Louisiana, as a religion instructor.

Jael Kerandi completed her BS in finance and marketing with minors in business law and leadership in May 2021. Kerandi is originally from Nairobi, Kenya, but grew up in Minneapolis, and she served as the first Black undergraduate student body president at the University of Minnesota.

Rosamond S. King (PhD, New York University) is the Carol L. Zicklin Honors Academy Chair and professor of English at Brooklyn College, part of the City University of New York. Her teaching focuses on Caribbean and African literature, creative writing, performance studies, and sexuality. King is the author of the award-winning *Island Bodies: Transgressive Sexualities in the*

Caribbean Imagination and the poetry collections *All the Rage* and *Rock | Salt | Stone* (Lambda Literary Award). You can find more information at www.rosamondsking.black.

Cato T. Laurencin earned his BSE in chemical engineering from Princeton; his MD, magna cum laude, from Harvard Medical School; and his PhD in biochemical engineering/biotechnology from MIT. In receiving the Spingarn Medal, he was named the world's foremost engineer-physician-scientist. Laurencin pioneered the novel use of polymeric biomaterials for treating musculoskeletal conditions. In recognition of his breakthrough achievements, the American Institute of Chemical Engineers created the Cato T. Laurencin Regenerative Engineering Founder's Award. Laurencin is the first surgeon in history elected to membership in the National Academy of Medicine, the National Academy of Engineering, and the National Academy of Sciences. He is the first person to receive both one of the oldest/highest awards of the National Academy of Medicine (the Walsh McDermott Medal) and the oldest/highest award of the National Academy of Engineering (the Simon Ramo Founder's Award). The American Association for the Advancement of Science awarded him the Philip Hauge Abelson Prize given "for signal contributions to the advancement of science in the US." Laurencin is the recipient of the National Medal of Technology and Innovation, America's highest honor for technological achievement, awarded by President Barack Obama in a ceremony at the White House.

Jewell Stewart Lay received her EdD in leadership for organizations from the University of Dayton. Her research interests include social support network formation among Black women, sanctuary space formation, and interpersonal connection.

Tamorah Lewis (MD, PhD) is a practicing neonatologist and physician-scientist. Her research program in neonatal pharmacology is supported by external funding, and she leads an active research program advancing precision therapeutics in the neonatal ICU. Dr. Lewis is also passionate about anti-racism in medicine and diversification of the biomedical workforce. She cocreated a curriculum for her local School of Medicine to teach anti-racism in medical education.

Timothy E. Lewis is an identity politics scholar and researcher, social justice activist, and associate professor of political science. Lewis received his undergraduate degrees (in political science and history) from Tuskegee University and his PhD in political science from the University of Missouri–St. Louis. He is the first Black American to earn tenure in the Department of Political Science at Southern Illinois University Edwardsville.

Charisse L'Pree (PhD, University of Southern California) draws from critical media studies and psychology to focus on how media affects the way we think about ourselves and others, as well as on how we use media to construct and affirm identity. Her most recent textbook describes how satire can disrupt processes of marginalization. In her spare time, she podcasts at criticalandcurious.com about pop "trash," or content that academics have largely discarded.

Christine Lynn McClure (EdD, University of Pittsburgh) is a senior research scientist in the Department of Health Policy and Management, School of Public Health, at the University of Pittsburgh. Her current research interests include the intersectional experiences of women of color in various contexts, including higher education, healthcare, public health, and child welfare, to inform the creation of more equitable spaces, policies, and practices.

Thelma "Pepper" G. McCoy (PhD, MSW, LMSW) has an educational and academic background that encompasses psychology, counseling, and interdisciplinary social work research, as well as full-time faculty experiences. She possesses a passion for and well-honed expertise in providing evidence-based research and practice, proactive support to first-generation, marginalized, and economically disadvantaged students to help them succeed in college and to graduate in a timely manner. Moreover, her primary research interests are focused on health disparities, post-traumatic stress, and the psychopathology of trauma and resilience with a particular interest in BIPOC population-based behavioral mental health, wellness, and recovery.

Anisha Melton has a BA in psychology with a double minor in business administration and communication and social interaction from the State University of New York at Oswego. Her research and professional interests include analytics, professional development and training within human resources, and college or academic advisement.

Laura D. Oliver (PhD, Louisiana State University) is an assistant professor of performance studies at Xavier University of Louisiana. She is also an award-winning performance artist, a published scholar, and a traveling guest speaker. Oliver's research is primarily focused on Black performance methods, storytelling, spoken word poetry, African American theatre, Black feminism, and digital performance. She is the creator of the *Black Performer's Toolbox*.

Ijeoma Nnodim Opara (MD) is a double board-certified assistant professor of internal medicine and pediatric physician, scientist, and activist in Detroit, Michigan. Her mission in life is to eliminate white supremacism in healthcare and public health while centering Black brilliance, abundance, and joy. She serves in a leadership capacity in multiple organizations, including as the founding director of Health Equity and Justice in Medicine; the faculty director for Healing Between the Lines; a cofounder and codirector of the Global Health Alliance and Global Urban Health Equity curriculum; "Racism and Health" section editor for *PLOS Global Public Health* journal; member of the White House Health Equity Leaders Roundtable; and creator of Antiracism in Action Roundtable, an Afrocentric think tank. Her research focuses on asset-based approaches to dismantling structural and social determinants of health in healthcare and public health.

Christopher R. Ortega (PhD, University at Buffalo, SUNY) is an associate professor of communication and media studies. His research focuses on new communication media and the role they play in society. Ortega currently serves as the cochair of the President's Council on Inclusive Excellence at SUNY Cortland.

Tameka Porter (PhD, George Mason University) is an affiliate scholar at George Mason University and the executive director of the Division of Assessment, Accountability and Performance Reporting at the Maryland State Department of Education. Her research interests include postsecondary access, culturally responsive education, educator and student well-being, and college matching. She serves on the American Educational Research Association's Culturally Sustaining Data Use Committee of the Data-Driven Decision Making in Education Special Interest Group.

Bentley Porterfield-Finn (MA, Colorado State University) is an organizational professional and doula working in the maternal health space. Her scholarship highlights the imperative of critically centering identity in supportive communication scholarship. Her research interests include investigating the intersections of health communication, social support, and identity, particularly as they pertain to maternal health and birth equity.

Amardo Rodriguez (PhD, Howard University) is a professor in the Communication and Rhetorical Studies Department at Syracuse University. His research interest is in postcolonial theory, specifically in post-colonizing communication studies. His most recent book-length monographs are *Communication: Colonization and the Making of Discipline* and *Notes from the Margins: Reflections on Regimes of Knowledge and Power*. He has also published papers in such journals as *Journal of Race and Policy*, *Journal of Latino/Latin American Studies*, *Cultural Studies/Critical Methodologies*, and *International Journal of Discrimination and the Law*. Rodriguez teaches in areas related to communication theory and inquiry and is the book review editor for the *Journal of Race and Policy*.

Nadia A. Sam-Agudu (MD, Mayo Clinic Medical School) is director of the Global Pediatrics Program and faculty in the Division of Pediatric Infectious Diseases of the Department of Pediatrics at the University of Minnesota Medical School. She provides mentorship and strategic leadership for global health research for trainees and mentees in the United States and West and Central Africa. Dr. Sam-Agudu is also associate dean of the Office of Diversity, Equity, and Inclusion for medical students at the University of Minnesota Medical School. Her research focuses on implementation science for the prevention and control of HIV and other infectious diseases among children in African countries.

Kerri-Ann M. Smith (EdD, Binghamton University, SUNY) is an associate professor of English at Queensborough Community College (CUNY) and the Inaugural Faculty Fellow for Diversity, Equity, and Inclusivity in the Office of Academic Affairs. Her work centers on culturally responsive pedagogy.

Valorie Diane Thomas is a scholar, speaker, consultant, writer, and meditation practitioner for more than twenty years. Her interdisciplinary scholarship and teaching center Black feminism, decolonial theory, Indigenous spirituality, literature, visual arts, media, liberatory somatics, and embodied social justice. She is from South Central Los Angeles, went to public school, and was taught to advocate for education and collaborative work that supports young people.

Paris Wicker (assistant professor, University at Buffalo, SUNY) applies sociological and equity-based perspectives to study the success and well-being of Black and Indigenous students, faculty, and staff in higher education, across the academic life course. Prior to her doctoral journey, Wicker worked for ten years as a higher education practitioner within college admissions and student affairs.

A. Lamont Williams (PhD, Florida State University) is an assistant professor of sport management and entertainment in the Department of Kinesiology at San José State University. Williams is a scholar-activist whose research interests are interdisciplinary in nature, covering critical theories, mental health, social justice, activism, and intercollegiate athletics.

Evelyn B. Winfield-Thomas (PhD, Southern Illinois University Carbondale) is the executive director of Institutional Equity and special assistant to the president at Western Michigan University. She is a professor in the College of Health and Human Services and a licensed psychologist. Her research focuses on cultural and psychosocial issues impacting Black women. She coined the term "hair stress" and published on the concept, which relates to Black women's hair care practices. Professional interests include mentoring, coaching, consulting, and leadership/professional development.

Andraya Yearwood (BA in Spanish language and literature with dual minors in political science and women's and gender studies) has research and professional interests involving social activism, sociolinguistic studies, and queer theory to investigate how oppressive systems, both politically and culturally, utilize language to further marginalize Black queer and Indigenous communities.

ABOUT THE EDITOR

Shardé M. Davis is an associate professor in the Department of Communication and a faculty affiliate of various research institutes at the University of Connecticut. Her research examines the way Black women leverage communication in the sistah circle to invoke collective identity, erect and fortify the boundaries around their homeplace, and backfill the necessary resources to return to white/male dominant spaces in American society. These ideas have been published in over forty peer-refereed articles and invited book chapters and are best represented in her framework known as the Strong Black Woman Collective theory. Her research was formally recognized with the 2018 American Postdoctoral Fellowship from the American Association of University Women and the 2019 Ford Foundation Postdoctoral Fellowship. In addition to her program of research, Dr. Davis created #BlackintheIvory, the viral Twitter hashtag that extended a timely opportunity for Blackademic TRUTH-tellers to share personal instances (and engage in necessary conversations) regarding anti-Black racism in academia. She is also the inaugural recipient (2021–22) of the Faculty of Color Working Group Fellowship funded by the Andrew W. Mellon Foundation and the Humanities Institute at the University of Connecticut to write and edit this book.

INDEX

golden handcuffs, 215

González, Carmen G., 12, 54; *Presumed Incompetent I*, 12, 101; *Presumed Incompetent II*, 12

graduate school, overview, 43–44. *See also* undergraduate life, overview

Graham, Nathan Lee, 129

Green, Carlton E., 239; "Racial Trauma Toolkit," 239

Green, Kay Marshall: *A Body Made Home*, 216; *Gender Trappin'*, 216

Gregory, Steven, 209

grief, 215

Gutiérrez y Muhs, Gabriella, 12; *Presumed Incompetent I*, 12, 101; *Presumed Incompetent II*, 12

hair, 20, 88, 178–81, 186, 202. *See also* incident examples

Hall, Edward T., 224

Hamilton, Charles V., 2; *Black Power*, 2

Hannah-Jones, Nikole, xi, 230

harassment, 97–99

Harris, Adam, 236; "The Death of an Adjunct," 236

Harris, Angela P., 12, 54; *Presumed Incompetent I*, 12, 101

Harris, Thomas, 126

Harvard Political Review (magazine), 13–14

Harvard University, 3–4

hate crime, 119–21, 230. *See also* anti-Black racism in academia, overview; anti-Black violence

HBCUs (historically Black colleges and universities), 34, 35, 40, 52, 68, 204

healing, 14, 15, 201, 237–39, 241

Heavy (Laymon), 91

Hersey, Tricia, 43; *Rest Is Resistance*, 43

hidden disability, 91–93. *See also* incident examples

hiring process incidents, 52, 56, 147–48. *See also* incident examples

history lecture incident, 60–61. *See also* incident examples

home, redefining, 124

hooks, bell, xiv, 7, 12, 173, 223; *Feminist Theory*, 14; *Yearning*, 7, 238

hostile research environment, 97–99. *See also* incident examples

Hughes, Langston, 130

Hunter, Thea K., 236

Hurston, Zora Neale, 144, 199, 224

HWCUs (historically white colleges and universities), 46

hypervisibility, xiii–xv, 1, 73, 132, 176

identity affirmations, 251

illness, 209–10, 216, 235–36. *See also* mental health

imposter syndrome, 68–69, 71, 73, 102, 214–15

incident examples, 226–37; academic lynching, 165–68; angst professor, 152–54; anti-abortion protest, 27–28, 230; aversive racism, 188–89; book awards and lack of recognition, 155–57; bullying, 52, 130, 141, 144–45; classroom discussions as teachable moments, 185–87; in the dining hall, 25–26; EEO investigations, 140–42; faculty advisor as obstacle, 31–32, 62–63, 65–67, 94–95; group representation, 33; hair choices, 20, 88, 178–81, 186; hidden disability, 91–93; in hiring process, 52, 56, 147–48; during history lecture, 60–61; hostile research environment, 97–99; in-class group work, 53–55; lynching, 73–74, 119–21; misogynoir, 134–36; national identity, 88–90; organizational naming, 164; plagiarism accusation, 65; in post-classical sociological theory, 75–76; professor on intelligence and race, 34; professor on South Central LA, 57; reverse racism accusation, 83–87; in theatre performance, 70–71; while waiting for appointment,

mental health, 41, 67, 98–99, 100,
102, 235–36. *See also* anxiety;
panic attacks; post-traumatic slave
syndrome; post-traumatic stress
disorder; race-based traumatic
stress theory
mentorship, 62, 100, 127–30, 169–70,
171, 201, 232
meritocracy, 139
microaggressions, 20, 33, 45, 58–59,
62, 77, 175–77, 186–87, 235. *See also*
incident examples; *and names of
specific acts*
Milner, H. Richard, IV, 75
Minneapolis Police Department, xiii, 22
Minority Coalition, 45
misogynoir, 134–36, 170, 229. *See also*
Black women; incident examples
MIT (Massachusetts Institute of
Technology), 37–40
monochronism, 224–25
moral imperative, 218–21
Morehouse College, 126
Morrill Act, 37
Morrison, Toni, 184; *Beloved*, 222
Muslim students, discrimination
against, 149

naming, 164, 185
Nap Ministry, 43
Nappy Hairstories (production), 71
narcolepsy, 91
National Aeronautics and Space
Administration, 109
National Center for Faculty
Development and Diversity, 207
national identity, 88–90. *See also*
representation
National Institutes of Health, 109
National Science Foundation, 50, 109
natural hair. *See* hair
negative energy, 110
Niemann, Yolanda Flores, 12; *Presumed
Incompetent I*, 12, 101; *Presumed
Incompetent II*, 12

Northwestern University, 124

Obama, Michelle, 17; *The Light We
Carry*, 17
Obama Presidency Oral History
project, 208
offer letter, 116–18
Okobi, Chinedu, 149
Omi, Michael, 1
overt vs. covert racism, 4, 7, 14, 77, 146,
166, 230, 232–33, 234, 239. *See also*
anti-Black racism in academia,
overview

Palmer, Arnold, 109
panic attacks, 41, 98, 166. *See also*
mental health
paralysis, 119–21
pay parity, 170–72
Pearl Milling Company, 185
PepsiCo, 185
performance spaces, 70–72
perspective affirmations, 246
plagiarism incident, mistaken, 65.
See also incident examples
poetry, 151
police brutality, xi–xiii, 20, 21–22,
149, 192. *See also* anti-Black
violence
police divestment, xiii
political encounters, 42
positive energy, 245. *See also*
affirmations
post-classical sociological theory
course, 75–76. *See also* incident
examples
postdocs, 97–98, 176, 199
postdoctoral fellowship, 124, 128, 129
post-traumatic slave syndrome, 237.
See also mental health
post-traumatic stress disorder, 130–31,
166, 236–37. *See also* mental health
Poussaint, Alvin Francis, 237
power dynamics, 52, 58–61, 73. *See also*
incident examples

predominantly white institutions, 31, 82, 104, 194–96, 204, 205
Presumed Incompetent I (Gutiérrez y Muhs, Niemann, González, and Harris), 12, 101
Presumed Incompetent II (Niemann, Gutiérrez y Muhs, and González), 12
Princeton University, 17
"professionalism," 86, 130
Project Interphase, 37
pro-life protest, 27–28
promotion affirmations, 249–50
Public Enemy, 45; "Don't Believe the Hype," 45
PWIs (predominantly white institutions), 31, 82, 104, 194–96, 204, 205

queerness and academia, 35, 175–76, 215–16, 227. *See also* LGBTQIA+ representation

race-based traumatic stress theory, 236, 237. *See also* mental health
race labor, 194–96
racelighting, 235
racial battle fatigue, 235–36, 237
racial caste system, 4
racial climate survey, 33
racial comfort, 46
racial ladder, 47–48, 50, 113–15
"Racial Trauma Toolkit" (Institute for the Study and Promotion of Race and Culture), 239
racism. *See* anti-Black racism in academia, overview
racism, internalized. *See* internalized racism
racist branding, 185
rage, xi, xii, 119, 150, 173, 185–86, 231
redlining, 23
Reed, Sean, 192
reframing, 232, 246. *See also* counterstorytelling
regenerative engineering, 109

reparations, 173–74, 238
representation, 23, 33, 35, 186–87
resilience, 10, 14, 42, 63, 101, 111, 123–25, 199, 237. *See also* adaptability; courage
resistance, 63–64, 94–96, 140–43, 237
respectability politics, 139, 237
responsibility, as concept, 78
Rest Is Resistance (Hersey), 43
"Rethinking Racism" (Bonilla-Silva), 47
reverse racism accusation, 83–87. *See also* incident examples
Rice, Tamir, xii
Robinson, Michael, 2–3
Rockquemore, Kerry, 207; "Do You Need an Exit Strategy?," 207
Ross, Kihana Miraya, 6; "'Be Real Black for Me,'" 6
running (sport), 91, 93

Saenz, Rogelio, 49
safe space, 71, 105, 243
Sawyer, Mark Q., 209
Science Translational Medicine (journal), 109
self-advocacy, 28, 100–105, 131, 171–72, 219–20
self-care, 100, 238
self-preservation, 54, 62–64, 238
self-worth, 43, 170–71, 201, 203
Seton Hall University, 138
sexual assault, 80, 149
sexual harassment training, 58–59
sickness, 209–10, 216, 235–36. *See also* mental health
silence, 21, 63, 80–82, 131, 147–48, 149, 159, 199, 201
Simmons, Ruth, 3
1619 Project, xi
skills affirmations, 250
slavery, 2–4, 37, 173, 179, 236–38, 239
Slavery, Race, and Memory project, 3
Smith, William, 236
sociology departments, 47
Solórzano, Daniel, 5

welcome, defined, 210
"Welcome to rage" project, 150
well-being, as social justice, 100
West, Cornel, 230
White, Deborah G., 227; *Telling Histories*, 227
white aversive racism, 188–90
white gaze, 181, 191
whiteness, 46–50, 71, 130, 157, 175
white privilege, 173–74, 179–80, 188–90
white racial terrorization, 130–31
white supremacy, 6, 44, 86, 104, 119–21, 130–31, 150, 175, 224, 228. *See also* anti-Black racism in academia, overview

white women's tears, xii
Wilder, Craig Steven, 3; *Ebony and Ivy*, 3, 4, 37
Williams, Patricia, 235
Williams, Serena, 198
Winant, Howie, 1
"working twice as hard to be seen as half as good," as concept, 21, 78, 114, 197
writing affirmations, 248–49

Yale University, 3
Yearning (hooks), 7, 237–38
Yosso, Tara, 4, 5

To my father, Richard Waiss,
and to my spiritual father, St. Josemaría Escrivá—
both taught me to have a great love
for Mother Mary.